IN HITLER'S OWN WORDS . . .
this shocking document reveals—

- Hitler's personal reaction to Mussolini's overthrow and the fall of Italian Fascism

- Why Hitler considered August 15, 1944, the worst day of his life

- The inside story of the attempt on Hitler's life

- Why Hitler considered his defeat in the Normandy campaign the result of treason

- Hitler in the last horrifying days of his regime

- And other first-hand insights from Hitler's top-secret military conferences

NEVER BEFORE HAS A BOOK SHOWN
WITH SUCH DOCUMENTED AND DAMNING
DETAIL
THE EVIL CORE OF NAZI GERMANY!

HITLER
DIRECTS HIS WAR

Translated and edited by
Felix Gilbert

CHARTER
NEW YORK

AWARD BOOKS ARE PUBLISHED BY
UNIVERSAL-AWARD HOUSE, INC.
DISTRIBUTED BY ACE BOOKS
A DIVISION OF CHARTER COMMUNICATIONS INC.
A GROSSET & DUNLAP COMPANY

Published by arrangement with Oxford University Press, Inc.

Charter Books
A Division of Charter Communications Inc.
A Grosset & Dunlap Company
360 Park Avenue South
New York, New York 10010

i

2 4 6 8 0 9 7 5 3 1
Manufactured in the United States of America

EDITOR'S NOTE

The documents in this book were first translated by the Army for official use, but the translation has been thoroughly revised and modified for this edition. The German text contains frequent repetitions of sentences and of single words, suddenly broken-off sentences, and even ungrammatical expressions—especially when Hitler himself is speaking. The translation has tried to reproduce the effect of the original, and when the meaning of the English text is not clear, it reflects the ambiguity of the German text.

A short dash (—) indicates a sudden interruption of a sentence, but no omission of words of the manuscript. An ellipsis (. . .) indicates the omission of a few words or sentences at a place where the manuscript was burned and the full sentence was therefore no longer comprehensible. A long dash (——) indicates an omission by the editor of a longer passage. Such omissions were made either because the meaning of the omitted passage was not clear or because the topic discussed seemed of no general interest or represented an unnecessary interruption in the trend of the discussion.

Rank and titles have generally been given in their English form in the main text and in their German form in the footnotes. Officials mentioned are usually identified either in the footnotes or in the index or List of Participants.

The *Atlas of the World Battle Fronts in Semimonthly Phases (Supplement to the Biennial Report of the Chief of Staff of the United States Army, 1943-45)* and drawings in A. Guillaume's *La Guerre Germano-Soviétique* were used as sources for the maps, which have been adapted to the special requirements of the text. Germany military maps are still classified and therefore not available.

The full titles of books mentioned in the footnotes will be found in the Bibliography.

The transcript of the original record is in the possession of the Library of the University of Pennsylvania, and in his work the editor has had the active support of Dr. Charles W. David, Director of the Library. Dr. David and Dr. Conyers Read, of the History Department of the University of Pennsylvania, suggested the publication of the manuscript and followed its preparation with the greatest interest and with helpful comments and advice. Friendly assistance was also received from Mr. Rudolf Hirsch, Assistant Librarian, Preparation Division, University of Pennsylvania Library. Mention must be made of the cooperation and interested support of Dr. Kent Roberts Greenfield, Chief Historian of the Department of the Army, and of the continued assistance of Captain Frank C. Mahin, of the same office. Thanks are due also to Major General Maxwell D. Taylor for placing the official translation of the record at the disposal of the editor.

Mr. George Allen, the discoverer of the manuscript, Dr. Stephen J. Herben, Dr. Caroline Robbins, and Mr. Adolph G. Rosengarten, Jr., helped in various ways, and the editor owes a special debt of gratitude to Mr. John L. Clive, Dr. Gordon A. Craig, and Mr. Arthur K. Solmssen.

F. G.

Bryn Mawr
August 1950

CONTENTS

FOREWORD

As soon as the 506th Parachute Infantry of the 101st Airborne Division occupied Berchtesgaden on Saturday, 5 May 1945, I proceeded there to open the Divisional Counter-Intelligence office and begin the task of clearing the Nazi element out of the town's local government. On Sunday, 6 May, I set up my office in the Hotel Bellevue, which until only a week before had served as the district Party Headquarters. I had hardly put my typewriter down when men began to come in to me to be interrogated for positions in the local government. In the afternoon of 7 May the Military Government Team, which was located in the same building, sent me two men with a recommendation that I give them special attention. These men, Herr Gerhard Herrgesell and Dr. Hans Jonuschat, wanted to place themselves at the disposal of the Americans, since they thought they had information which would be of use to us.

I talked with Herr Herrgesell first, and was amazed to learn that he had been a stenographer for the Military Conferences (*Lagebesprechungen*) which had taken place twice daily all through the war at Hitler's headquarters (*Fuehrerhauptquartier*), and that he had actually attended the last conference to be held with all the major figures present, on 22 April 1945. While I was still interrogating him, Special Agent Eric Albrecht, who had been sent to our Division on detached service to work with me, arrived from our previous camp at Miesbach. He listened to Herr Herrgesell's story with equal amazement. After he had gained an impression of the information this man and his colleagues could give us, we discussed what we should do with them.

9

Contemporary policy of the Counter Intelligence Corps (CIC) would have required us to arrest them and send them back to some internment camp, where they would have been crowded in with *Ortsgruppenleiter,* sergeants of the SS and others who were being imprisoned with such energy and to so little purpose by the average CIC team. However, we decided to keep the men at Berchtesgaden, since we felt that in them we had a living link with Hitler and an important source of information not otherwise quickly to be obtained and which we could use in our work. In view of the fact that the very small area in which we were stationed yielded Julius Streicher, Dr. Robert Ley, Fritz Sauckel, Franz Ritter von Epp, Hitler's sister Paula, his personal physician Morell, most of his household, and a score of generals and other important persons, as well as tons of documents, our decision to ignore the usual procedure and keep the men at our disposal, but free, was perhaps almost historic. At any rate, it was surely justified by the uniqueness and importance of the documents that were consequently preserved.

Having reached our decision, we told Herr Herrgesell to bring in all his colleagues on the following day so that we could talk to them at length. Accordingly, he and Dr. Jonuschat returned the next day with Dr. Kurt Peschel, head of the stenographic service at Hitler's Headquarters, Herr Ludwig Krieger, director of the same service at the Reichstag, Dr. Ewald Reynitz, and Herren Heinz Bucholz, and Karl Thöt. Dr. Kurt Haagen, the remaining member of the group, refused to come with them, but I was able to interrogate him later and found that he had nothing to add to what we had learned from the others.

For the next two days Mr. Albrecht and I talked to these men as much as we could, in between our other work. We found that they had collectively sat in on every conference Hitler had held with his High Command (*Oberkommando der Wehrmacht*) from September 1942 to 22 April 1945. Six of them had been flown from Berlin to Munich and then driven to Berchtesgaden on 20 April, and Herr Herrgesell and Dr. Haagen had joined these on the morning of 23 April. One of them, Herr Buchholz, had been present when the attempt of 20 July 1944 was made on Hitler's life; Herr

Krieger had been a stenographer for Col. Walter Nicolai, head of German espionage during World War I; and Herr Herrgesell had been present at Hitler's Headquarters when Roosevelt's death was announced. It was an exciting experience to listen to these men discuss the most important and most secret affairs of recent German history and clear up matters which had puzzled us for months. They were, moreover, very willing to talk, and their experiences were of such absorbing interest that not only we but the representatives of the major American news services spent hours in questioning them.

In the course of our interrogations we learned from Herr Herrgesell that one set of the minutes of the conferences which they had taken down in shorthand had been brought from Berlin to Berchtesgaden in the middle of April, in anticipation of the possibility that the government might be transferred to the 'Alpen Redoubt' for its last stand, and that it had been burned by SS troops near the village of Hintersee, about five miles from Berchtesgaden. Since Mr. Albrecht was busy elsewhere at the moment, I picked up a driver and went out with Herren Herrgesell, Peschel, and Buchholz to visit the place and determine more fully what had happened. We bounced over a dirt road a short distance beyond Hintersee until we came to a 'motor pool' where a number of damaged cars belonging to the Luftwaffe were parked. First we searched in a large garage where the documents were said to have been stored, but we found practically nothing of interest there. Then we went a short distance to a large hole in the ground, some twenty feet in diameter and three or four feet deep. Here lay the remains of Hitler's own copy of the minutes of his conferences, a mass of charred paper perhaps two feet deep. With the aid of the stenographers I began to search the ashes to determine whether we could find anything that had escaped destruction. After digging about for a few minutes I came upon what Herr Herrgesell told me was a complete stenographic original of a whole conference, then another, and then quite a few typescripts which had been charred around the edges. After finding a dozen or more conference records that were intact, or only partly destroyed, I decided to take them back with me to Ber-

chtesgaden and to continue the search the next day. I went
out again twice, once with Mr. Albrecht and once alone, and
on each occasion recovered additional fragments.

All in all we were able to recover the remains of fifty-one
conferences, some complete, or practically complete, some
consisting of only a few charred pages. Most of the fragments were in shorthand, still wrapped in their original ma-
nila envelopes; the rest were typewritten copies and bore the
word *Fuehrerkopie* at the top of each first page. All told,
they filled about 800 typed pages, and covered conferences
from December 1942 to 23 March 1945. Another set of the
minutes of the conferences, which is said to have been left in
Berlin in the German Army Archives, may be presumed to
have been completely destroyed. A third set, which was in
the custody of Brigadier General Walter Scherff, historian of
the *Oberkommando der Wehrmacht*, was completely burned
shortly before the arrival of the Americans in the Berchtesgaden Area. It is therefore altogether probable that the
charred remains we recovered from the pit beyond Hintersee
represent all that has survived of an immensely important
historical document of over 200,000 pages.

As soon as I returned to Berchtesgaden, I discussed with
Mr. Albrecht what we should do with the fragments. Since
many of them were charred and would stand little handling,
we decided to set up offices in the Hotel Bellevue, where the
stenographers could re-transcribe them. We acquired
typewriters, bought paper, took food from captured 'Wer-
wolf' supplies, and made all necessary arrangements so that
the men could work comfortably and with every inducement
to do a good job.

Since Hitler had put Dr. Perschel in charge of making the
original record, we let him continue as head of the group.
This arrangement worked out well, though it was not in
accordance with the more fervent contemporary conceptions
of 'denazification.' In addition, we let him bring in as typists
several women who had originally worked on the notes in
Berlin and who were familiar with the system and arrangement of the material. The result was that less than a month
after these people stopped working for Hitler we had them
working for us, reconstructing the same records they had

prepared for him. The stenographers worked on the
documents for a period of two months, dispensing with the
typists after work had been finished on the complete and
nearly complete portions. First the stenographers reconstructed the record in longhand, using their memory and their
knowledge of the subjects under discussion to fill the gaps of
single words and parts of words which had been destroyed by
fire. Since they were very intelligent and quite familiar with
the subject matter, they were able to supply many missing
words and phrases, though they always put these supplied
portions in brackets. They made six copies of the reconstructed record, a number we thought would be sufficient for the
Army's needs. Herr Buchholz acted as librarian for the
group, keeping a catalogue of all the conferences and putting
them together.

After the work had finally been completed, I turned the
original charred remains and four copies over to a Documents Team, which in turn sent them to Wiesbaden for
use in the Nuremberg trials. I gave one copy to the G-2
Section of the 101st Airborne Division for its archives and
retained the sixth to go with my collection of the interrogations Mr. Albrecht and I had made at Berchtesgaden. The
extracts here translated were made from this copy, now
(along with the rest of our Berchtesgaden papers) in the
possession of the Library of the University of Pennsylvania.

> GEORGE ALLEN
> formerly, T/3, MIS,
> 101st Airborne Division.

INTRODUCTION

'The Fuehrer practically lives in a concentration camp. Whether the guards before his General Headquarters are furnished by the SS or by some Prisoner of War Camp—the effect is the same. The loneliness of General Headquarters and the whole method of working there naturally have at long last an extraordinarily depressing effect upon the Fuehrer. He hasn't the slightest opportunity for relaxation, and as long as he is awake he is surrounded by work and responsibility.' This is one of the many passages in Goebbels' *Diaries* in which the Minister of Propaganda remarks on the manner in which, during the war, Hitler cut himself off from all his former associates and interests and closed himself in at his headquarters with his military advisers. The center of Hitler's activities became then the daily conferences on the military situation, which took place twice every day and which were frequently supplemented by special meetings with individual commanders and discussions of particular strategic problems. A full record of these meetings would be of the highest significance for the history of the Second World War and of Nazi Germany. Unfortunately only a very small part of the record has been saved, and the surviving fragments are in a very bad state of preservation. But this loss is somewhat compensated for by the fact that what is preserved are stenographic records. It is uniquely authentic material; the reader is able to reconstruct a completely accurate picture of the discussion that went on in these conferences, and to gain a most lively impression of the personalities responsible for the conduct of war on the German side. Because of the importance of this source for the understanding of the mentality of the German war leaders, the publication of the most significant of these records will be of interest not only to historians and military experts, but to all those who have lived through the tragic and dramatic years of the Second World War.

I

The most lively and detailed description of the daily conferences on the military situation is contained in the book of memoirs of an eyewitness, a young German officer named Gerhard Boldt. After long service at the front, he had been called back and assigned to the Army General Staff during the last winter of the war, and in February 1945 Guderian, who was then Chief of the Army General Staff, took him along with him to one of the conferences. By then the German armies, in the East as well as in the West, had been forced back over the German frontiers, and Hitler's headquarters were in Berlin, so that the conferences took place in the New Chancellery.

In earlier times, this building had been a kind of Nazi show place, the center of ostentatious displays intended to impress foreign statesmen with the extent of German power. At the time of Boldt's visit these glories had departed. The rigors of Allied bombing had reduced much of it to rubble and only that part which contained Hitler's personal quarters was still intact. In order to reach the wing in which Hitler was living the officers had to walk through a number of dark corridors and side rooms, because the direct route was impassable. At each passage SS Guards were stationed and controlled the legitimation papers of the officers. When they entered the room before Hitler's study, another still more rigid control by a number of SS officers and SS Guards armed with automatic pistols took place. Guderian and his companions had to hand over their arms and to open their briefcases, which were thoroughly examined to see whether they contained weapons or explosives—such measures having been introduced as routine after the attempt on Hitler's life on 20 July 1944, when Count Stauffenberg had taken a time bomb to one of the conferences in his briefcase. The SS men did not go as far as to make a bodily inspection, but their

eyes wandered carefully and searchingly up and down the
tightly fitting uniforms of the General Staff officers.

The door leading from this antechamber to Hitler's study
again was protected by three heavily armed SS officers. After
a report had been received that Hitler's study was empty, the
General Staff officers were permitted to enter. Hitler's study
was a hall rather than a room. The long wall opposite the
door of the antechamber was broken by a large number of
tall but narrow windows, and by a glass door leading into the
garden of the Chancellery. Along the two sidewalls on the
right and left a few tables with heavy leather-upholstered
chairs were placed, but in comparison to its large size the
furniture of the room was sparse. The whole area was dominated by a writing desk and chair, heavy pieces of furniture
which stood near the middle of the wall opening on the
garden.

On the occasion described by Boldt, the officers stepped to
the large desk and placed on it a number of maps, one above
another, the one at the top showing the section of the front
which Guderian intended to discuss at the beginning of his
report. They then returned to the antechamber, which had in
the interval filled up. Besides the representatives of the various branches of the Armed Forces who were the regular
participants in these conferences, a number of Nazi bigwigs
like Goering were present. They were making use of the
well-furnished buffet which had been placed in this room,
eating sandwiches and drinking coffee or cognac. After some
time, Hitler's chief adjutant appeared and announced that the
Leader was ready for the conference.

The officials assembled in the antechamber formed a line
in accordance with their military rank and filed into Hitler's
study. The Leader received them standing in the middle of
the room and greeted each one with a handshake. Then he
sat down at his writing desk in front of the maps. It had been
decided that a report on 'the situation in the West,' i.e. on the
latest developments along the Western and Southern fronts,
should be taken up first. Since direction of these operations
was in the hands of the Armed Forces High Command
(OKW), it was the function of Jodl, who was chief of
operations in the OKW, to present this report. To Boldt, Jodl

appeared as a virtuoso in adjusting his performance to
Hitler's moods. He knew that Hitler disliked it if anyone
talked loudly in his presence, so he reported quietly and in a
subdued voice. In February 1945, after the loss of the Battle
of the Bulge, the outlook for the Germans on the Western
front was not auspicious, and Jodl had to apply all his
ingenuity to keep Hitler in a good mood; he slid quickly over
unpleasant facts like withdrawals in Italy, and emphasized
insignificant successes like the capture of two prisoners of
war by a patrol of four men. With the exception of Goering,
who threw in a few words, Jodl was hardly interrupted, but a
few joking words by Hitler after Jodl had finished showed
that he had succeeded in satisfying the Fuehrer.

The German troops on the Russian front were under
control of the Army General Staff; the next report, on the
situation in the East, therefore, was presented by Guderian,
the Army Chief of Staff. He lacked Jodl's ingratiating manner and spoke without flourishes, concisely and to the point.
Hitler listened to Jodl's and Guderian's reports, sitting at his
desk and studying the maps to which the speakers frequently
referred. After the completion of these reports, which represented the most important business of the conference, the
participants changed places and moved around more freely.
While the succeeding report, on the struggle in the air, was
being given, Goering, the Commander-in-Chief of the Air
Force, and his Chief of Staff placed themselves close to
Hitler's desk and listened attentively to what was said by the
representative of the Air Force. The officers of the Army
General Staff and of the Armed Forces High Command
moved into the background and talked among themselves in
low voices. Guderian got involved in a lively discussion with
Doenitz, the Commander-in-Chief of the Navy. When the Air
Force report had been finished, the Chief of Staff of the
Navy gave the report on the naval situation, and it was now
Doenitz's turn to take his stand directly in front of Hitler on
the other side of his desk.

With this naval report, the regular routine of the meeting
was completed; the question that remained was whether any
general issue had arisen which needed to be discussed and
decided. Now emerged what had been the object of the

dialogue between Doenitz and Guderian, because Doenitz asked for Hitler's decision concerning the withdrawal of the German troops in Courland for which a co-operation of land and sea forces was necessary. But the expected discussion did not materialize. Hitler rejected Doenitz' proposal rather brusquely; he said that such an operation would result in too heavy losses of material and would have undesirable political repercussions, particularly in Sweden. He made one concession, however, namely that he would consider the withdrawal by sea of one division, but he cut all further discussion short by closing the conference.

While Bormann alone remained with Hitler, the others now filed back into the antechamber. There the various adjutants began to telephone. The higher officers and officials sat down and continued the discussion of the military situation, smoking, drinking, and again enjoying the refreshments displayed on the buffet. It had been more than three hours since the General Staff representatives entered the Chancellery, but another half hour had passed before this discussion broke up and the officers, after passing again through endless corridors, stood once more on the pitch dark streets of the city in ruins.

Boldt's account should not be considered as entirely typical of all of the conferences the records of which are published in the following pages. Some of the meetings covered were not regular daily conferences but special meetings with individual army commanders, convoked to decide on a particular urgent issue. Furthermore, it will be recalled that before the winter of 1944/5 Hitler's headquarters was not in Berlin but on the Eastern front, in Vinnitsa and Rastenburg. In the conference described by Boldt an unusually large number of high Nazi dignitaries residing in Berlin could be present, while previously the participation of such party dignitaries had been an exception; although it appears that whenever any of them was visiting Hitler's headquarters he received an invitation to attend. When a foreign dignitary was present, the conferences sometimes degenerated into a completely unreal show for his benefit; in some cases even inaccurate maps were produced. Among themselves the German officers called this a 'show-off session' (*Schaulage*). Nevertheless, in general features Boldt's[1] picture is accurate, and the ːedure he describes was usually followed.

ːeitel and Jodl, the two key figures in the Armed Forces High Command, were regular participants. They were present in a double capacity: as Hitler's chief military advisers, because the Armed Forces High Command, after its formation in 1938, was his personal military cabinet, and as commanders of the operations of the Western front, which were controlled directly by the Armed Forces High Command. Consequently Jodl himself generally reported on the situation in the West and only on rare occasions did he relinquish this task to his deputy, Warlimont. In addition to these chief figures of the Armed Forces High Command, representatives of the staffs of the three armed forces—Army, Navy, and Air Force—were always present in order to report on events in their respective fields. Air Force and Navy were usually represented by high staff officers, although on some occasions their chiefs of staff themselves were in attendance. In the case of the Army, the Chief of Staff—first Zietzler, then Guderian—was always present: his special duty was the report on events on the Eastern front, since the Eastern front was controlled by the Army General Staff. Each of these high staff officers was accompanied by one or more adjutants. Moreover Hitler himself had personal adjutants from each of the branches of the Armed Forces—Army, Navy, Air Force, SA, and SS—and these men too attended the conferences. Another regular participant was the representative of the Foreign Office at Hitler's headquarters—Ambassador Hewel. Finally, if special questions of supply or equipment were scheduled for discussion, officials of the agencies in charge of these questions—of the staff of the Home Army, of the Ministry of Armaments and War Production—attended. Thus, it must be assumed that a group of nearly 20 persons were generally present at Hitler's daily military conferences.

This is of importance for the understanding of the text of

---

[1] Brief statements on the procedure of the 'situation conferences' were also given by Jodl, Wagner, and Winter at the Nuremberg Trial; see *The Trial of the Major War Criminals,* vol. XV, p. 296, vol. XIII, p. 464, vol. XV, p. 605.

the minutes, as they are handed down to us. They are frequently marked by sudden and apparently irrelevant remarks, comments that refer to topics previously debated but long since passed by in the discussion. Occasionally we even find single sentences that have no apparent relation to anything that has been discussed. If we keep in mind the large number of participants at these conferences, the tendency of the whole group to break into sub-groups and to conduct separate discussions, the constant coming and going, and the frequent arrival of new reports and telephone messages—and if we also recall the inevitable strain upon the official stenographers and the speed at which they were forced to work in order to make a complete record of discussions—the lack of consistency in the text becomes understandable. It would be very easy, for instance, for a stenographer who was attempting to follow the main discussion at Hitler's desk, to overhear and to incorporate in his record a remark made in the background.

The description given by Boldt also clarifies the manner of organization of these conferences. They were divided into two parts: the first part contained the reports on the daily military occurrences, presented by the representatives of the Navy, Air Force, and Army—of the Army divided into two parts, one on the Eastern and one on the Western front. No set rule regarding the sequence of these reports existed. Apparently the order depended on circumstances and Hitler's personal decision. The second part of the conferences was devoted to a more general discussion, involving far-reaching strategical decisions, or questions of supply and equipment, or political problems bearing on strategy.

The following selections from the surviving records draw their bulk from the second parts of the conferences. The early parts of the protocols are reproduced only in a few instances—more or less as samples. This is not meant to imply that those parts of the conferences in which the daily progress reports were presented are not extremely interesting and valuable, particularly to the military historian: if they were complete they would present a detailed documentation of the German evaluation of the changing military picture and of Hitler's conduct of the war. But because out of something like 200,000 pages only 800 have been preserved, and because these pages are frequently preserved only in fragmentary form, the value of these parts of the protocols is considerably decreased. Since usually not more than one day of the conferences in an entire month is preserved, and this frequently in mutilated form, we do not get more than isolated glimpses. Because the daily character of these conferences brought it about that the reports and discussions referred frequently to matters mentioned in previous meetings, it is not uncommon to come upon passages that are meaningless because they are separated from their contents. Moreover, it should be remembered that, in making their reports, the officers constantly refer to maps spread out on Hitler's desk; they speak of 'above' and 'below,' 'to the right' and 'to the left'; without knowing what they are pointing out on the map, it is very difficult, and frequently quite impossible, to understand what they are talking about and what is the bearing of the discussions.

The second parts of the protocols, however, do not suffer much from such limitations. Since single topics of a more general character are discussed here, these accounts are more or less self-contained; and when their state of preservation is relatively satisfactory, the main lines of the discussion and the points in which Hitler was particularly interested emerge clearly. Moreover, while in the initial parts of the conferences, it was usually the reporting officers who were the main speakers, it was Hitler himself who held the center of the stage in the second. Thus, because of the incomplete state of preservation of these protocols, their value for us is somewhat different from what might have been expected; they throw less light on the details of the German military conduct of the war than on Hitler's approach to the problems of war and on his general political philosophy. With regard to these their value is unique. We receive his views not in the broken or reflected light of witnesses, but precisely in the form in which he expressed them—the very words he spoke.

It is clear that, because only a small portion of the records has been preserved, and because the surviving parts are frequently very badly preserved, it would make no sense to publish a translation of the entire material. What is presented

here is a selection of those parts which seemed particularly
revealing with regard to the German conduct of war and
Hitler's war leadership. From what has been said before, it
should be evident that most of the published material comes
from the second parts of the conferences, although a few
particularly interesting records of the first parts are also
included, so that the reader will be able to get an impression
of the entire procedure at Hitler's daily military conferences.

II

It would be going too far to
claim that a study of these documents will solve the enigma,
which, despite all revaluations and interpretations, the rise
and fall of Hitler still presents. Yet it can hardly be ques-
tioned that these reocrds will have to be carefully weighed in
any attempt to evaluate his military leadership or to explain
his hold over the German people, and it may be appropriate
to point out some aspects of these problems on which they
shed new light.

Hitler's relation to his generals—the question whether his
active participation in the conduct of the war was of advantage or disadvantage for Germany, and whether the outcome
of the war would have been less disastrous for Germany if
the campaigns had been conducted entirely by the professionals in accordance with the traditions of the Prussian General
Staff—has always been regarded as a crucial issue in judging
Hitler's war leadership. Since most of the Nazi leaders have
perished but many of the generals have survived, the thesis of
the professional officers that all the defeats have to be
ascribed to Hitler and all the success to the professionals is
strongly represented in interviews and interrogations and has
prevailed in many books dealing with the events on 'the other
side of the hill.' Typical is the book recently published by
Halder, former chief of the German Army General Staff, on
Hitler as War Lord. In a somewhat changed form, this repre-
sents a revival of the stab-in-the-back legend. It is therefore
of great importance to have, even if only in a spotty and fragmentary form, Hitler's case in his own words. It should be
noted immediately, however, that, with regard to this problem,

the value of these records has limitations. They begin in
December 1942, at a time when the last stage had been
reached in the long and rather varied development of Hitler's
relationship to the generals. For many years—indeed, since
the end of the First World War when he had begun his political career as a propaganda agent for the Reichswehr in Munich—Hitler had been very anxious to appear as an obedient
servant of military interests; and the Reichswehr generals had
considered him as a useful instrument to reawaken the military spirit of the German people and to promote the cause of
rearmament. Even after Hitler came to power this relation
remained fundamentally unchanged for quite a while, although
it is likely that Hitler resented the patronizing attitude of the
generals. The great turning point came in 1938 with the
dismissal of the Reichswehrminister Blomberg and Chief of
the Army Fritsch, and with the abolition of the post of
Reichswehrminister and the creation of the Armed Forces
High Command under Keitel as Hitler's deputy. The significance of these events lies in the fact that through them Hitler
asserted his paramount authority over the military.

But even after 1938, Hitler's authority over the army was
not undisputed; the relationship was rather that of an uneasy
equilibrium. The Army Chiefs of Staff, first Beck and later
Halder, represented the old Reichswehr tradition, which
brooked no political interference in military questions; and
they were able to assert themselves at various crucial moments, as in the decision to arrive at an understanding with
Russia in order to avoid a two-front war, or the decision to
postpone until 1940 the attack upon France, which Hitler
had originally planned for the fall of 1939. The decisive
change that made Hitler really supreme over military affairs
came only during the war, and—strangely enough—not
through German military successes, but as a result of the
relative failure of the first summer campaign against Russia
in 1941. When winter was approaching the generals believed
it necessary to make a large withdrawal of the German
armies to the line from which the advance had started.
Hitler, on the other hand, maintained that the German armies must make a stand and defend the positions which they
had attained. In the end Hitler prevailed, and even his most

bitter critics were obliged to acknowledge that his decision was probably correct. For the German armies proved able to hold the advanced positions, and it remains on open question whether the withdrawal which the generals had advocated might not have given the Russians the opportunity of transforming the German retreat into a military catastrophe. From this time on Hitler was convinced that his grasp even of purely military and strategical questions was far superior to that of the generals; he no longer felt any hesitation in overruling them and in dismissing them if they objected to his decisions. In December 1941 Brauchitsch was removed and Hitler himself took over the direct field command of the German armies. In the following fall Halder, the Army Chief of Staff, followed Brauchitsch into retirement because he had insisted on the withdrawal of the German armies from Stalingrad. With the removal of these two men the two chief representatives of traditional military thinking at Hitler's headquarters were eliminated.

It may be noted here in passing that we owe the existence of the stenographic records of the daily military conferences to the clash between Hitler and Halder. Because of a dispute between the two men about what had really been decided at one of the conferences, stenographers were installed in the conference room and charged to take down every word that was spoken. The first month from which such a record of Hitler's daily conferences has been preserved is December 1942, and by that time the struggle between the Fuehrer and the generals had ended with Hitler having arrogated to himself the entire direction of the war and having surrounded himself with men who believed in his military genius. Thus the two chiefs of the Army General Staff who appear in these documents—Zeitzler and Guderian—cannot be regarded as representing the typical Prussian General Staff outlook in contrast to Hitler's, and we do not find in the conference records any clear representation of the traditional Prussian Military point of view. It is known that in the course of time Zeitzler lost his initial enthusiasm for Hitler's military genius, and indications of this fact can be found in the records. In the conference after the fall of Stalingrad he appears as a subservient 'yes-man,' while later in the summer of 1943 in

the conference with Kluge and particularly in the conference
of December 1944, in which Manstein's suggestion of a
withdrawal of the southern wing of the Russian front is
debated, he is inclined to defend the view of the army group
commanders as against Hitler. But he does not go beyond
trying to arouse Hitler's understanding of the view of the
army commanders. He acts as a kind of buffer or mediator,
but he does not stand out as the clear representative of a
different school of military thinking. Thus for the most part
the records show Hitler surrounded by his own subservient
creatures. But if we do not get a clear clash of contrasting
points of view, we are compensated by seeing Hitler revealing his outlook on military problems frankly and without
restraint.

In many respects these documents provide a striking illus-
tration of the justice of the accusations the generals have made
against Hitler's conduct of the war. He left hardly any freedom
to his field commanders and tried to keep even the smallest
details in his own hands. This tendency became gradually
stronger. Although he always kept an over-all check on movements, at the end not even the smallest unit was permitted to
be moved without Hitler's express agreement.

Secondly, the documents confirm the criticism that Hitler's
first reaction to any suggestion of a withdrawal was invari-
ably to suspect that it was motivated by lack of courage, and
that his most usual attitude toward such proposals was to
reject them offhand. Finally, it may be observed that, although hardly any direct opposition to Hitler's strategic views
was expressed, there was a substratum of tension between
him and the professional officers. This becomes evident if one
compares the freedom of discussion that existed when one of
Hitler's favorites like Rommel was around, with the cool
correctness in conferences with men like Kluge or Guderian.

Despite such confirmation of some of the chief accusations
that have been made against Hitler, these records make his
attitude more comprehensible than the criticism of the professionals allows it to be. In general terms, the military thesis
is that Hitler acted entirely by intuition, that he was inacces-
sible to rational considerations and did not brook contradiction. It cannot be said that this impression is born out by

these documents. In those conferences in which a serious
strategical problem was considered—as in that with Kluge in
the summer of 1943 or in the conference on the necessity of
a retreat in the East in December 1944—Hitler appears to
weigh at great length all the different aspects of the problem
and only after such rational consideration to arrive at a
definite decision. An example may be cited to demonstrate
that the professional officers frequently seemed more intran-
sigent than Hitler—that they were unable or unwilling to
grasp the logic of views contradictory to their own. Boldt,
who may be taken as a representative of the traditional point
of view of the General Staff officer, reports that Guderian
suggested that Manstein, who had been dismissed after the
collapse of the southern wing of the German Eastern front in
the spring of 1944, should be re-employed, and that Hitler
rejected this suggestion brusquely, more or less because of
personal pique against an unsuccessful general. This question
is discussed in the conference records, but the text indicates
that Hitler offered a fairly convincing argument in support of
his position, namely that in the desperate situation in which
Germany was involved in 1945 it was necessary to scrape
together the last reserves of manpower and supplies, and that
people like former free corps commanders who had experience in improvisation would be more useful than a general
who was trained to operate with large numbers of fully
supplied and equipped divisions. Thus, in reading Hitler's case
as it emerges from the records, it would appear that it is an
oversimplification to view the contrast between him and the
generals as one between professionals who act on the basis of
rational considerations and a madman acting on the basis of
intuition. The conflict arose rather from a fundamental difference of thinking. It was the contrast between professionals
who excluded all but military and strategic considerations
and the non-professional who viewed military considerations
only as part of a more general picture, between the perfect
exponents of a great tradition of military thought and a man
who, despite grudging acknowledgment of the values of this
tradition, did not consider it adequate in the emergencies of
modern war.

What Hitler found lacking in the professionals' approach

to war emerges clearly from the conference records. He considered three aspects of modern war as of decisive importance. One is morale. He talks about few things so frequently as about his own experiences as a common soldier in the First World War, and he derives from these personal experiences many of his views of what the soldiers need, what good leadership means, and what a soldier is able to achieve under good leadership. Secondly, Hitler places great emphasis on making full use of modern techniques. It has been previously reported that he was not only deeply interested in new weapons but that he had astonishing knowledge of the details of the processes that went into their making. The conference records confirm these reports. Hitler also appears as much concerned with the problem of the extent to which modern techniques had transformed the general character of war; it is interesting to read his argument why it is necessary to maintain advanced lines in Russia; in the age of tanks and airplanes he regards a country without space as lost. The third factor is politics. When questions like the retreat on the southern wing of the Russian front are discussed, political considerations such as repercussions on Turkey or Rumania weighed most heavily with him. Emphasis on such factors as these, or at least a different evaluation of their importance, formed the chief dividing line between Hitler and the generals.

In stressing the fact that Hitler's opinions are based on more than mere intuition, on a definite concept of modern war, it is not intended to imply that he was always right or that his concept was clearly superior to that of the professionals. When, shortly after his capture, Halder was asked for his views on Hitler's military leadership, he expressed an opinion that, though very much in contradiction to his recent book, must probably be considered as a much more balanced and penetrating evaluation. He said that Hitler's gifts for technical details and for over-all strategy were remarkable, but that he lacked the capacity of operational thinking, which has to combine these two approaches in order to give them practical meaning. Though formulated in purely military terms, this evaluation jibes to a large extent with what emerges from these records: namely the division of Hitler's

interest between very general issues, like the bearing of
politics and morale on war, and minute details of equipment
and supply.

Naturally Hitler was most successful when his ideas were
offset and balanced by those of the professionals, as in the
first years of the war. When this counterweight was removed,
as from the fall of 1942 onward, this became a handicap
instead of an advantage. The conferences indicate that until
March 1945, Hitler believed in a successful outcome of the
war. This belief was based partly on the expected effects of
the new technical weapons, namely jet planes, and partly on
political considerations, namely the necessity of a collapse of
co-operation between East and West. Certainly this belief
was based on a great amount of self-deception, of psychological unwillingness to face the facts; but it was fortified by his
customary emphasis on the necessity of recognizing the importance of the political factor; and because he had met such
obstinate opposition to this political view, it had gained in his
mind a quite exaggerated importance. He was unable to
realize that, effective as such an approach had been while the
military situation was favorable, a situation had arisen in
which it was no longer sound.

In calling attention to the fundamental conceptions that
determined Hitler's ideas on the conduct of war and to his
differences with the generals, it is not intended to minimize or
deny the strange nature of his psychology. His differences with
the generals would have been less important, and probably
less dangerous for the German conduct of war, if he had not
upheld his views with the obstinacy of an *idée fixe*, he
appears to have been obsessed by them. The abnormal character of the working of his mind emerges with devastating
clarity. For many, this psychological aspect—and the light
these frank revelations of his psychology throw on the reasons for his power over other men—will constitute the chief
interest of these documents. There is no doubt that these
conferences are entirely dominated by the personality of
Hitler; in reading the protocols one seems to get an almost
physical feeling of an unhealthy and unpleasant atmosphere.
In translating them one of the greatest difficulties—and one
which I am afraid has not been met with complete success—

was to indicate the differences between Hitler's language and that of the other participants. Hitler's sentences are badly constructed, he is very repetitive, his language is extremely vulgar. The impression of vulgarity is a penetrating and pervading one.

Next to vulgarity, meanness appears as one of the outstanding features of Hitler's character. A most striking example of this is shown on the occasion when Kluge was vehemently pleading that his forces should not be denuded of tanks in favor of other sections of the front. In his argument he inadvertently used the term 'junk' to indicate that the tanks presently under his control were in bad condition. Hitler immediately seized upon this incautious utterance to invalidate the whole of Kluge's argument, intimating that, since Kluge considered his tanks valueless, he would not suffer from their loss. This streak of meanness in Hitler's character shows itself also in petty insistence upon being right in all circumstances, even in the smallest details. Such dogmatism is all the more incongruous in view of the fact that it was clearly not supported by adequate factual knowledge. It is almost incredible that a man responsible for the fate of a whole nation could be so fundamentally misinformed about political events and forces as Hitler appears to have been—to take only one example—in his remarks about the United States, where he talks of the non-existence of a farming population, the possibility of an arraignment of Roosevelt before the Supreme Court, and the factors that determined the entry of the United States into the war.

Accidental information, gained from a motion picture like the *Grapes of Wrath* or from a chance remark by a visitor, like that supposedly by the Duke of Windsor—as long as it corresponded to his bias and preconceptions—was readily accepted as conclusive proof of an elaborate theory. It should be noted, however, that Hitler's information about political events and forces was extremely uneven. When he talks about countries and situations with which he was personally acquainted—Germany, Italy, or even France—his remarks are frequently interesting and penetrating. But whether he had personal knowledge of the topic discussed or not, his statements are always delivered in an equally definite and

apodictic way. Yet even these features—and the always low
moral and frequently low intellectual level of his thinking—
do not fully explain the somewhat morbid atmosphere that
dominated the conferences. It would seem that the records
contain material that demands the diagnosis of a trained
psychiatrist, for even the layman is struck by the strange
attraction that talking about deaths and sacrifices seems to
have had for Hitler. His delight in launching forth on lengthy
descriptions of the horrors of war; the high emotional pitch
to which he is able to raise himself at the slightest provoca-
tion, and the seemingly endless stream of speeches leave an
impression of strangeness and abnormality.

The insight into Hitler's psychology which these records
afford may seem to make an understanding of his rise to
power and his hold over the German people still more
difficult to attain. This is not quite correct, however. For if
we examine his utterances in regard to his general philosophy, we find—beside the usual tenets of Nazi philosophy,
namely of the superiority of the German race, of the evilness
of the Jews, et cetera—a few more general basic assumptions
that may throw some light on the mainsprings of his power.
One basic assumption is that of the purely egoistic character
of man, and the complementary idea that man can be led by
playing upon his egoistic instincts. The most striking and
callous instance of this is perhaps his statement after Kluge's
suicide: that he was particularly shocked by this treason, as
he had believed Kluge's personal loyalty secured by the
presentation to him of a large estate. On the other hand,
Hitler assumes that such materialistic egoism of men can be
overcome only by a high emotionalism, by the imposition of
an hypnotic will, not by rational persuasion. Hitler frequently
recalls incidents from the time when the Nazis were strug-
gling for power and when in his opinion only his unbreakable
will kept the Party together and led it to triumph over
seemingly hopeless odds. This period was—the fact emerges
clearly from the conferences—Hitler's decisive political training school and formed his entire outlook about the operation
of political forces.

Within the framework of such simple and primitive views
about the forces determining men's actions, utter brutality

was the best and strongest weapon. Within such framework there was no room for the intertwining of individual freedom and necessary order, of interests and moral obligations, of cultural tradition and need for social changes—the fabric of which modern Western society has been formed. But because these relationships have become increasingly complicated in modern society, the man who abandoned the weaving of these strands into a meaningful whole and simply cut the Gordian knot seemed to offer a solution of otherwise insoluble problems. Hitler's strength lay in the fact that he was indeed what one of the greatest historians has declared to be the most deadly danger of modern civilization—'a terrible simplifier.'

PARTICIPANTS

ASSMANN
  Kapitän zur See
  Navy adjutant at Hitler's headquarters
BELOW, NICOLAUS VON
  Oberst
  Air Force Adjutant at Hitler's headquarters
  Present during the last days in Hitler's Berlin bunker
BODENSCHATZ, KARL HEINRICH
  General der Luftwaffe
  Liaison Officer between the Commander-in-Chief, Air
    Force, and Hitler's headquarters
  Wounded in the explosion at Hitler's headquarters on 20
    July 1944
BORGMANN
  Oberstleutnant
  Army Adjutant at Hitler's headquarters
BRAUCHITSCH, BERND VON
  Oberst
  Chief-Adjutant to Goering
BREUER
  Generalleutnant
  Staff Officer, Army Group 'E,' Aegean area
BRUDERMUELLER
  Major
  Staff Officer, Armed Forces High Command (OKW)
BUECHS, HERBERT
  Major
  Second Adjutant to Jodl
BUHLE, WALTER
  General der Infanterie

Section chief, Organization Division, in Army General Staff (OKH)

Wounded in the explosion at Hitler's headquarters on 20 July 1944

BURGDORF, WILHELM

General der Infanterie

First Deputy Chief, later Chief (1944), Army Personnel Office, Chief Adjutant of the Armed Forces with Hitler

CHRISTIAN, ECKARD

Oberstleutnant, later General der Luftwaffe

Operations Branch, General Staff Air Force, later its Chief

Present during the last days in Hitler's Berlin bunker. Married Hitler's secretary

DARGES, FRITZ

SS-Obersturmbannfuehrer

SS Adjutant to Hitler, 1943

Later commanded 5th SS Division

DOENITZ, KARL

Grossadmiral

Commander-in-Chief, Navy, from 1943

Succeeded Hitler as head of the German state in 1945

ENGEL, GERHARDT

Oberstleutnant

Army Adjutant to Hitler, 1937-44

FEGELEIN, HERMANN

SS-Gruppenfuehrer

SS representative at Hitler's headquarters

Eva Braun's brother-in-law, present in Hitler's bunker during the siege of Berlin

Executed by Hitler's order in the Chancellery garden after trying to escape

FREYTAG-LORINGHOVEN, FREIHERR VON

Major

Adjutant to Krebs

Present in Hitler's Berlin bunker up to the end of April 1945

GOEHLER

SS-Sturmbannfuehrer

GOERING, HERMANN
Reichsmarschall
Participated in these conferences in the capacity of Commander-in-Chief, Air Force

GUDERIAN, HEINZ
Generaloberst
Commanded 2nd Panzer Army in Russia until the end of 1944
Inspector General of Panzer Troops
Chief of Army General Staff (OKH), 1944-5

GUENSCHE
SS-Hauptsturmfuehrer
Hitler's SS Adjutant
Present in Hitler's Berlin bunker during the last days, officiated at Hitler's cremation, and is believed to have committed suicide to avoid capture by Russian troops

HEUSINGER, ADOLF
Generalleutnant
Chief of Operations Section, Army General Staff (OKH)
Wounded in the explosion in Hitler's headquarters on 20 July 1944

HEWEL, WALTER
Ambassador
Representative of the Foreign Office at Hitler's headquarters
Present at Hitler's cremation, probably committed suicide

HIMMLER, HEINRICH
Reichsfuehrer SS
Reichsminister of the Interior
Chief of Replacement Army
Commanded Army Group 'Vistula,' 1945

JESCHONNEK, HANS
General der Luftwaffe
Chief of Staff, Air Force, 1942-3

JODL, ALFRED
Generaloberst
Chief of Operations Staff, Armed Forces High Command (OKW)

JOHANNMEIER, WILLI
   Major
   Member of Army Personnel Office
   Left Hitler's Berlin bunker just before Hitler's death, bearing a copy of Hitler's will

JOHN VON FREYEND
   Major
   Adjutant to Keitel

JUNGE
   Hauptmann
   Sent to Rome on 26 July 1943 with instructions for Kesselring and Ruge regarding the developments in Italy

KEITEL, WILHELM
   Generalfeldmarschall
   Chief of the Armed Forces High Command (OKW)

KLUGE, GUENTHER VON
   Generalfeldmarschall
   Commanded Army Group 'Center' in Russia, 1943
   Commander-in-Chief, West, July-August 1944
   Committed suicide after being relieved of his command because of his part in the conspiracy of 20 July 1944

KOLLER, KARL
   General der Luftwaffe
   Chief of Staff, Air Force, 1945

KRANCKE
   Vizeadmiral
   In charge of naval defenses in western Europe

KREBS, HANS
   General
   Last Chief of Army General Staff (OKH), 1945

KUECHLER, GEORG VON
   Generalfeldmarschall
   Commanded Army Group 'North' in Russia

LANGEMANN
   Oberstleutnant

LOEHR, ALEXANDER
   Generaloberst
   Commanded 12th Army, later Army Group 'E' in the Aegean area

MAIZIÈRE
 Oberstleutnant
 Member of Army General Staff (OKH)
NEURATH, CONSTANTIN ALEXANDER VON
 SS-Sonderfuehrer
 Member of German Diplomatic Corps in Rome
 On special mission to North Africa and Italy in 1943
 Son of former Foreign Minister
PUTTKAMER, K. J. VON
 Kapitän zur See
 Navy Adjutant at Hitler's headquarters
ROMMEL, ERWIN
 Generalfeldmarschall
 Commanded 'Afrikakorps' until 1943
 Charged with the preparation of invasion defenses
  throughout occupied Europe
 Commanded an army group in northern Italy
 Commanded Army Group 'B' in France, 1944
 Was forced to commit suicide, October 1944
SCHERFF, WALTER
 Oberst
 Official historian of the German Army
SCHMUNDT, RUDOLF
 Generalleutnant
 Chief of Army Personnel Office
 Killed in the explosion at Hitler's headquarters on 20 July
  1944
SCHUSTER
 Metereologist
SPEER, ALBERT
 Minister of Armaments and War Production
SUENDERMANN, HELLMUT
 Representative of the Reich Press Chief at Hitler's head-
  quarters
VOSS, HANS
 Vizeadmiral
 Liaison officer between the Commander-in-Chief, Navy,
  and Hitler's headquarters
 Present in Hitler's Berlin bunker at Hitler's death
 Subsequently captured by Russian troops

WAIZENEGGER, HEINZ
   Oberstleutnant
   Staff officer, Armed Forces High Command (OKW)

WARLIMONT, WALTER
   General der Artillerie
   Deputy Chief of Operations Staff, Armed Forces High
      Command (OKW) till November 1944

WESTPHAL, SIEGFRIED
   Generalleutnant
   Chief of Staff, Army Group 'C' in Italy, 1943-4
   Chief of Staff to Commander-in-Chief, West, 1944

WINTER, AUGUST
   Generalleutnant
   Successor to Warlimont as Deputy Chief of Operations
      Staff, Armed Forces High Command (OKW),
      November 1944

ZANDER, WILHELM
   SS-Standartenfuehrer
   Assistant to Martin Bormann, Chief of Nazi Party
      Chancellery
   Left Hitler's Berlin bunker just before Hitler's death, bear-
      ing copies of Hitler's will and wedding certificate

ZEITZLER, KURT
   Generaloberst
   Chief of Army General Staff, 1942-4
   Dismissed after 20 July 1944

I

NORTH AFRICA AND STALINGRAD

1 DECEMBER 1942

This conference lasted from
8.20 P.M. until 9.15 P.M.

Participants: HITLER,
BODENSCHATZ, BUHLE, JODL,
KEITEL, KRANCKE, AND SPEER

At the time of this meeting, the German military situation was undergoing a serious crisis. On the Eastern front, the Russian winter offensive had achieved its first great successes, the German attack in Stalingrad had not only been halted, but the Russian army had succeeded in breaking through into the rear of the German 6th Army on the north and south, effecting its complete encirclement. In addition the Russians had started offensives in the central sector of the Eastern front at Rzhev and Velikie Luki. In North Africa, the German 'Afrikakorps' had retired for more than 700 miles after the decisive defeat at El Alamein and was trying to take up defensive positions at El Agheila. The Anglo-American troops, which had landed in French North Africa, were pushing toward Tunis and Bizerte. The difficult situation was reflected in the change from Halder to Zeitzler as Chief of the Army General Staff. This was announced on 11 December, but had actually taken place two months earlier on 25 September, when Halder had urged the abandonment of the Stalingrad operation.

The meeting begins with Jodl's report on the situation on the Eastern front, this report is supplemented through information given by Zeitzler over the telephone. It is followed by a report on naval operations in the Black Sea, which prompts Hitler to express indignation about the inability of the German motor-torpedo boats to engage the Russian Black Sea Fleet.

41

JODL: Military Commander, France, reports: yesterday
fairly quiet. No visible change in attitude of the population. No incidents among the demobilized French soldiers.[1] A raid on a town hall in the department Seine-
Loire. The French police succeeded in capturing six armed
participants, all of whom belong to a terrorist group.

HITLER: Good. The police[2] is all right. We'll use the
police and work only with them. Himmler knows his police. He makes them use shady means, and gradually they
become dependent on him. This will become an alliance
with the police.
JODL: They make a very good impression.
HITLER: The police are hated more than anything else in
the country and seek support from a stronger authority
than their own government; that's us. It will come to a
point where the police will beg us not to leave the country.
JODL: The number of French workers recruited to work
in the Reich passed 200,000 a few days ago.[3]
HITLER: That's also increasing. First of all, these people
haven't got anything left; and in addition they tell themselves 'at least there isn't any more danger of war for us.'
They don't want war. Why should they? They all have the
feeling that no matter what may happen, the whole war
was madness.
JODL: May I add something more on the question of leadership in Africa:[4] of course that's a question of organization. This is a very touchy point with the Italians; before
long they will say 'Of course we must have full command

---

[1] After the Anglo-American landing in North Africa, the German
Army occupied 'Vichy France'; on 27 November, German troops had
entered the harbor of Toulon, but the French succeeded in scuttling
the warships anchored there. Hitler, explaining these actions in a letter
to Pétain, had also pronounced his intention of demobilizing the small
army which had been allowed France by the Armistice of 1940.
[2] Hitler means the French police.
[3] In exchange for the return of French prisoners-of-war, Frenchmen
were drafted to work in Germany.
[4] Jodl alludes to the question whether the creation of a unified command in Africa, comprising the Eastern (Libya) and Western (Tunisia)
fronts, had become necessary. Officially, Rommel had always operated
in Libya and Egypt under the Italian High Command.

in this theater of war.' Up to now they haven't raised this question.

HITLER: In the first place, at the moment we're handling the show. Secondly if we do start another offensive, you can be sure there will be no Italians in it.

JODL: That's also the reason why they never speak of the fact that we are quietly in command in that theater. They have never said a word about it.

HITLER: How can they? Since we have at least four of our motorized divisions there—another one is practically over there if one adds up the parachutists, et cetera—that makes five divisions, together with the two infantry divisions, that makes seven divisions. With seven divisions we're running the war alone anyway. They're not running it. From the point of view of supplies, it is also our show, although they do handle the crossings; but there again, we have contributed the shipping space, ever since we defeated the French; if we hadn't beaten the French we wouldn't even have the shipping space. When this business is cleaned up—

KRANCKE: —then we can give them Tunisia, and we'll take Algeria.

HITLER: Then they can put that completely under their administration.

BODENSCHATZ: Except for the anti-aircraft, which we'll have to handle ourselves.

KEITEL: —and the supplies. I ought to mention the anti-guerrilla operations again. An order about this came in yesterday.[5]

---

[5] The following discussion refers to anti-guerrilla operations in the eastern occupied territories which had been placed under the command of SS-Obergruppenfuehrer von dem Bach-Zelewski. In the Nuremberg Trial, Jodl made the following statement about this discussion: 'It was on 1 December 1942: As the Tribunal will remember, a directive in regard to combating the guerrillas was issued on 11 November by the Armed Forces Operations Staff. . . In that directive, which was issued on 11 November, I had written the sentence: "The burning down of villages as a reprisal is forbidden, because it necessarily only creates new partisans."—The draft of that instruction remained in the Fuehrer's hands for weeks. He always objected that this instruction would hamper the troops in ruthlessly combating the guerrillas. As at that time I had already issued that instruction and he still had not given his approval, I

HITLER: I consider a kind of introduction necessary: Fundamentally, and this has to be hammered into everyone's head, whatever leads to success is right in the conduct of anti-guerrilla operations. That's the point of departure. If someone does something not exactly in accordance with regulations, but achieves complete success, or if someone is faced by an emergency he can only deal with in the most brutal way, he's entitled to use any measure that promises success. The goal must be the annihilation of these gangs and the restoration of order. Otherwise we'll come to the same point as we did in domestic politics with the so-called Self-Defense Law.[6] This law had the final result that no policeman or soldier in Germany dared to use his weapon. Because that was such an elastic law, everyone had to ask himself: 'Should I be unlucky enough to kill the other fellow, I'll be in the hole. If he kills me, I'm also in the hole. How can I manage it to disable him without hurting him, and at the same time not be disabled myself?' That was the famous elastic clause of the Self-Defense Law through which it came to the point where the man under arms was always the fall-guy, whether he was a policeman

---

[6] Hitler probably refers to the decree of the Prussian Minister of the Interior of 11 July 1928, which established general rules for the use of fire arms by the police. Firing was permitted only if no other means could have the desired effect, and only in so far as it was necessary to achieve the desired effect. No firing on children was permitted.

---

became rather rude; and when he once more came with lengthy explanations of his fighting experience, his experience of fighting the Communists in Chemnitz, I said, in order to break the ice at last, "My Fuehrer, what people do in battle does not come into this instruction at all. As far as I am concerned, they can quarter them or they can hang them upside down." If I had known that the Russian gentlemen have so little sense of irony, I would have added, "and roast them on the spit." That is what I said and I added, "But in this instruction we are concerned with reprisals after the battle, and they must be prohibited." —Then there were roars of laughter from all the officers present, and also from the Fuehrer; and he gave me permission to issue that directive; and the testimony of a witness, General Buhle, who was present, will confirm that to you.' See The Trial of the Major War Criminals, vol. XV, p. 545, and, for Buhle's testimony, p. 558. But it must be added that, on 16 December 1942, Keitel issued a top-secret directive for 'The Combating of guerrillas,' in which it was stated that 'the troops have the right and the duty to use, in this struggle, any and unlimited means, even against women and children, if only conducive to success.' Ibid. vol. VII, p. 489.

or a soldier; it was always the same. The clearest example of this was the incident at Zabern.[7] But the police had the same thing over and over again. On the one hand there was the order, 'You must do such-and-such'; on the other the threat of breaking the Self-Defense Law. Therefore, I think we have to add an introduction: 'Despite everything else, it is the supreme duty to see to it that these gangs are wiped out. Therefore, everything which has helped to wipe out these gangs will ultimately be considered justified; conversely, everything which does not serve in the destruction of these guerrillas will be considered wrong.' That way, everybody has freedom of action. Otherwise, how could he help himself in many instances? What can they do if these swine take cover behind women and children? I myself saw that in Chemnitz, where the Red swine spat at us and held children in front of them while they were doing it. We were completely defenseless. God help us if we had touched those children.

It's the same thing with the fight against the guerrillas. If they shove women and children to the front, the officer or the sergeant must be able to fire regardless. The only thing that matters is fighting his way through and rubbing out the gang. The troops must have complete backing. One can give them general instructions; but in addition one has to back them completely, so that the poor devils won't have to think: 'Afterwards I'll be made responsible!'

What else would you do? The swine are in a house and barricade themselves in, and in the house there are also women and children. Can the man set fire to the house or not? If he does, the innocent will be burned too. There shouldn't be any question about it. He must set fire to it. One should not say: 'That's not his decision, that's up to his officer.' No, if the poor devil is standing there with six or seven men, what can he do? That was just the tragedy with the police—everything was up to the officer. When was a policeman ever backed up by his officer? The poor

[7] Hitler alludes to the famous incident of November 1913 in the Alsatian town of Saverne (Zabern), where the provocative behavior of a German officer led to demonstrations by the population in consequence of which martial law was declared.

devil was always left high and dry. That's why the French
police officials attach themselves to our German police;
because for the first time they are being backed up. That
has never happened to the French police before. When
there was shooting at those disturbances in Paris,[8] it cost
the French police officials their heads. They were called on
the carpet for it. On the one hand they had been ordered to
protect the Chamber and to break up the demonstrations.
How could they protect the Chamber, when the others
were advancing? Had the others advanced and had the
police failed to protect the Chamber, they would have
been punished for failure to act. Well, they did fire, and so
they were punished for firing.

One has to be incredibly careful in things like that, not to
put the blame on the little fellow. Also one has to picture
the mentality of the fighter. It is all very well for us at the
green table to say that reason must be the decisive factor.
'How can you be so unreasonable? Didn't you think about
it, man? Haven't you given it a thought?' The poor devil
can't think about it, he's fighting for his life, for his very
existence. And it is precisely the little guy, the little non-
com who has tried to fight his way through the mess, he
has shot into it and massacred so and so many women,
because he couldn't see any other way of getting through
the place.

JODL: It doesn't say anything about that here. They can do
what they want in battle; they may hang them, hang them
upside down or quarter them; about that there is nothing
here. The only limitation concerns reprisals after the battle, in areas where the gangs have been operating. And
that is a measure which even the Reichsfuehrer[9] regards
with caution because he says: 'I have got to be careful not
to increase the guerrilla areas and drive the whole male
population away.' Because such news travels from village
to village, and then two thousand more men whistle off

---

[8] Hitler alludes to the demonstrations of 6 February 1934 in Paris,
which resulted from the Stavisky scandal; a number of people were
killed or wounded, and the government resigned. The dismissal of the
Prefect of the Police Chiappe had preceded the riots and was rather
one of their causes than their consequence.

[9] Himmler, Reichsfuehrer of the SS.

into the guerrilla areas. Otherwise nothing is said about what is permitted and what is not. It only deals with experiences in reconnaisance and troop commitments.

HITLER: But in addition we must state positively that if they consider it necessary, in order to do their duty, to proceed with the strongest measures, they are absolutely in the right, and will be backed up under all circumstances later on.

JODL: It is meant more for the command level, because the SS has more experience in these matters anyway.

HITLER: They do have the greater experience. But just listen to what is said about the SS, because they have that experience. It's always said that they are brutal.

JODL: That's not true at all. They do it very skillfully; they do everything with sugarplums and the whip, as it's done everywhere else in the world.

HITLER: Well, the people forgive them for the sugarplums, but not for the whip.

KEITEL: All this doesn't matter much in the partisan country. We are glad that everyone co-operates so well now. Everything will be done together and placed under a uniform command. Bach-Zelewski did everything on his own initiative, using police as well as troops of the local division.

HITLER: That Bach-Zelewski is one of the cleverest persons. Even in the party I only used him for the most difficult things. When the Communist opposition in a locality seemed too strong to break down, I brought him there and he beat them into pulp.

The conference ends with a short discussion about tank production.

12 DECEMBER 1942

This conference lasted from
    12:45 P.M. until 3 P.M.

Participants: HITLER,
    BODENSCHATZ, BUHLE, CHRISTIAN,
    HEUSINGER, HEWEL, JODL, KRANCKE,
    WARLIMONT, AND ZEITZLER

The meeting begins with a report by Zeitzler about the Eastern front. A very long and detailed discussion takes place, in which single points—like the questionable reliability of allied troops (Italians, Rumanians, Georgians, Armenians)—are taken up at length. The discussion centers on the military situation at Velikie Luki and Stalingrad; although Hitler agrees with Zeitzler on the seriousness of the situation, he insists on the impossibility of retreat from Stalingrad, saying that this would involve sacrificing 'the whole meaning of the campaign' and that 'too much blood has been shed.' Then Jodl launches his report on the African theater. He is interrupted by Hitler.

HITLER: I've received another report saying that there is a
    retreat in progress here.[1]
JODL: Yes, that's right. There is no doubt that the enemy
    has begun his first major attack here, which he probably

[1] The following discussion refers to Rommel's retreat from the position before El Agheila, which the British 8th Army was preparing to attack both from the front and by a flanking movement from the south. Describing these events, Montgomery's chief of staff, Sir Francis De Guingand, states in his book *Operation Victory*, p. 221: 'In order to reduce our casualties to a minimum, a big artillery and bombing programme was laid on to start on 12 December, and this was to coincide with a policy of large-scale raids. These activities would also draw attention away from the out-flanking movement. The enemy must have thought this was the big attack, for on the 13th he began to withdraw.'

wants to continue on the 13th. Our air reconnaissance confirms that he had his air force ready, and that he had moved his bases up. He has his main fighter group, with 130 single-engined and 120 twin-engined planes in the area north of Agedabia, plus 100 single-engined and 40 twin-engined planes in the area between Sollum and Marina. In addition, the total number of intercepted radio messages indicates that his condition is just as it was before the El Alamein offensive, and he is now ready to attack here. The Air Chief Africa is also of the opinion that the English offensive aimed at Tripoli will commence within the next few days. Our own forces are weak in comparison as long as the main body is in Sicily. Essentially they are too far away from the final position.

HITLER: Who said that was the final position?

JODL: The Duce has given that order.

HITLER: The conference the Reichsmarshal had wasn't that clear.[2]

JODL: Rommel says the same thing in his telegram.

HITLER: What does he say?

JODL: He says: 'Troops in the area ... will be drawn back into the final position.' There is the word 'final.' So the over-all situation allowed him to count on that.

Now to continue: Although he repulsed all attacks yesterday, including those from the south, Rommel says that the attacks will doubtless be continued here today, and that he can't afford an engagement that would use up his fighting strength, particularly since the enemy attacks also from the south, though with weak forces. His fuel situation is such that he can't conduct offensive and mobile operations, but was just able to withdraw into this position. He has to stay here until the 15th, so that he will be mobile

[2] Goering, who alone possessed the military rank of Reichsmarschall, had been in Rome on 30 November for a conference with Mussolini at which, according to Ciano's *Diaries*, p. 550, he had promised to send three German Panzer divisions to Africa, and at which it was agreed that the final stand for the protection of Tripoli would be made not at El Agheila, but at Buerat. This is confirmed by the report of a conference of Goering with the Italian military leaders, given in Cavallero, *Comando Supremo*, p. 404-6. The Buerat position was taken by the British 8th Army on 15 January 1943.

again. Therefore he can't commit himself to anything.
Considering the fuel situation, that's understandable. If he
were mobile, if he could drive around the way he wants,
he could slip out of any encirclement.

HITLER: I really must say that that huge army of his must
have had fuel to come back here from the El Alamein.
They didn't do that on water. In all that time, they had
practically no fuel. If they had brought up the fuel instead
of going back for it, they could have operated out in front.
There's no doubt about that. Because it would have been
simpler to operate in front with a couple of divisions. In
the last analysis it is only the tanks and a little artillery.
They've covered 1500 kilometers, taking along household
goods and everything else they could get their hands on. Of
the men we lost there, it is certain that 50 per cent were
lost during the retreat, which means that the real losses up
front were probably extraordinarily low. There is no doubt
that probably failure to push through the first offensive
under the impact of the sinking of the 4,000-ton steamer
was wrong.[3] That's the impression Kesselring had, as well
as Ramcke who said: 'We can't understand why we didn't
get further, the English were in complete rout; all we
would have had to do was to drive on and to push in from
some flank.'

But I really think one shouldn't leave a man in a
position of such heavy responsibility too long. That gradually demoralizes his nerves. There is a difference, if one is
in the rear. There, of course, one keeps one's head. These
people can't stand the strain on their nerves. One should
really carry out the principle of not leaving a man in the
theater of war too long. That makes no sense. It's better to
relieve him. Then someone comes in fresh, who wants to

---

[3] The sinking of German supply ships played a decisive role in Rommel's failure to pierce the British position at El Alamein and in his
decision to abandon the offensive on 2 September 1942; for details see
Cavallero, *Comando Supremo*, especially pp. 319-20, where the importance of the sinking of the *Sant' Andrea* is stressed. See also Ciano's
Diaries, pp. 519-20. There, on p. 521, is the notice that Kesselring, then
chief of the German Air Forces based in Italy, went to Berlin to complain about Rommel's handling of this attack. Ramcke was commander
of the 2nd German Parachute Division.

earn his laurels and is relatively fresher. I am therefore
determined that, as soon as the first wave is passed, we
shall relieve a number of generals who are perfectly all
right; we'll simply order them—even a fieldmarshal—to
take a furlough so that they will return to the front
completely relaxed.

You've got to imagine the situation. He has always got
to spar around with all kinds of miserable elements out
there. So it's no wonder that after two years he loses his
nerve. . . Then things which to us in the rear don't appear
so terrible seem unbearable to him. Last winter we had
cases where people up front simply lost their nerve under
catastrophic weather conditions; they said, 'It's easy for
them in the rear to talk, they don't have to stay in this
weather.' That's right, too. But we should also guard
against exposing people constantly to the same conditions.
If I expose a high staff to three weeks of mortar fire, I
can't be surprised if they lose their nerve. That's the reason
for *Der Feldherrnhuegel*.[4] Except in case of final decisions, where the general has to seize the flag because
everything is at stake, he must be in the rear. You can't
command for any length of time surrounded by the roar of
battle.

One thing is certain: in this comparatively narrow
area[5] one person must be able to survey the whole battle
line. He doesn't even have the necessary communications;
he has to depend upon instinct. But if you do that for two
years, eventually your nerves go to pieces. That's the
Reichsmarshal's impression, too. He says that Rommel has
completely lost his nerve.

Add to that the tragic distractions with the Italians; the
eternal uncertainty. We are expecting that, too. I didn't
sleep last night; that's the feeling of uncertainty. If I had a
German front, it would still be possible that something
might happen, but I would have the feeling that it could be
made up again. At least a whole army wouldn't fall apart

---

[4] *Der Feldherrnhuegel* (The General's Hill), a well-known comedy by
Rhoda-Rhoda which lampoons generals who direct battles from a safe
hill in the rear.
[5] Of the North African theater of war.

in one day. The Russians have announced[6] the capture of
94,000 prisoners—Axis forces; they hardly captured any
Germans, just Rumanians. The first air-reconnaissance reports said that huge gray columns are moving over there—
apparently all prisoners—and others are coming back
again, so that one can't know whether they are Russians or
Rumanians. Once a unit has started to flee, the bonds of
law and order quickly disappear in the course of the flight
unless an iron discipline prevails. It's a thousand times
easier to storm forward with an army and gain victories,
than to bring back an army in an orderly condition after a
setback or a defeat. It was perhaps the greatest feat of
1914 that it was posible to bring back the German army
after the idiocy of the Marne business, to turn them
around again on a definite line and restore them to order.
That was perhaps one of the greatest feats. You can do
that only with superb, disciplined troops.

JODL: We succeeded in doing that with the German troops
here, too.

HITLER: We succeeded with the Germans, but not with the
Italians, and we won't succeed with the Italians, anywhere.
Therefore, if anybody breaks through down there, there
will be a catastrophe. If a man lives under this pressure
constantly, he'll gradually go to pieces.

JODL: We only had the Italian 8th Army on a small sector
of our front,[7] but his[8] whole front is Italian.

HITLER: Perhaps it would have been better to have recalled
him right away and to have sent down some other tough
guy with strict orders to hold.

JODL: I think one can't say anything against his measures
here. It's like asking a man who has been nourished on a
little bread and milk to participate in the Olympics. He
hasn't received anything in weeks. In the East they scream
if they are two trains short.

[6] Hitler refers to the special Soviet announcement of 12 December
that 'in the period 19 November to 11 December our troops captured
72,400 prisoners. In the same period 94,000 enemy officers and men
were killed in the Stalingrad area.'
[7] The Russians had driven through the sector held by the 8th Italian
Army near Stalingrad.
[8] He means Rommel's.

He has the intention—and this is forced upon him by the fuel situation—to operate step by step in order to gain time for the fortification of this line.[9] There were still parts of the XXI Corps here, which have now received orders to move in at this point. He is going to wait right here until the English have established a new line. They have to build a new line and bring up artillery. That will take a few days.

HITLER: Let's hope so.

JODL: Of course the English know that a large part of our forces has been detached to the rear. That may have been the reason why they attacked somewhat earlier here.

HITLER: How much of this huge German supply column is he putting into the line? Is that all heading for Tripoli?

JODL: No, on the contrary, six or seven days ago he reported that he had combed out all supply columns, as far as possible, and brought the men into the line.

HITLER: Because in a position like that, ten to twenty thousand Germans, shoved in between the Italians, might give some staying power; with the Italians alone it is impossible.

JODL: He also reports that all kinds of mining operations, especially on the Via Balbo,[10] have been and are being carried out intensively.

HITLER: The mining is very difficult because one can only do it behind oneself and on the retreat one doesn't have time, so the enemy sees every mine in the road.

JODL: No, also in front of the line. What he needs is an improvement in the gasoline situation, since he doesn't have freedom of movement. If the enemy succeeds in getting at him from the south, he's in a very difficult position. The lighter traffic out of the base at Sfax is heavier than before. Single lighters are not being reported.

HITLER: Up to now it hasn't been running at all.

JODL: Single lighters were always running. At any rate Kesselring felt greatly relieved this morning; he claimed

[9] Evidently the Buerat line.

[10] The Via Balbo is the coastal road in Italian North Africa, running along the coast from Tunisia to Egypt.

that since yesterday a great weight had been lifted from his mind with regard to the whole supply problem.

HITLER: There you have the two greatest extremes. Rommel has become the greatest pessimist and Kesselring a complete optimist. That's amazing progress.

KRANCKE: It can't just be lighters; we had seventy motor packets on the coast.

JODL: Naturally there are always small boats running there. Only up to now they have had nothing with which to complete the transport. That's changed only now, through the arrival of some units in Sousse and Sfax. Therefore the traffic is running, and Kesselring emphasizes again and again that in this situation the most important thing for him is the continued operation of these small boats, lighters, etc.

HITLER: I can only say that the ships in Marseilles and also in Toulon must be used, and we must under all circumstances do away with all safety measures, and just build ships. It doesn't make a damned bit of difference. In the past there weren't any safety measures, and there wasn't any compartmenting either, and the ships sailed just the same. I don't know what kind of compartmenting they had forty or fifty years ago when the first iron ships appeared. I want to see one of those old blueprints. They sailed all over the world. Now, suddenly, a lighter has to have compartments. If it's hit by a torpedo, it'll sink anyway, with or without compartments. That's right, isn't it?

KRANCKE: Yes, sir.

HITLER: That takes a lot of material. The point is, the people should get life preservers. Life preservers are easier to build than compartments. They have to jump into the water anyhow. And then mount some good quadruple guns—those are the best compartments for a lighter.

> [There is continued discussion of the supply problems of the African front. The possibility of an English invasion of the Eastern Mediterranean is considered and dismissed as unlikely. Christian reports on air operations.]

CHRISTIAN: Yesterday the enemy made a few large-scale daylight attacks on France.[11]

At first several of their fighter units involved our fighters in a sort of running fight, and then they flew in with 17 planes over Rouen to the south of Paris, and, since there was a comparatively low ceiling, they got most of their planes out again. Two four-engined aircraft were shot down by fighters near Paris, and also three Spitfires. There was some damage only near Rouen, for instance a French children's home was hit; actually only damage to civilians.

HITLER: Those are the honorable Allies; there's no help for them.

JODL: One could play that up in the French newspapers.

CHRISTIAN: At night there were a few nuisance raids in this area with single planes, without any damage being reported, mostly they didn't even drop bombs. One plane was shot down, here. There are further reports on the attack on Sunderland.[12]

HITLER: The English report that six planes were over the city. How can they say such a thing so boldly.

CHRISTIAN: 16 aircraft at heights between 700 and 2,000 meters. Three 1,000-kg HE bombs, 48 large incendiary HE bombs, and 540 incendiary bombs were dropped into the city area. Three large fires in the vicinity of the ... shipyards.

HITLER: I can believe that the English are lying; but that they just say there were only six planes and hardly any damage after a major raid like that seems unbelievable to me.

CHRISTIAN: Sixteen planes are not very much.

HITLER: They claim there were only six.

JODL: It depends on whether they intend to circulate this in

[11] The British Air Ministry and the U.S. Army announced on 14 December 1942: 'USAAF heavy bombers attacked targets at Rouen on Saturday afternoon. The weather was bad and results were not seen. Squadrons of Allied fighters supported and covered this operation. Strong opposition was encountered from enemy fighters, 14 of which were destroyed by the bombers and 4 by fighters. 2 bombers and 4 fighters are missing.'

[12] On 13 December, the German communiqué stated: 'During the night a bomber formation attacked the important port and shipbuilding center of Sunderland [in England].'

the foreign press or at home. They couldn't hide such a thing very well in their own country.

HITLER: Up to now they haven't done that. They haven't denied the damage. One can't do that. One can't risk it. That caused bad blood here at the beginning of the war and a few times thereafter, when, on the basis of Air Force reports, it was announced that there had been very small damage, when actually there had been great damage. I don't know what kind of a local impression that made in the Rhineland, where the Air Force itself issued such reports. Now that has been stopped. Now only accurate reports are used. It was especially shameless in Cologne. The people will bear anything; but if the official High Command communiqué announces no damage, or only insignificant damage, and acutally 9,000 houses are destroyed or damaged, that of course is fantastic.

The principle is applicable here, too: one has to train all of them to report the most brutal truth. For it is easier to bear the most brutal truth, no matter how disgusting it is, than an embellished picture which doesn't correspond with the truth.

The conference ends with Christian reporting further on air operations in Africa and Russia.

1 FEBRUARY 1943

This conference began 12.17
P.M.; the closing time is not
indicated in the manuscript.

Participants: HITLER,
BUHLE, CHRISTIAN, ENGEL,
JESCHONNEK, JODL, KEITEL,
AND ZEITZLER

*A special communiqué of the
Soviet Information Bureau published in the night of Sunday, 31 January to Monday, 1 February 1943, announced that the Russian 'forces on the Don front between
27 January and 31 January completed the annihilation
of the German troops surrounded west of Stalingrad', it
stated on 31 January the Russian forces had 'captured
Fieldmarshal Paulus, commanding the group of German
forces before Stalingrad, consisting of the 6th Army and
the 4th Tank Army, his chief of staff, Lieutenant-General
Schmidt, and the whole of his staff.' The Russian report
listed the various captured generals by name, among others
Lieutenant-General von Seydlitz, commander of the LI
Army Corps.*

*The following stenographic report of the meeting held by
Hitler under the impact of this news is very badly
preserved, sentences are frequently incomprehensible. Nevertheless the publication of this record, even in incomplete
and fragmentary form, seems justified in view of the great
interest which must be felt in Hitler's reaction to the
defeat at Stalingrad.*

*The meeting starts with a discussion between Hitler and
Zeitzler on the possibility of a German withdrawal from the*

*Donets Basin, where the advanced German positions were
threatened by Russian attacks from the north and the
southeast. Hitler wants to think over this problem but is
reluctant to make the decision, because he feels that
without the use of this industrial region he would not be
able to resume offensive action in the East. The discussion
then turns to Stalingrad.*

HITLER: They have surrendered there formally and absolutely. Otherwise they would have closed ranks, formed a
hedgehog, and shot themselves with their last bullets. When
you consider that a woman has the pride to leave, to lock
herself in, and to shoot herself right away[1] just because
she has heard a few insulting remarks, then I can't have
any respect for a soldier who is afraid of that and prefers
to go into captivity. I can only say: I can understand a
case like that of General Giraud; we come in, he gets out
of his car, and is grabbed.[2] But—

ZEITZLER: I can't understand it either. I'm still of the
opinion that it might not be true; perhaps he is lying there
badly wounded.

HITLER: No, it is true ... They'll be brought to Moscow,
to the GPU right away, and they'll blurt out orders for the
northern pocket to surrender too.[3] That Schmidt will sign
anything. A man who doesn't have the courage, in such a
time, to take the road that every man has to take some
time, doesn't have the strength to withstand that sort of

[1] Hitler returns to this reference to a woman's suicide three times in
the course of this conference. The version of the story varies each time.
In addition to the two published passages, another mention is made in
an omitted part of the record: 'Such a beautiful woman, she was
really ... first class. Just because of a small matter, insulted by a few
words, she said, "Then I can go. I'm not needed." Her husband
answered, "Why don't you?" so the woman went, wrote farewell letters,
and shot herself.' It is impossible to judge whether this event really
happened or if it is a figment of Hitler's imagination.

[2] Hitler refers to General Giraud's capture by German troops in the
French campaign of 1940. Giraud later escaped from German imprison-
ment and was brought to North Africa.

[3] A small part of the German forces, under the command of Generalleutnant Streicher of the XI Corps, was still holding out north of Stalingrad at this time. This unit surrendered on the day following this conference.

thing. He will suffer torture in his soul. In Germany there has been too much emphasis on training the intellect and not enough on strength of character . . .

ZEITZLER: One can't understand this type of man.

HITLER: Don't say that. I saw a letter . . . It was addressed to Below. I can show it to you. An officer in Stalingrad wrote: 'I have come to the following conclusions about these people—Paulus, question mark; Seydlitz, should be shot; Schmidt, should be shot.'

ZEITZLER: I have also heard bad reports about Seydlitz.

HITLER: And under that: 'Hube— The Man.'[4] Naturally one could say that it would have been better to leave Hube in there and bring out the others. But since the value of men is not immaterial and since we need men in the entire war, I am definitely of the opinion that it was right to bring Hube out. In peacetime in Germany, about 18,000 or 20,000 people a year chose to commit suicide, even without being in such a position. Here is a man who sees 50,000 or 60,000 of his soldiers die defending themselves bravely to the end. How can he surrender himself to the Bolshevists? Oh, that is—

ZEITZLER: That is something one can't understand at all.

HITLER: But I had my doubts before. That was at the moment when I received the report that he was asking what he should do.[5] How can he even ask about such a thing? From now on, every time a fortress is besieged and the commandant is called on to surrender, he is going to ask: 'What shall I do now?' . . .

ZEITZLER: There is no excuse. When his nerves threaten to break down, then he must kill himself.

HITLER: When the nerves break down, there is nothing left but to admit that one can't handle the situation and to shoot oneself. One can also say the man should have shot himself just as the old commanders who threw themselves on their swords when they saw that the cause was lost.

[4] Generaloberst Hube was then Commander of the XIV Panzer Corps.
[5] During January Paulus had declined a Russian demand for surrender on instructions from Hitler.

That goes without saying. Even Varus[6] gave his slave the
order: 'Now kill me!'

ZEITZLER: I still think they may have done that and that
the Russians are only claiming to have captured them all.

HITLER: No.

ENGEL: The extraordinary thing is, if I may say so, that
they have not announced whether Paulus was badly
wounded when he was taken. Tomorrow they could say
that he died of his wounds.

HITLER: Do you have exact information about his being
wounded? ... The tragedy has happened now. Maybe it's a
warning.

ENGEL: The names of the generals may not all be correct.

HITLER: In this war, no more fieldmarshals will be made.[7]
All that will be done only after the conclusion of the war.
I won't go on counting my chickens before they are
hatched.

ZEITZLER: We were so completely sure how it would end,
that granting him a final satisfaction—

HITLER: We had to assume that it would end heroically.

ZEITZLER: How could one imagine anything else.

HITLER: Together with such men, in such surroundings,
how could he have brought himself to act differently. If
such things can happen, I really must say that any soldier
who risks his life again and again is an idiot. Now if a little
guy is overwhelmed, I can understand it.

ZEITZLER: It's much easier for the leader of an outfit.
Everyone is looking at him. It's easy for him to shoot
himself. It's difficult for the ordinary soldier.

HITLER: — This hurts me so much because the heroism
of so many soldiers is nullified by one single characterless
weakling—and that is what the man is going to do now.
You have to imagine, he'll be brought to Moscow—and
imagine that rattrap there.[8] There he will sign anything.
He'll make confessions, make proclamations. —You'll see:

[6] Commander of the Roman legions which were defeated by German
tribes in the Teutoburg Forest (A.D. 9).

[7] The promotion of Paulus to the rank of Generalfeldmarschall was
announced on 31 January, the day before this conference, and the last
day of the defense of Stalingrad.

[8] Hitler refers to the prison in Moscow in the Liubianka Street.

they will now walk down the slope of spiritual bankruptcy
to its lowest depths. One can only say that a bad deed
always produces new evils. —— With soldiers, the fundamental thing is always character, and if we don't manage
to instill that, if we just breed purely intellectual acrobats
and spiritual athletes, we're never going to get a race that
can stand up to the heavy blows of destiny. That is the
decisive point.

ZEITZLER: Yes, in the General Staff, too. For the first time
I have given General Staff stripes to an administrative
officer who had not received General Staff training, because he had worked out the retreat of his division fabu-
lously well from the General Staff point of view. It doesn't
really matter whether he took the eight weeks' training
course. That had its effect right away. I just sent down the
order: 'As of today, you are a General Staff officer.'

HITLER: Yes, one has to take brave, daring people who are
willing to sacrifice their lives, like every soldier. What is
Life? Life is the Nation. The individual must die anyway.
Beyond the life of the individual is the Nation. But how
anyone could be afraid of this moment of death, with
which he can free himself from this misery, if his duty
doesn't chain him to this Vale of Tears. Na!

[*After some discussion about the official attitude
to be taken on the subject of the Stalingrad surrender, Zeitzler withdraws. After he has left,
Christian, Buhle, Jeschonneck, Jodl, and Keitel
arrive. Jodl reports on the most recent developments in North Africa, the Balkans, and at sea,
the meeting ends with a report by Jeschonnek on
air operations, but before this topic is taken up,
there is another mention of Stalingrad.*]

JODL: In regard to the Russian communiqué, we are
checking that to see if there isn't some kind of error in it.
Because a single mistake—for instance a general who
couldn't have been there—would prove that everything
they published was taken from a list they captured somewhere.

HITLER: They say they have captured Paulus, as well as
Schmidt and Seydlitz.

JODL: I'm not sure about Seydlitz. It isn't quite clear; he
may be in the northern pocket. We are ascertaining by
radio which generals are in the northern pocket.

HITLER: Certainly, he was with Paulus. I'll tell you something: I can't understand how a man like Paulus wouldn't
rather go to his death. The heroism of so many tens of
thousands of men, officers, and generals is nullified by such
a man who lacks the character to do in a minute what a
weak woman has done.

JODL: But I am not yet certain that that is correct—

HITLER: This man and his wife were together. Then the
man fell sick and died. The woman wrote me a letter and
asked me to take care of her children. She found it
impossible to go on living, in spite of the children. . . .
Then she shot herself. That's what this woman did, she had
the strength—and soldiers don't have the strength. You
will see, it won't be a week before Seydlitz and Schmidt
and even Paulus are talking over the radio. . .[9] They are
going to be put into the Liubianka, and there the rats will
eat them. How can one be so cowardly? I don't understand
it.

JODL: I still have doubts.

HITLER: Sorry, but I don't. You know, I don't believe in
these wounds that Paulus is supposed to have received
either. That doesn't seem to fit. . . . What hurts me the
most, personally, is that I still promoted him to fieldmarshal. I wanted to give him his final satisfaction. That's the
last fieldmarshal I shall appoint in this war. You must not
count your chickens before they are hatched.

I don't understand that at all. . . So many people have
to die, and then a man like that besmirches the heroism of
so many others at the last minute. He could have freed
himself from all sorrow and ascended into eternity and
national immortality, but he prefers to go to Moscow.
What kind of choice is that? It just doesn't make sense. . . .

[9] Hitler's prediction was sound, for these generals, captured at Stalingrad, spoke over the Moscow radio for the National Committee of Free
Germany. Hitler's 'week' is a small miscalculation; the movement did
not get under way until July 1943.

It is tragic that such heroism is so terribly besmirched at the last moment.

JESCHONNEK: I consider it possible that the Russians have reported this on purpose. They are such clever devils.

HITLER: In a week they'll be on the radio.

JESCHONNEK: The Russians would even manage to let someone else speak for them.

HITLER: No, they themselves will speak on the radio. You'll hear it soon enough. They'll all speak personally on the radio. They'll ask the people in the pocket to surrender and they'll say the most disgusting things about the German Army. You have to realize that they will be brought to Moscow and put into the Liubianka, to be 'worked over'——

[*The surrender of Stalingrad was announced from Hitler's headquarters on 3 February 1943, in the following manner: 'The battle for Stalingrad has ended. True to their oath to fight to the last breath, the 6th Army under the exemplary leadership of Fieldmarshal von Paulus has been overcome by the superiority of the enemy and by the unfavorable circumstances confronting our forces.'*]

5 MARCH 1943

This conference lasted from
12.30 P.M. until 1.30 P.M.

Participants: HITLER,
CHRISTIAN, HEWEL, JODL,
PUTTKAMER, AND ZEITZLER

*The meeting opens with a long,
detailed report by Zeitzler on the events of the previous
days on the Eastern front and on the German troop
dispositions there; after giving this report, Zeitzler leaves,
and Jodl speaks about the situation in North Africa, the
Mediterranean, and the Balkans; Hitler makes few comments on these reports. Jodl then discusses the situation in
the Far East, including the disposition of American troops.*

JODL: The Japanese are convinced that the European theater will remain the center of gravity in 1943.

HITLER: That doesn't exactly please me.

JODL: The evacuation of Guadalcanal[1] has succeeded.

HITLER: You can't count too much on what the Japanese
say. I don't believe a word of it.

JODL: One shouldn't believe anything they say. They are the
only people who can tell you absolutely anything with a
perfectly straight face.

HITLER: They stuff you with lies, and all of their statements
are based on what later turns out to be deception.

HEWEL: Public opinion in America is very inclined to
consider the Pacific the main theater of war.

HITLER: I have read a comment by Dieckhoff.[2] He denies

[1] The remnants of the Japanese landing forces had been withdrawn
from Guadalcanal on the night of 7-8 February.
[2] Last German ambassador in Washington.

that quite flatly. There's not the slightest truth in it. If you want to win over the Americans, you have only to announce: (1) The war is fought for American interests; (2) liquidation of the British Empire; and (3) the principal enemy is Japan. Then you have the great majority on your side. The Jews don't agree with all of these points, but the others are in the great majority. The English are beginning to complain more and more about political developments and are terribly worried that these are turning against their Empire.

HEWEL: It would be interesting to find out how the American divisions in North Africa are. Neurath flew in from Tunis last night.[3] He has interesting things to tell. He has interrogated American prisoners, and he says it's unbelievable. . . . Most of them have come over to make money, and to have new experiences, and to see something new, to take part in something. There's not a trace of political conviction. They are rowdies who'll take to their heels very quickly; they won't be able to weather a crisis. He says he spoke with hundreds of them. Not one of them had political faith or a strong political conviction.

HITLER: That will never become another Rome. America will never become the Rome of the future. Rome was a community of farmers.

HEWEL: But the Americans do have good human material somewhere.

JODL: Only superficially.

HITLER: Not as much as we have been told. It is concentrated in a few areas which are known to Europeans. . . . The farmers are terribly run down. I have seen photographs. You can't imagine anything as miserable and as degenerate as the farmers; a completely uprooted mob, wandering all over the place.[4]

---

[3] SS-Sonderfuehrer von Neurath had been on a special mission to Africa; on him, see list of participants. The battle of the Kasserine Pass in which Rommel had thrown back the American forces had occurred in the second half of February.

[4] It appears that Hitler is thinking of the movie *Grapes of Wrath*, which he is said to have seen several times.

CHRISTIAN: They have no spirit, no inner pride.

JODL: They have nothing like that.

HEWEL: Just look at their war posters. They are completely impossible.

HITLER: There is no doubt that the Anglo-Saxons, the English are the best.

JODL: One has the feeling that the English are fighting for their country and their Empire. One never has this feeling about the Americans.

HITLER: That may be the reason why the English say that they can always handle the Americans.

HEWEL: That's a frivolous attitude. They won't be able to handle them because they will become dependent on them economically and in every other way. But politically and militarily they feel so superior to the Americans that they say: 'In ten years we will make up that.' One hears that from many Englishmen. I consider that very frivolous.

HITLER: But on the other hand, Jodl, one thing is clear and that is the great strength that lies not only in the size of the population but simply in the magnitude of the national territory. Just look at the Chinese Empire. They've been fighting there for five years. Part of the country is occupied, but the structure as a whole is still standing.

JODL: It is holding out almost without weapons.

HITLER: If we can't increase our space, it will mean our end. Space is one of the most important military factors. You can conduct military operations only if you have space. Only he who has space can survive the wars of the future. That was the misfortune of the French. In a single drive last year, we occupied more territory than in our whole Western offensive. France was finished off in six weeks, but in this huge space one can hold on and on. If we had had a crisis like this last one, on the old German border along the Oder-Warthe curve, Germany would have been finished. Here in the East we were able to cushion the blow. We have a battlefield here that has room for strategical operations.

JODL: Things have changed; at the time of the Roman wars, Germany was space. In the Middle Ages they marched all over Germany on foot, and now in the age of tanks and planes—

HITLER: In a fast plane one can fly over the whole old Empire in 1¼ hours.

JODL: While the Rusian space is a space that even the airplane can't handle. One can see that in the industrial region in the Urals. We can't reach it.

CHRISTIAN: Flying time from Cologne to Koenigsberg is 2½ hours.

HITLER: If you make 600 kilometers per hour in your plane, it takes 1¼ hours from Stettin to Munich. Before the war, Germany was to the world what Schleiz-Greiz[5] was to the German states. A ridiculous situation when you compare it with the rest of the world. The others have whole continents—America, East Asia, or Russia. And then Australia—where seven milion people have a whole continent. This was one of the wildest suggestions: the Prince of Windsor[6] was saying at that time that we Germans should really settle north Australia. He always advocated our getting it. Then we would have settled it, and one fine day the English would have pocketed it.

HEWEL: Australian agriculture is entirely German. The German element in Australia has been the most creative by far.

HITLER: That's quite clear. That's why he wanted to have us there, but I said no. We are not interested. Australia for the Australians.

[*The discussion continues to speculate on the possibilities of advances in the Far East, and on the nature of Japanese military equipment; Hitler, who becomes very optimistic about the Japanese prospects, remarks that their secrecy makes it impossible to get any exact information. Chris-*

[5] Schleiz-Greiz, a tiny German state in Thuringia, used in the vernacular as an example of smallness.
[6] The Duke of Windsor visited Germany in the fall of 1938, but Hitler can hardly be considered to be a reliable reporter of the conversations which then took place.

tian then reports on the previous day's air attacks on Germany and on the activities of the German Air Force, a few remarks by Hitler indicate that he is very critical of the Air Force's inactivity in the West, particularly over the British Isles.

II

THE FALL OF MUSSOLINI

The following five meetings are all concerned with the Italian crisis of the summer of 1943, covering the events leading to Mussolini's overthrow and Hitler's reaction to the fall of Fascism. When the first conference took place, on 20 May 1943, German and Italian resistance in Tunisia had ceased. With the exception of increasing Allied air activity over German and Italian territory, the military situation in Europe remained relatively quiet until the beginning of July. Then the German Army started a summer offensive on the central sector of the Eastern front, in the region around Orel and Kursk. This offensive failed after heavy fighting and led to a Russian counter-offensive in the same region, which resulted in the capture of Orel and Belgorod by the Russian Armies at the beginning of August. At the same time a decisive turn of events took place in July. On 10 July the invasion of Sicily had started, and when Mussolini was overthrown on 25 July the Axis hold on that island was restricted to the northeastern corner, the shrinking triangle Cefalù-Messina-Catania. All these events had important repercussions on the German hold over the Balkans, not only because parts of the Balkans were occupied by now unreliable Italian troops, but also because these developments gave hope and encouragement to Balkan partisans, who increased their activities.

20 MAY 1943

This conference lasted from
1.19 P.M. until 3.30 P.M.

Participants: HITLER,
BREUER, GUENSCHE, HEWEL, KEITEL,
LANGEMANN, LOEHR, NEURATH,
ROMMEL, SCHERFF, SCHMUNDT, AND
WARLIMONT.

HITLER: You were in Sicily?

NEURATH: Yes, my Fuehrer, I was down there, and I
spoke to Roatta,[1] whom I have known since the days
when he was the leader of the attaché group in Rome.
Among other things he told me that he did not have too
much confidence in the possibility of a defense of Sicily.
He claimed that he is too weak and that his troops are not
properly equipped. Above all, he has only one motorized
division; the rest are immobile. Every day the English do
their best to shoot up the locomotives of the Sicilian
railroads, for they know very well that it is almost impossible to bring up material to replace or repair them, or not
possible at all. The impression I gained on the crossing
from Giovanni to Messina was that almost all traffic on
this short stretch is at a virtual standstill. Of the ferries
there—I think there were six—only one remains. This one
was being treated as a museum piece; it was said that it
was being saved for better purposes.

HITLER: What are the 'better purposes'?

NEURATH: Well, my Fuehrer, sometimes the Italians explain, 'when the war is over'; others say, 'you never know

[1] General Roatta was commander of the Italian 6th Army in Sicily at
this time and soon afterwards became Chief of Staff of the Italian
Army, a post he held during the entire period of the Italian collapse
and surrender.

what's going to happen next.' At any rate, this one ferry
has not been operating. It may be that there is something
wrong with the engine, but the German officers with
whom I talked denied that.

The German troops in Sicily have undoubtedly become
rather unpopular. That can be explained very easily because the Sicilians hold the view that we have brought the
war to their country. First we have eaten up everything
they had, and now we are going to cause the English to
come themselves, although—and I must emphasize this—
the Sicilian peasant really wouldn't mind that. He thinks
that this will end his suffering. It is understandable that the
simple peasant prefers what looks most attractive in the
near future to long run considerations. The general opinion
all over southern Italy is that the war will be over when
the English come, and that the presence of the Germans
just delays this.

HITLER: What is the Italian Government doing to counter
  this attitude?

NEURATH: My Fuehrer, as far as I know the prefects and
  officials who are still around are not doing much about it;
  whenever I directed their attention to it and complained
  that German soldiers were being cursed in the streets, I
  was told that they didn't know what to do about it, since
  this represented the popular view. They said, 'That's how
  the people feel. You have made yourselves unpopular; you
  have requisitioned things and eaten up all our chickens.'——
  But I do think that the officials could make more of an
  effort, and make examples of the more flagrant cases.

HITLER: They won't take action.

NEURATH: It is very difficult. They just won't take action.
  The Sicilian temperament is different from the north Italian. But on the whole it is very unpleasant to see how they
  let things slide.

The threat to Sicily from the air, that is the air superiority,[2] is extremely strong. There's no doubt about it. I
don't think I'm saying anything new with that. Palermo is
badly flattened—large parts of the town, many beautiful

[2] Of the enemy.

old buildings, and most of all, the harbor. Several officers have told me that the English got the harbor into a state in which they won't be able to use it themselves. The English raid on Cagliari in Sardinia was quite a different thing; there the city and the warehouses were destroyed, but the harbor installations and the moles as such were still in fairly good condition.

HITLER: That's the report—

WARLIMONT: That is the same thing Admiral Ruge reported.[3]

NEURATH: And then, my Fuhrer, the Italian Crown Prince is down there as Commander-in-Chief of the Italian troops——it is significant that he holds frequent inspections down there, and that General Roatta spends a lot of time with him. On the staff of General Roatta there are quite a number of officers—Italian staff officers—who are known to be rather Anglophile. Some of them have English wives, others have English connections of some sort.

HITLER: Well, what did I always tell you?

NEURATH: My personal opinion is that, as far as I know him,[4] I wouldn't trust him as far as the other side of the street.

HITLER: No.

NEURATH: I have always considered him very foxy.

HITLER: Foxy? He is the Fouché of the Fascist revolution, a completely characterless spy. He's really a spy.

NEURATH: He is a born stoolpigeon, the prototype of one. Personally I'm convinced that he is up to something. The German officers down there agree that it has become noticeable how he increasingly makes use of the Crown Prince, how he increasingly tries to find some common basis with him that would be acceptable when the English descend on Sicily. I can't judge to what extent he is able to carry out such a plan, but I do believe that he is a dangerous gambler.

HITLER: My opinion exactly.

NEURATH: And he is the absolute ruler of Sicily, there's no

---

[3] Vizeadmiral Ruge was the German representative on the Italian Navy Staff and commander of the German naval forces in Italy.
[4] He means Roatta.

doubt about that. He managed that well. His headquarters is in Enna. I repeatedly found that everyone jumps through his hoop, and everybody said about General Roatta that nothing can be done without his permission.

HITLER: Did you discuss this matter with Kesselring?[5]

NEURATH: I told it to General von Rintelen,[6] my Fuhrer.

HITLER: One has to be very careful. Kesselring is a terrific optimist, and we must be careful that in his optimism, shall we say, he doesn't misjudge the hour when optimism must give way to severity.

NEURATH: The German Air Force in Sicily is certainly having a hard time; the attacks are so heavy that, I suppose, the casualties on the airfields will be correspondingly high. Sometimes they can't even take off any more —— In Rome itself the mood varies, my Fuhrer. It is very unpleasant; we are, of course, wise to the plutocratic clique, which, naturally, thinks along English lines. The people expect that the measures which the Duce is carrying out with great energy[7] will bring about a more just distribution of the burden of the war. But on the other hand, I am afraid these measures should have been instituted earlier. The people have become so accustomed to black-marketing and racketeering that it is extremely difficult to wipe it out in one stroke. This action will certainly not increase his popularity.

HITLER: How can you eliminate this in a country where the leading elements of the armed forces, as well as of the state, et cetera.—where the whole thing is a mass of corruption? Have you been in northern Italy too?

NEURATH: No, my Fuehrer, I only passed through there.

HITLER: How long were you in Rome?

NEURATH: I was in Rome for seven days—— In general the impression Rome leaves is still—

HITLER: Prewar?

NEURATH: Prewar, yes; there is no doubt about it. You

[5] Kesselring was Commander-in-Chief, South, at this time, i.e. he was in charge of the German forces in Italy.

[6] German military attaché in Rome from 1936 to 1943.

[7] Under the impact of the Tunisian defeat, Mussolini had tightened controls and begun to purge the Fascist party.

were always surprised when you came from Africa and
found the streets looking as if nothing had happened during the last two years. And their excuse is always, 'We are
a poor people; we have neither the clothing nor the boots
for soldiers, so that it is better to let them walk the streets.'

HITLER: If they had only given them to us as a labor force,
we could have put them to work.

ROMMEL: That doesn't suit the plutocrats; we would have
'spoiled' them.

NEURATH: In the eyes of the Italians, our progressive
social policies would have 'spoiled' their people.

HITLER: Altogether, how many Italian workers do we have
now in Germany? Do you know that, Hewel?

HEWEL: We had 230,000; after June they were to be
gradually released.

HITLER: After June?

HEWEL: I'm not quite sure; I will find out.

HITLER: You can do that later.

KEITEL: Call up Sauckel.[8] He'll know exactly.

HITLER: And Roatta himself? Anyway, my opinion is definite: this war has been consistently sabotaged from the
beginning by a certain group in that country. From the
beginning. Originally it was sabotaged in 1939. Through
this sabotage, those people succeeded in preventing the
entry into the war. That means the thing could have been
avoided; if the Italians had declared their solidarity with
Germany at that time, which they were obligated to do on
the basis of the treaties, the war wouldn't have broken out.
The English wouldn't have started it; and neither would
the French. Because it was this way with the English: as
soon as the Italians decided that they would stay out of the
war, the decision was sent to London and two hours later
the English hastily signed the assistance treaty with Poland.[9] They had not signed it before. It was signed two

---

[8] Commissioner General of Labor Supply and District Leader of
Thuringia.

[9] In March 1939 the British Government had given an assurance to
the Polish Government that Great Britain would come to the assistance
of Poland if Poland's independence was threatened; then negotiations
began with the purpose of transforming this one-sided guarantee into a
Mutual Assistance Pact. This Pact was signed on 25 August 1939, two

hours after the interview. We've had the same experience
again; every memorandum I wrote to the Duce immediately reached England. Therefore I only wrote things I absolutely wanted to get to England. That was the best way to
get something through to England quickly.

NEURATH: This sort of trafficking with England is still
going on. The night before last, on the train, the submarine
commanders based in Spezia told me that they had proof
that every morning from 8 to 10 o'clock there was contact
between the battleship *Vittorio Veneto* and Malta. A German counter-intelligence officer came to investigate the
situation, and is supposed to have been arrested on suspicion of espionage when they noticed that he had found out
about it. That's a true story.

HITLER: Isn't anyone here from the Navy? Never mind—.
We have to watch out that the submarines in the Aegean—

KEITEL: I have already made a note of it.[10] We'll include
everything in that. New thoughts will occur all the time.

HITLER: The ships and all that stuff, primarily the submarines.

KEITEL: All of the auxiliary ships are included in our
notes.

WARLIMONT: On the southern coast of France—

HITLER: As long as they are on the southern coast of
France, they can stay there, but not in Italian ports, in
Spezia, et cetera. Guensche, measure the air distance from
England to Munich on the map, and also from Corsica to
Munich. I'm sure this Roatta is a spy.

NEURATH: It's the same story with the 'Goering.'[11] The
sad thing is that we can get them out of Sicily only if those
gentlemen down there co-operate.

---

[10] This exchange seems to refer to the preparation of an over-all directive concerning the disposal of troops, ships, and air forces in case
of an invasion.

[11] The Herrmann Goering Division, which had been destroyed in
Tunisia, was being re-activated in southern Italy, France, and Sicily;
parts of it subsequently participated in the Sicilian campaign.

---

days after the signing of the Nazi-Soviet Non-Aggression Treaty. Hitler
seems to have several times expressed the view that war would have
been avoided if Ciano had not told the British that Italy would stay
neutral; see Rahn, *Ruheloses Leben*, p. 138.

HITLER: We must consider whether we should really move the whole 'Goering' Division over.[12] I think perhaps we shouldn't.

KEITEL: It has been my opinion from the beginning that we should keep them in southern Italy.

ROMMEL: They won't be able to get back again. I don't believe what Fieldmarshal Kesselring said, that they will be able to cross back over the Straits under pressure from the enemy. Perhaps single men would get back, but not the equipment and the bulk of the division. That will go down the drain.

KEITEL: Yes, that will go down the drain. My original suggestion was to pull back parts of the 'Herrmann Goering' Division to southern Italy, so that we would keep the Division available as such; and not to send more of it over. Is it possible to repair the ferry?

NEURATH: That can be done easily, sir.

HITLER: There you are!

NEURATH: It is even possible to get along without the ferry.

HITLER: That's right: the ferries are not decisive. The decisive thing is the will.

NEURATH: The state the ferries are in is typical.

HITLER: Where there is a will, there is a ferry. Of the twenty or thirty barges we and the Italians used, 60 per cent of ours were always in condition, and only 10 per cent of the Italians'. There was always something wrong with theirs. It was probably the same with the tanks; I have seen how quickly the Italian tanks melted away in battle. After two or three days there weren't any Italian tanks any more; they were all in the repair shop. Surely that's a matter of will.

SCHMUNDT: The distance from England to Munich is 1,000 kilometers, and from Corsica to Munich, 750 kilometers.

HITLER: Another point—write this down—is the ammunition allowance for the anti-aircraft we have down there. It must be handled in such a way that it can be stopped at

[12] He means 'over to Sicily.'

any time, and so that they do not have too much on hand. Only very little.

WARLIMONT: Yes. You mean the anti-aircraft we gave to the Italians?

HITLER: I mean all of it.

ROMMEL: Wouldn't it be possible, my Fuehrer, to have the Italians send more of their troops over to Sicily to hold it in our place?

HITLER: Of course, anything would be possible. The question is if they *want* to defend it. If they really wanted to defend it, anything could be done. What worries me is not that it cannot be done—there is no doubt that it can be defended, if it is seriously attempted, then we could move troops over there—but what does worry me is that they don't want to defend it; we can see this lack of determination. The Duce may have the best intentions, but they will be sabotaged. I have read Bastianini's speech. There is no question but that it is a stinking speech. This speech is—I don't know if you've read it—

KEITEL: No, I haven't. I just saw a short notice this morning that he had spoken.

HITLER: A telegram came. I have it in my room—The speech has somewhat the following tone: Italy and Germany are fighting for justice, et cetera, the others for injustice, and any unconditional surrender would be unbearable for the Italians—more or less along those lines—and Italy will rally around her king, and will defend her army and her king. At the word 'king' there was demonstrative applause by certain people in the Senate. There!

GUENSCHE: My Fuehrer, from the northern tip of Corsica to Munich it is 600 kilometers, and from southeast England to Munich 800 kilometers.

[*Ambassador Hewel submits the telegram containing the speech given on the previous day in the Italian Senate by Under-Secretary of Foreign Affairs Bastianini. Hitler reads it aloud and intersperses it with critical remarks. He takes particular exception to Bastianini's statement that the*

Italians had 'no wish to destroy or humiliate France . . . The victors aimed at a settlement of all the questions left open.']

HITLER: How can he say such a thing! The French say they were not beaten by the Italians. All in all a lousy speech, a very lousy speech, and it strengthens my feeling that a crisis of the type we have discussed[13] can suddenly develop there at any moment.

[*Generaloberst Loehr, commander of the Army Group 'E' in the Aegean area, who had been for conferences at Hitler's headquarters, takes leave, it emerges that the repercussions of an Italian collapse on the Balkan area had been discussed with Loehr. Hitler remarks that 'fortunately, I have a good nose for such things and am usually able to smell in advance what can happen'; he indicates that he considers 'the holding of the Balkans as absolutely decisive, because of copper, bauxite, chromium, as well as because of the necessity of making sure that an Italian collapse would not develop into an uncheckable debacle.' Then Ambassador Hewel submits a memorandum*].

HEWEL: These are just a few ideas of mine.

HITLER: Those two worlds are nothing new. They were always there, even at the time of his Abyssinian war. If I had taken a stand against Italy then, it would have collapsed immediately . . .

I remember that I got the correct impression at that reception in Rome;[14] that there were two different worlds became strikingly apparent. On the one side, the undoubted warmth of the Fascist reception; on the other,

---

[13] In previous military conferences; for instance the possibility of an Italian defection was envisaged in a conference of the previous day, 19 May. Then Hitler had said that, under such circumstances, he would have to use 'his old SS divisions, who are propagandists. If they get down to Italy, there will be complete fraternization with Fascism in the briefest time.'

[14] Hitler refers to his state visit to Italy in the first week of May 1938.

the definitely ice-cold atmosphere of the military and court circles—people who are actually nondescript, or just cowards. All people who have property of more than 250,000 marks generally become cowards in my eyes, because they want to live on their interest and keep their 250,000 marks. They lose all their courage. If a man has one or two millions, one doesn't have to worry about him; people like that don't start revolutions or anything else. They are opposed to every war, even if they see that their people are starving. It doesn't matter to them. They are the lords of creation. If everyone got his proper share in such a country, if, at least, everyone received his allotted rations, then even the people in England might be sympathetic about the possibility of imperial expansion. But that isn't the case now; those people live like kings. They don't miss anything; they have everything, and only the poor have to suffer. In Rome I saw what Fascism is like. It could not prevail over the court circle. That reception at court—I really shouldn't talk about it—is the sort of thing that is nauseating according to our standards. But it is the same way at the Duce's. And why? Because the whole court clique has wormed its way in there. Ciano is no different. I was supposed to take the Countess Edda Ciano in to dinner. Suddenly Philipp rushed in with his Mafalda, and the whole program was upset.[15] Great excitement; I had to sit next to Mafalda. What do I care about Mafalda? As far as I'm concerned, she is the wife of a German Oberpraesident, period, that's that. On top of that, her intellectual qualities aren't such that would charm you—to say nothing of her looks. That gave me an insight into the conditions there. The Fascists and the Quirinal crowd are all jumbled together . . .

For me the most important question is: What is the state of the Duce's health? That's the decisive factor about a man who has to make difficult decisions. And secondly,

[15] Princess Mafalda, daughter of the King of Italy, was married to Prince Philipp of Hesse, an SA-Obergruppenfuehrer, who, under the Nazis, became governor (Oberpraesident) of the Prussian province Hesse-Nassau. Princess Mafalda died in a German concentration camp, where she was put after the Italian surrender.

how does he judge Italy's chances in the event of a waning
of the Fascist revolution or of the Royal House? Those are
the two problems. For either the Royal House supersedes
the Fascist revolution—how would he judge the prospects
of his people in that case?—or how does he judge them if
the Royal House alone should take over the power [sic].
It's hard to say. In Klessheim[16] he made a remark while
we were having dinner together; he suddenly said: 'My
Fuehrer, I don't know; I have no successor in the Fascist
revolution. A chief of state can be found to succeed me,
but no one who will continue the Fascist revolution.'—
That is certainly a tragedy. His misfortune began back in
1941, when we were at the second headquarters in the railroad viaduct during the Russian campaign.[17]

KEITEL: Oh yes, down in the Galician area, where the big
tunnel was.

HITLER: At night we spoke about the Russian commissars;
there can't be two powers, et cetera. Then he became very
thoughtful. And then while I was eating with him on the
train, he suddenly said to me: 'What you say is true,
Fuehrer, that one shouldn't have two powers in one army;
but what do you think, Fuehrer, what can you do, if you
had officers who entertain reservations toward the regime
and its philosophy of the state? They say they have reservations because they are officers, and the moment you
reason with them by appealing to the idea of the state or
the interest of the state, they say: "We are monarchists
and obey the King." ' That's the difference. That was
already his problem in 1941. And it was even more pronounced in 1940, or 28 October. . .[18] Suddenly he said

[16] The meeting at Klessheim, near Salzburg, took place on 29-30 April
1942. There are detailed reports about this meeting by Mussolini and
Ciano in the *Hitler-Mussolini Correspondence*, pp. 119-22, and in
Ciano's *Diaries*, pp. 477-80. Of course these reports do not mention the
remark to which Hitler refers, but contain rather striking statements by
Hitler, showing his belief that he enjoyed the special protection to
providence.

[17] The Hitler-Mussolini meeting on the Russian front took place from
25 to 29 August 1941. For a report on this meeting see Ciano's *Diplomatic Papers*, pp. 447-52.

[18] Conference between Hitler and Mussolini at Florence on 28 October 1940, the day when the Italian attack upon Greece commenced.

to me; 'You see, I trust my soldiers but not my generals; I can't have confidence in them.' The man told me that on the very day on which he started his offensive against Greece or Albania. The question is how he feels physically; if the Duce were fifteen years younger today the whole thing would be no problem, but at the age of sixty it is more difficult. But in my opinion those two worlds have always existed. The one world was not removed and so continued to spin its web. I hear the same thing from all of our people down there. Probably tonight—what's his name?

KEITEL: Djurisic.[19]

HITLER: —will be with the King. Perhaps it will turn out that this robber baron is a relative of the Royal House. Yes, it would be very difficult for an ordinary citizen to marry off his daughter if father steals sheep and has been locked up so and so many times.[20] But in court circles that is no disgrace; instead it's a great honor. The princes vied for these princesses, although actually Nikita was nothing but a tramp who had escaped from Austria, exacted blackmail time and again, and played Italy and Austria against each other. He even used the World Postal Union for fraud, and tricked the Austrian state out of 1¾ million kronen; the Emperor had to pay for that out of his private purse. A huge scandal, but that doesn't matter in high society.

The Conference ends with a few remarks by Keitel, who submits to Hitler the draft of a directive concerning the military measures to be taken in case of an invasion.

[19] Chetnik Leader under Mikhailovich, who co-operated first with the Italians and then with the Germans.
[20] This refers to the fact that the Queen of Italy was the daughter of King Nikita of Montenegro.

25 JULY 1943

The starting time of this
conference is not indicated
in the manuscript;
it ended at 2.12 P.M.

Participants: HITLER,
BUHLE, CHRISTIAN, DARGES,
HEWEL, JODL, JUNGE, KEITEL,
PUTTKAMER, WARLIMONT, AND
ZEITZLER.

*This record is fragmentary. The
beginning is missing. The extant part starts with Zeitzler
reporting on the situation on the Eastern front and submitting the reports the army groups have sent in. Hitler's and
Zeitzler's words show serious concern about the lack of
reserves on the Eastern front. They want to order Kluge,
commanding the Army Group 'Center,' to give up some of
his reserves in order to reinforce Manstein, commanding
the Army Group 'South.' Then Zeitzler leaves and Jodl
reports on the situation in Sicily and Italy, with many
details about the number of troops and tanks available
there; Hitler intersperses remarks, sharply critical of the
Italian Royal House. Jodl is followed by Junge and Christian, who reports on naval and air operations in the Mediterranean theater of war. Then Warlimont reports on
fighting against partisans in the Balkans. Junge and Christian give reports on naval and air activities in the West and
North. Christian describes a project to mine English rivers
from airplanes, which Hitler receives with skepticism.*

HITLER: I have already told you, when we discussed this a
few days ago, that terror can only be broken by terror.

One has to counter-attack, everything else is nonsense. In my opinion all this mining is worthless, it gives no lift to our people and it doesn't affect those people over there either. Maybe you think it has a psychological effect on the German people if the enemy has losses through mines. It doesn't impress them a bit. There is no use now in talking about enemy ships being sunk. It is quite a different business when in one night, in Hamburg, a hundred thousand people have to be evacuated and shipyards are destroyed.[1] That's a much greater loss. We can't act irresponsibly any longer. In my opinion we should use our planes for attacking them directly, especially since they are putting so many planes into the air.

CHRISTIAN: My Fuehrer, that is just why we have come to the conclusion that it is of no use to make a terror raid on a small town with 50 planes; that makes no impression at all. Instead one has to use those 50 planes to achieve an indirect result, so that they have to divide their forces and can't come with 500 planes at once. In my opinion this is the only way.

HITLER: . . . I don't think that you can do that. We've reached the point where we have to be glad if our men even find London. Today they tell me, 'We hope to find London all right.' That's a damned shame, and I'm going to tell the same thing to the Reichsmarshal; and I'm not going to mince words. ——

[There follows a brief exchange about the possibility of attacking English airfields. Hitler denies the usefulness of such operations.]

[1] The immediate cause of this discussion was the series of Allied air raids on Hamburg, which had started the night before. This extended attack commenced the saturation raids on German cities, which continued until the end of the war. The whole discussion is interesting in view of the debate among the German leaders how these air attacks could best be countered. According to Speer, Hitler and Goering believed that 'enemy bombing attacks could only be removed by complying with same by counter-attacks.' Speer considers this view the reason for Germany's fatal error of concentrating aircraft production on bombers instead of fighters. (*U.S. Strategic Bombing Survey*, 'Speer Interrogation.')

HITLER: Terror can only be broken by terror. That they attack airfields moves me little. But if they smash our cities in the Ruhr—. And the enemy is so sensitive. A few bombs with the new explosive, and those people were terrified: 'The Germans have new weapons.' I don't know why everyone wants to handle them with kid gloves. We can only stop this business if we get at the people over there. Otherwise our own people will gradually go crazy. Eventually the time will come when our people will lose all confidence in the Air Force. It is almost partly gone, anyway. You can't just tell them: 'We've dropped mines over there.' If they appear over Hamburg, it doesn't matter if they have 400 to 500, or only 200 or 300 planes. But we are handling them with kid gloves. It is going to work only if we attack their cities systematically. But all the time I am told things like 'We couldn't find that place' or 'We don't have enough planes'; but then it turns out we do have enough to do something else. The next time I am told, 'That would have no effect. We must use mines.'— Then I'm told, 'That anti-aircraft was too strong'; on the other hand I'm told, 'The anti-aircraft has no effect at all'—the usual excuse I got to hear is, 'We can't find it.' You can't find London! A God-damned shame! And now some ass tells me, 'My Fuehrer, when they fly from England to Dortmund, their new radar enables them to make a direct hit on a building 500 meters wide and 250 meters long.' Complete ass! But we can't find London, which has a diameter of 50 kilometers and is 150 kilometers from the coast. Don't think I'm saying this just to you; I told the others the same thing. It's not your fault; you're just my adjutant. I'm going to tell the responsible officers too.

CHRISTIAN: I'm still of the opinion that we just don't have the 400 to 500 planes available needed to affect the enemy to the same degree.

HITLER: That's not true.

CHRISTIAN: Our planes can't carry that much.

HITLER: But the enemy has to fly further. We only have to

fly one-fifth as far as they do. To get to Hamburg they
have to fly 600 kilometers, or even more.

JUNGE: At least 800.

HITLER: Mostly over the sea. We have only a short distance from our starting fields, so that should balance it. If
we use the high-powered bomb, it will have a great effect.
The important thing is to make them feel something. It
seems to me that if there are 50 bombers over the center
of Munich it is quite enough; not a single person can sleep
that night. At any rate, it is better for you to put 50 of our
planes over a city like that than to drop mines. That's a lot
of tripe! They just fly a plane over them and bang!—up
they all go anyway.

CHRISTIAN: Our night fighters are lined up here, and their
night fighters are as tight as—

HITLER: But you yourself say they can't fly on a day like
that; so that if you can't reach their airfields, at least you
can hit the towns—

CHRISTIAN: On days when the enemy is making raids, he
can't use his night fighters.

HITLER: Fine. Instead of monkeying around, let's attack,
get ready here, and pick out a target—it doesn't matter
what target. We can't go on this way. Eventually the
German people will go nuts. When I hear that we have
committed 50 hit-and-run bombers, so and so many mine
laying planes, or have attacked an airfield somewhere or
other, then I consider that a poor joke. That is avoiding
the only effective method. Terror can only be broken by
terror, and in no other way. . . But the decisive thing is
that the English will stop only if their cities are knocked
out, and for no other reason. These other measures might
delay them for a night, but they won't stop unless their
cities are knocked out. That's clear. I can only win the war
if I destroy more of the enemy's than he destroys of ours;
by teaching him the terrors of war. That's always been the
way, and it's the same thing with regard to air war. ——
Do we have a report about how many aircraft losses the
enemy admits, what he has to say about Hamburg?

CHRISTIAN: I'll have somebody find out.

HITLER: Don't we have the 12.8 battery there?

CHRISTIAN: We don't as yet have a picture of the civilian casualties.

HITLER: One of the 10 districts reports 800 dead so far. I would write here:—

CHRISTIAN: 'Considerable and extensive destruction?'

HITLER: 'Great destruction.'[2] But believe me, even if it was 'only' 200 planes, the population expects us to do something over there. This is no time for fooling. This experimenting around— 'Today we'll throw mines, tomorrow we'll try something else'—won't help any more. The population now demands reprisals. I hear these wonderful tales that the Heinkel 177 will be ready after all; that it will be able to fly at night. Now we can make a raid on London with 100 Heinkels. Each one can take six 1000-kilo bombs, and everything else as well. The Reichsmarshal, or rather his pilot, and my pilot, Bauer,[3] say we should let them try once when the ceiling has closed down. They claim they can take a fully loaded JU-52 back and forth—nothing will happen—and drop the whole works on London.

CHRISTIAN: That's what I said back in 1940.

DARGES: The English report that they had dropped 2000 tons of bombs, and that 12 of their bombers are missing.

HITLER: I want to know the exact points at which these 13 [sic] were shot down.

CHRISTIAN: Yes, but that takes longer now because we don't allocate any gas for that. They just send people out with bicycles.

HITLER: That has to be done, or else you won't be able to make a report. You'll have to send them out with bicycles.

[Jodl submits a report on the commitments of all German forces until the fall, including the

---

[2] Reference is to the drafting of the daily German Army communiqué. This communiqué, published 26 July, states about the raid on Hamburg: 'The population again suffered heavy losses. Great destruction was caused in residential quarters.'

[3] Gruppenfuehrer Hans Bauer, Hitler's pilot-in-chief.

> *creation of special striking forces in northern
> Italy and the Balkans. The discussion of this
> report follows, and then is interrupted by Hit-
> ler.]*

HITLER: Have you any news, Hewel?

HEWEL: Nothing definite yet, Mackensen[4] has only sent a
telegram saying that we should say that the Reichsmarshal's[5] trip is no longer certain in view of events. But
more exact information is expected. Up to now he has
heard that the Farinacci group has finally persuaded the
Duce to call a meeting of the Fascist Grand Council.[6]
That was originally scheduled for yesterday but has been
postponed until 10:00 p.m. because no agreement on the
agenda had been reached. He heard from different sources
that the meeting was extraordinarily stormy. Since the
participants are sworn to secrecy, he hasn't heard anything
authentic yet; only rumors. One of the most persistent
rumors he heard was that attempts were made to persuade
the Duce to install a Chief of Government—specifically a
Prime Minister in the figure of the politician Orlando,[7]
who is 83 years old and who played a role in the First
World War; the Duce is then to become President of the
Fascist Grand Council. These are all just rumors. We have
to wait. It is also said that this morning at 10 o'clock the
Duce and a number of generals went to the King, and are

---

[4] German ambassador in Rome.

[5] Goering was scheduled to go to Rome to congratulate Mussolini on
his sixtieth birthday (29 July).

[6] This is a rather simplified version of the events, leading to the last
meeting of the Fascist Grand Council. Although such a meeting had
been demanded by the pro-German Farinacci, who wanted to intensify
the Italian war effort, it was equally urged by those Fascist leaders, like
Grandi, who wanted to end the war. When, after the establishment of
the Badoglio government, Mussolini's chief supporters were arrested,
Farinacci succeeded in escaping to the German embassy and was flown
to Germany. His reception at Hitler's headquarters, on 27 July, is described in Goebbels' *Diaries*, p. 412.

[7] Orlando, the well-known Italian statesman, pre-Fascist Italian Prime
Minister, played a role in preparing the fall of Mussolini. See Badoglio,
Italy in the Second World War, p. 43.

still there. They are receiving one celebrity after another. Among others, Buffarini[8] is there.

HITLER: Who's that?

HEWEL: Buffarini is a Fascist. . . It is also said that the Duce, strongly under the influence of the meeting in northern Italy,[9] is firmly decided to continue the war. That is all we have received so far. Glaise[10] hopes that he will hear something from Buffarini, who is with the Duce now. Then this afternoon—

HITLER: That fellow Farinacci is lucky he pulled that trick in Italy and not on me. If he had done something like that with me, I would have handed him over to Himmler immediately. What's the use of councils like that? What do they do except jabber?

HEWEL: As I said, Mackensen emphasizes that these are just rumors. But at any rate, there is a real crisis, and Mackensen feels that one shouldn't do anything with regard to the Duce's birthday, especially since the Duce has repeatedly told him that he would prefer not to have it mentioned. In view of the crisis, one should be particularly careful about that. However, he is still trying to get more information. To have the Reichsmarshal appear down there at this time—well, I'll get more information.

HITLER: Well, I don't know about that. The Reichsmarshal has been through many crises with me. He is ice cold in time of crisis. At such a time one can't have a better adviser than the Reichsmarshal. In time of crisis the Reichsmarshal is brutal and ice cold. I've always noticed that when it comes to the breaking point he is a man of iron without scruples. So you can't have a better one; a better one can't be found. He has been through all crises with me; through the worst crises; that's when he is ice cold.

[8] Buffarini-Guidi, Undersecretary in the Ministry of the Interior, member of the Fascist Grand Council, supported Mussolini to the end.

[9] Refers to the meeting between Hitler and Mussolini at Feltre, 19 July 1943.

[10] Probably General von Glaise Horstenau, German Military Plenipotentiary in Croatia; no other references to his presence in Rome at this time have been found.

Every time it got really bad he became ice cold. Well, we'll see.

[*The discussion again turns to Jodl's report, about which a few remarks are made. Then Keitel brings up another matter.*]

KEITEL: My Fuehrer, a report has come in from the area of the Military Commander, Belgium-Northern France. In the last few days the security police have taken major action against the Belgian Communist party. They raided the printing shop and arrested the leaders. Since they had already penetrated the organization, they have been able to arrest the secretariat, 53 of the chief functionaries, 22 of their leading men, and have confiscated all of their equipment—weapons, ammunition, all of their propaganda material, files, all sorts of things. In other words, a big affair; one could really call it a knockout blow. The security police believe that in the Command Area Belgium-Northern France they have reached the point where everything is under control. The co-operation is good; very intensive and therefore fruitful.

HITLER: You know, when we first came to power our police weren't at peak efficiency and for the following reason: important as the right political attitude may be, that is not enough; a good knowledge of crime is necessary, experience in criminal matters; and unfortunately some of the crime experts belonged to the old police force. It was a hard job to screen them all to find the decent ones, and it didn't quite succeed. In that 'Rote Kapelle'[11] business they discovered that one bastard in there had been in contact with foreigners since 1933. I have to admit one thing about our enemies; by the time they dissolved the Allied Control Commissions[12] they had installed their cells in the whole machine of the state, in the machine of

[11] The 'Rote Kapelle' (Red Chapel) was a minor anti-Nazi group in Germany, with contacts in Russia. Consisting of higher members of the civil service, particularly in the Air Ministry, it was uncovered by the Gestapo in 1943, and 78 of its members were executed.
[12] He means 'after the First World War.'

the party, everywhere in public offices, in the economic world, in administration.

KEITEL: They were operating all right.

HITLER: So the Control Commission could go home all right. Actually the cells continued to function and were in contact with their embassies, consuls-general, attachés, et cetera. They functioned splendidly. There was no need for a Control Commission any longer. They functioned splendidly. They even had people in the police. In 1933 the police was handicapped by the fact that it was full of National Socialists with the best intentions but very little police experience. They had no training in criminology. Now ten years have passed, and these people have acquired experience and knowledge. They are now on the same high level as the police of the Latin countries, which have always had a good state police. Even in the Austrian Empire, in Russia, and in France they always had a good state police. Now we have that too, and we can see the results. Now there is hardly anything on which the police are not completely informed. Naturally it requires big organization and large resources.

HEWEL: Large resources and many young people.

HITLER: Young people who are adventurous, but also great resources. One can't get anywhere with rewards of 100 or 200 marks. To bribe such a person, you have to deal in larger sums. . . One has to be very careful. Our people have to be arrested and locked up along with others, so that the others don't notice what they are. They are even tried and convicted along with the others. Actually, though, they are our agents. The others must never realize who has sold them out. Do you have anything else?

PUTTKAMER: No.

25 JULY 1943

This conference lasted from
9.30 P.M. until 10.13 P.M.

Participants: HITLER,
BODENSCHATZ, BUHLE, CHRISTIAN,
GUENSCHE, HEWEL, JODL, KEITEL,
PUTTKAMER, SPEER, WAIZENEGGER,
AND ZEITZLER.

*Zeitzler reports on the situation
in the East. Hitler asks him to be brief. The chief problem
under discussion is the freeing of troops by withdrawals on
the Eastern front. It is decided to ask Kluge to come to a
conference.*

HITLER: Do you know about the developments in Italy?

KEITEL: No, I just heard the end of your discussion.

HITLER: The Duce has resigned. It is not confirmed yet. Badoglio has taken over the government. The Duce has resigned.

KEITEL: Voluntarily, my Fuehrer?

HITLER: Probably by request of the King, under pressure of the court. I told you yesterday about the attitude of the King.

JODL: Badoglio has taken over the government.

HITLER: Badoglio, our most bitter enemy, has taken over the government. We have to decide immediately on a way to get our people to the mainland.[1]

---

[1] Hitler refers to the German troops fighting in Sicily. This conference, and the following conference with Generalfeldmarschall von Kluge, are to a large extent concerned with troop dispositions Hitler considers necessary due to Mussolini's fall from power. A short account of the position of the units most frequently mentioned in these con-

92

JODL: The decisive thing is: are the Italians going to continue fighting, or not?

HITLER: They say they will fight, but it is certainly treachery. We must realize that this is open treachery. I'm just waiting for information about what the Duce says. What's-his-name wants to speak with the Duce now. I hope he'll get hold of him. I want the Duce to come here right away if he can get hold of him. I want the Duce to come to Germany right away.

---

ferences may help the reader to understand them. The chief German units fighting in Sicily were the SS-Panzerdivision 'Herrmann Goering,' reorganized after its destruction in Tunisia and chiefly composed of very young troops, and the 15th Panzergrenadier Division, which had been put together from various units in Sicily, and had originally been named 'The Sicily Division.' In addition, parts of the 29th Motorized Infantry Division and of the 1st Parachute Division were in Sicily, other parts of these units were in southern Italy, and, of the 1st Parachute Division, also in France. On the Italian mainland, the chief German force was the 3rd Panzergrenadier Division, which had been transported from France to Italy in June, and was stationed north of Rome. Hitler's principal concern was to make sure of the Alpine passes dominating the access to Italy from Germany and France. For the securing of the lines from Germany to Italy, he had the 44th, 65th, and 71st Divisions, stationed at Tyrol and Carinthia, at his disposal; the accesses to northern Italy from France could be secured by the 76th, 94th, and 305th Divisions, stationed in southern France. Here the special problem was that these divisions had the additional task of replacing the 4th Italian Army, which had been occupying parts of southern France. Aside from this, Hitler wanted to send reinforcements to southern Italy and to the 3rd Panzergrenadier Division near Rome. For this purpose, the troops at his disposal were the 24th and 26th Panzer Divisions, and the 2nd Parachute Division, which were then being reorganized in France. For the action he was planning against the Italian Government, Hitler decided to use his politically most reliable unit, for which reason he ordered the 1st SS-Panzer Division 'Leibstandarte,' commanded by SS-Oberstgruppenfuehrer Sepp Dietrich, from the southern sector of the Russian front to Italy. This transfer would have left a gap in the southern sector of the Russian front. Since the Army Group 'South' had no reserves to fill this gap, troops had to be taken from the Army Group 'Center,' commanded by Kluge. This rather complicated operation made a conference with Kluge necessary. Among the units to be transferred from Kluge's command to Manstein's Army Group 'South,' the most valuable was the SS-Panzer Division 'Grossdeutchland,' which had come up from Army Group 'South' only a short time before. For further details about the military aspects of the Italian collapse, see the protocol of the conference between the German and Italian military leaders held at Feltre on 6 August, published in *Hitler-Mussolini Correspondence*, pp. 197-207.

JODL: If there is any doubt, there is only one thing to do.

HITLER: I have been thinking about ordering the 3rd Panzergrenadier Division to occupy Rome and to capture the whole government. ——There's only one thing to do; namely, try to get the men[2] on German ships, even if they have to abandon their equipment. To hell with the equipment. That doesn't matter. The men are much more important. I still expect news from Mackensen. After that we can work out the orders. But anyway they have to get out down there.

JODL: Yes.

HITLER: ——The most important thing at the moment is to secure the Alpine passes and to be ready to make contact with the 4th Italian Army so that we can get hold of the French passes immediately. That's the most important thing of all. We have to send down some units for that purpose, even the 24th Panzer Division.

KEITEL: That would be the worst thing that could happen to us—not having the passes.

HITLER: Has Rommel left yet?

JODL: Yes, Rommel has left.

HITLER: Where is he now? Still in Wiener-Neustadt?

KEITEL: That can be found out.

HITLER: Find out where Rommel is immediately.

[*At this point, Hitler uses a map to indicate in detail how various divisions are to be moved from France into the Alps.*]

HITLER: Is the 3rd Panzergrenadier Division near Rome complete?

JODL: It is there; but it is not entirely mobile, only in part.

HITLER: How many weapons and assault guns do they have?

BUHLE: The 3rd Panzergrenadier Division has 42 assault guns.

---

[2] He means the German troops in Sicily.

HITLER: Thank God, we still have the Parachute Division here. The fellows down here[3] have to be saved under all circumstances. They are of no use down here. They have to get back. Especially the paratroops and the men from the 'Goering.' Their equipment doesn't matter a damn. Let them blow it up or destroy it; but the men have to get back. There are 70,000 men there now. If flying is possible, the whole thing won't take long. They should hold a cover line and pull out from behind it. Except for side arms, let them leave everything behind. They don't need anything else. We can handle the Italians with side arms. ——The important thing is to get these units out of there, and to put the 'Leibstandarte' in motion.

ZEITZLER: Yes, I'll give the orders right away——First I have to bring up rolling stock.—— It will take two or three days to move it up. I'll start right away.

[*Zeitzler leaves.*]

JODL: We really ought to wait for exact reports about what is going on.

HITLER: Certainly, but still we have to plan ahead. Undoubtedly, in their treachery, they will proclaim that they will remain loyal to us; but that is treachery. Of course they won't remain loyal.

KEITEL: Has anyone spoken to this fellow Badoglio?

HITLER: In the meantime we've received the following report. Yesterday the Duce was with the Grand Council.[4] At the Grand Council there were Grandi, whom I have always called a swine, Bottai, and above all Ciano. They spoke against Germany at this Council; and specifically that there was no sense in continuing the war and that one must try to extricate Italy in one way or another. A few were opposed. Farinacci et cetera were probably also against that, but not so effectively as those who spoke for

[3] In Sicily.

[4] The facts given here about the last meeting of the Fascist Grand Council, although presented in a biased form, are substantially correct. These events and the first contacts between Badoglio and the Nazi Government are described in detail in books like Bonomi's *Diario di un anno*, Badoglio's *Italy in the Second World War*, and Bottai's *Vent' anni e un giorno*.

such a move. This evening the Duce let Mackensen know
that he would certainly take up this battle and not capitu-
late. Then I suddenly heard that Badoglio wanted to speak
to Mackensen. Mackensen told him that he had nothing to
say to him. Thereupon Badoglio became even more insis-
tent and finally sent a man—

HEWEL: Mackensen sent one of his men to Badoglio.

HITLER: He said that the King had just charged him with
the formation of a government after the Duce had laid
down his office. ——Now the minister[5] has ordered Mackensen to call at the Foreign Office. He will probably get
the official announcement there. I assume that all of this
is correct. Secondly, the minister wants to know if I
agree that Mackensen should go to see the Duce immediately. I told him that Mackensen should go to see him
right away, and try to persuade the Duce to come to
Germany. I would assume that he wants to talk to me. If
the Duce comes, that is all right. If he won't come, then I
don't know. If the Duce will come to Germany and will
talk to me, that is a good sign. If he doesn't come, or if
he isn't able to get away, or if he resigns because he doesn't
feel well, which wouldn't surprise me with such a bunch
of traitors—then one doesn't know. Although that so-and-so
declared immediately that the war would be continued,
that won't make any difference. They have to say that, but
it remains treason. But we'll play the same game while preparing everything to take over the whole crew with one
stroke, to capture all of that riffraff. Tomorrow I'll send a
man down there with orders for the commander of the 3rd
Panzer-grenadier Division to the effect that he must drive
into Rome with a special detail and arrest the whole government, the King and the whole bunch right away. First
of all, to arrest the Crown Prince and to take over the
whole gang, especially Badoglio and that entire crew. Then
watch them cave in, and in two or three days there'll be
another coup. ——How far are they from Rome?

JODL: About 100 kilometers.

[5] He means the German Foreign Minister Ribbentrop.

HITLER: 100? 60 kilometers. That's all they'll need. If he drives in with motorized troops he'll get in there and arrest the whole works right away.

KEITEL: Two hours.

JODL: 50 to 60 kilometers.

HITLER: That's no distance.

WAIZENEGGER: The division has 42 assault guns.

HITLER: Are they down there with the division?

WAIZENEGGER: Yes, with the division.

HITLER: Jodl, work that out right away.

JODL: Six battalions.

KEITEL: Ready for action. Five only partially ready.

HITLER: Jodl, work out the orders for the 3rd Panzergrenadier Division to be sent down, telling them to drive into Rome with their assault guns without letting anyone know about it, and to arrest the government, the King, and the whole crew. ——I want the Crown Prince above all.

KEITEL: He is more important than the old man.

BODENSCHATZ: That has to be organized so that they can be packed into a plane and flown away.

HITLER: Right into a plane and off with them.

BODENSCHATZ: Don't let the Bambino get lost at the airfield.

HITLER: In eight days the thing will be reversed again. —— And then I want to speak to the Reichsmarshal.

BODENSCHATZ: I will inform him immediately.

HITLER: The climax will come at the moment when we have mustered enough strength to go in there and disarm the whole gang. The motto of the whole operation must be that the traitorous generals and Ciano—who is hated anyway—are leading a coup against Fascism.

TELEPHONE CONVERSATION WITH REICHSMARSHAL GOERING.
[*The stenographers could not hear Goering's part of the conversation.*]

HITLER: Hello, Goering? I don't know—did you get the

news? Well, there's no direct confirmation yet, but there can't be any doubt that the Duce has resigned and that Badoglio has taken his place. In Rome it is not a question of possibilities, but of facts. —That's the truth. Goering, there's no doubt about it. —What? —I don't know, we are trying to find out. Of course that's nonsense. He'll keep going, but don't ask me how—. But now they'll see how *we* keep going—

Well, I just wanted to tell you that. At any rate, under these circumstances I think it would be a good idea for you to come here right away.[6] ——What?—I don't know. I'll tell you about that then. But adjust yourself to the fact that it's true.

[*End of the telephone conversation.*]

We had a mess like this once before.[7] That was on the day the *coup d'état* took place *here*. We changed things there, too. I only hope they didn't arrest the Duce. But if they did, it is even more important that we go in there.

JODL: That would be a different story though. In that case we would have to go in right away. Otherwise, the important thing is to get our troops over the passes. Else there might be units stationed there by the traitors, and then we can't get anything over anymore. The most important thing now is to get these jammed-up transports rolling again. That order was already given yesterday—to the effect that everything should be moved into northern Italy, even if it can't be moved on, so that we will get as much as possible into northern Italy.

[*The rest of the discussion is concerned with minute details of the planned operations in Italy, repeating to a large extent what has already been said. Mention is made of intelligence reports*

---

[6] Hitler asked all of his chief lieutenants to come to his headquarters for a meeting on the Italian crisis, see Goebbels' *Diaries*, pp. 406-12.
[7] Hitler alludes to the events in Belgrade in March 1941, when the Government, which had signed a treaty with Germany, was overthrown; Hitler then marched into Yugoslavia.

*from Cairo and Switzerland, which deal with
Allied invasion plans for Greece and the Italian
mainland. The discussion closes with a report on
air activity by Christian.]*

26 JULY 1943

This conference lasted from
12.25 A.M. until 12.45 A.M.

Participants: HITLER,
BODENSCHATZ, CHRISTIAN, HEWEL,
JODL, AND KEITEL

> *During these days, one confer-*
> *ence after another on the subject of the Italian crisis took*
> *place at Hitler's headquarters. The stenographic reports of*
> *most of these conferences were destroyed. The following*
> *comes from the report of a brief meeting on the night of 25*
> *July to 26 July; the chief topic of this meeting was the*
> *planned action against Rome, and it was chiefly concerned*
> *with the formulation of the orders and directives which were*
> *to be given to the German Commanders in Italy. Hitler*
> *makes some jokes about General Hube, who had reported*
> *that the situation in Italy was quite stable: 'You see how*
> *dangerous it is when "apolitical generals" get into such a*
> *political atmosphere.' Hewel asks about orders concerning*
> *the treatment of the Vatican.*

HEWEL: Shouldn't we say that the exits of the Vatican will
be occupied?

HITLER: That doesn't make any difference. I'll go right into
the Vatican. Do you think the Vatican embarrasses me?
We'll take that over right away. For one thing, the entire
diplomatic corps are in there. It's all the same to me. That
rabble is in there. We'll get that bunch of swine out of
there. . . Later we can make apologies. That doesn't make
any difference. . .

HEWEL: We will find documents in there.

HITLER: There, yes, we'll get documents. The treason will

come to light. A pity that the Foreign Minister isn't here. How long will it take him to draft the directive for Mackensen?

HEWEL: It may be finished.

HITLER: All right.

HEWEL: I'll check on it right away.

HITLER: Will that be a journalistic essay of twelve pages? I'm always afraid of that with you people. That can be done in two or three lines.—I've been thinking about something else, Jodl.[1] If our people in the East want to attack tomorrow or the day after—I don't know if the units have been gathered yet—I would recommend letting them do that. Because then the 'Leibstandarte' can still take part. For if they have to wait for the stock anyway—

KEITEL: The rolling stock.

JODL: That they could do, because it would be better if the 'Leibstandarte' leaves a secure position behind.

HITLER: Yes, that would be good. Then that one division, the 'Leibstandarte,' can be taken away. They must be moved first, but can leave their stuff there. They can leave a lot of their equipment over there; they don't have to take the tanks along. They can leave them over there, and get them replaced here. —By getting Panthers here, they will be perfectly well equipped. That's obvious; by the time the division is there, it will have its tanks.

HEWEL: I want to ask about the Prince of Hesse. He stands around all the time. Shall I say that we won't need him?

HITLER: I'll send for him and say a few words to him.

HEWEL: Of course, he bothers everybody and wants to know everything.

HITLER: One the contrary, we can use him as camouflage, as an impenetrable wall. That will be very good. In earlier times, when we planned something, we frequently surrounded ourselves with people who didn't know anything, which gave the other side the idea that since these people were around, everything would be all right. I'm afraid, though, that Goering might give himself away.

---

[1] The question, raised in this brief exchange with Jodl, is taken up at length in next day's conference with Kluge, published below.

BODENSCHATZ: I already told him that pointedly.

HITLER: One has to be very polite. I would start by giving him all the proclamations we have collected here. They have been made public anyway. Philipp can read those all right, they aren't dangerous. But be sure to give the order not to let him have the wrong thing.[2]

---

[2] As Goebbels reports in his *Diaries*, pp. 412-13, he was instructed by Hitler to take charge of Prince Philipp of Hesse.

26 JULY 1943

This conference lasted from
12.10 P.M. until 12.45 P.M.

Participants: HITLER,
KLUGE, SCHERFF, AND ZEITZLER

*This was an extremely active day
at Hitler's headquarters. In the morning a conference took
place in which Goering and Himmler participated; the
transcript is so badly mutilated that only the fact of its
concern with an examination of the over-all situation, aris-
ing from the Italian developments, can be deduced. This
conference was interrupted by a meeting with Fieldmarshal
von Kluge, who had flown in from the Eastern front. Although many parts of the discussion are not clear because
of references to maps stretched out on the conference
table, the map facing page 57 will make the general points
of discussion comprehensible. The transcript deserves publication because it shows the importance of the Italian
events for German strategic plans.*

HITLER: Did anything important come in, Zeitzler?

ZEITZLER: Nothing special, my Fuehrer.

HITLER: I don't know if you have been oriented about the
over-all position, Marshal.

KLUGE: Only by a radio report today.

HITLER: Well, the radio announcement is of course not
true.[1] Actually, this briefly is the situation: The developments I feared, and which I hinted at during the general
conference recently, have taken place. It is a revolt insti-
gated by the Royal House and by Marshal Badoglio, that

[1] The German radio first explained Mussolini's resignation as caused
by illness and as being purely an Italian internal affair.

103

is, by our old enemies. The Duce was arrested yesterday. He was summoned to the Quirinal for conferences, then was arrested inside the Quirinal, and was then abruptly dismissed by this decree. Then this new government was formed, which, of course, officially still declares that it will co-operate with us. Of course that is only camouflage to gain a few days' time in which to consolidate the new regime. With the exception of Jews and riffraff who are causing a commotion in Rome, there is no one behind the new regime, that is evident. But at the moment they are in, and it is absolutely imperative for us to act. I have always feared this development. That is the sole reason for my constant fear to strike prematurely in the East; because I always thought that the lid might blow off in the South. The English will take advantage of this, the Russians will cheer, the English will land; one might say that in Italy treason was always in the air. Under these circumstances, I considered it expedient to wait until several units were ready. After all, we do have units in the West. I am firmly determined to strike here with lightning speed, just as I did in the case of Yugoslavia.[2] I would estimate Italian resistance as nil. The Fascists will come over to us. Incidentally, we brought Farinacci over; he is with us. He is already in Munich, on his way here.[3] I don't know where the Duce himself is. As soon as I find out, I'll have him brought out by parachutists.[4] In my opinion that whole government is a typical *putsch* government, like that in Belgrade, and one day it will collapse, provided that we act immediately. I can't take actions unless I move additional units from the East to the West. In case your offensive can't be carried through, we must make plans for reorganizing your line. Are these your maps?

[2] See footnote 7 on page 98.
[3] See footnote 6 on page 88.
[4] From this time on, the planning for the operation that led to Mussolini's liberation by Skorzeny in September went ahead; the operation received the code name 'Eiche' and was placed under the general direction of Generaloberst Student, commanding general of parachute troops.

ZEITZLER: They are ours, marked according to reports.

HITLER: Will you please explain your over-all position to me. The point is I can't just take out units from anywhere. I have to take politically reliable units. That means, first of all, the 3rd SS Panzer Division, which I can only take from the Army Group 'South.' That means that you will have to send other units down, and one can free those units only by liquidating this whole business, by giving up this whole bulge. Perhaps the front should also be shortened at other, minor, places.

KLUGE: Well, my Fuehrer, the present situation is that a certain pressure from strong elements is being felt here. However, this has not had the full effect, because they[5] had trouble crossing the Oka River. Unfortunately, they were able to score a fairly deep penetration yesterday, in the area of the 34th Army.[6] However, this is being compensated by counter blows, although our own forces there are relatively weak. Here was the break-through, in the area of the 297th Division, which could be compensated somewhat by the withdrawal of the whole line.

HITLER: Are you on *that* line?

KLUGE: No, on *this* line.

ZEITZLER: The other map shows the exact position today. Up there is the withdrawal.

HITLER: Please show it to me on this map.

KLUGE: Well, the present situation is that yesterday there was a very strong attack here, although it was not as strong as we had expected. Rather, it was weaker and narrower, and although it resulted in a certain penetration, it could be stopped. Principally, there were large tank attacks—here there were 150 tanks, of which 50 were knocked out. The plan is now to go into this so-called Oka position, to cross over here, to shorten the Bolkhov bulge— tonight. I would like to take permission along right away to move the line away from Bolkhov and to shorten the

[5] He means the Russians; very frequently in this conference, 'they' or 'he' means the Russians.

[6] There is a mistake in the transcript; no German army numbered higher than 25 existed; probably he meant the 4th Army, which was fighting in this area.

whole business here. In general, our intention is to retreat here again, and then to move into this line. That's the immediate plan. After this minor withdrawal has been carried out, the general withdrawal should take place. In preparation for this movement—which has to take place in a very constricted area, especially here in the North—the 'Grossdeutschland' has advanced with its reconnaissance forces; has thrown back the enemy here; although it struck fairly heavy resistance here. I don't know how that is going to develop today. At any rate, they are to reach the edge of this land, which is marked as swamp. Actually that is no swamp; unfortunately it is terrain which can be crossed safely.

ZEITZLER: This morning the enemy made stronger attacks.

KLUGE: Has he attacked there?

ZEITZLER: Yes, and also an armored brigade.

KLUGE: We knew about that already yesterday. In this area the enemy has two infantry divisions—that is, two good ones—plus one armored brigade, and another armored brigade is being moved up.

HITLER: Tell me, where are those 100 Panthers?

KLUGE: They aren't there yet. They are just being assembled after having been unloaded.

ZEITZLER: The last trains were all there on the 26th.

KLUGE: They are there. Their crews are, too, though not all of them.

HITLER: And where are they?

KLUGE: In Berdiansk. Well, there is rather strong pressure here, which is not limited to this place but unfortunately also extends to this very weak salient, which, in my opinion, is the most dangerous place. It is held by some jumbled, miscellaneous troops that first tried to hold this line but have now been pressed back. The following development could become very unpleasant: if the enemy could take this road to the station at Reseta. We are still using that for moving from south to north. For that reason I have requested that the 113th Division be committed up here with the 4th Army, next to the Orel rail line and next to the highway.

ZEITZLER: The Fuehrer has already given permission.

KLUGE: —and to compensate for that, I would like to pull out two divisions; first one division was supposed to be sent *there* right away, and then another which we really also wanted to put into this locality, in order to strengthen this wing; because *here* we ought not to retreat one step more. That would be a very unpleasant development.

Here there are strong forces on the advance, which are far superior to our own—even tanks, but comparatively few of them; the mass of their tanks is pressing down in this direction, toward the 'Grossdeutschland,' and of course *here,* too.

HITLER: They must be gradually losing their tanks, too.

KLUGE: Certainly, that is clear. We have knocked out quite a number of them. Just the same, he is still attacking with strong tank units so that at present we have our hands full in coping with this crowd. That is the present situation.

Now we want to withdraw into this shortened Oka line, and on this basis the evacuation of Orel and everything that belongs to it is supposed to take place, and then—

ZEITZLER: Then the next point is the 'Grossdeutschland,' sir.

KLUGE: My Fuehrer, I still wanted to add that in order to create a sound foundation for further movements, Model[7] and I both feel that the attack of 'Grossdeutschland,' which is in progress, and another attack are necessary and would establish a solid line.

HITLER: I don't think that this will work any more. Will the 'Grossdeutschland' have to go through the woods?

KLUGE: Certainly not. That would have been forbidden. But the attack of the 253rd Division—

HITLER: I want to review the over-all situation again. The problem is to pull out a fair number of units in a very short time. This group includes, first of all, the 3rd Panzer Division, which I must take from the Army Group 'South,' which itself has to cover a very broad front. . . In other words, it is a very difficult decision, but I have no choice.

---

[7] Generaloberst Model was then commander of the 9th Army, belonging to Kluge's Army Group, 'Center.'

Down there, I can only accomplish something with crack formations that are politically close to Fascism. If it weren't for that, I could take a couple of Army Panzer Divisions. But as it is, I need a magnet to gather the people together. I don't want to give up the Fascist backbone, because in a short time we will rebuild so many things. I am not afraid that we can't manage that, if we can hold northern Italy.

Here is what they're doing in Rome. The *Messaggero* has published a disgusting article about the Duce, which will pierce every Fascist to his heart. One must not get the idea that the people as a whole are as vacillating as that crowd that has been bribed. That's the riffraff there, the Jews and such trash, who are looting Fascist party offices.

KLUGE: In Rome?

HITLER: We had the same thing here in Germany. But just these methods resulted in making fanatics out of the National Socialists. The same will happen in Italy. But I have to have units down there which come under a political banner. It is not enough for me to have just a good military outfit down there. . . The Fascists must join us. We will get them because of the fate that threatens them. In my opinion, within a very short time we shall raise divisions down there, composed not of regular soldiers, but of volunteers out of the regular divisions. You can't accomplish anything with their present army anyway, because it always runs away.

KLUGE: My Fuehrer, I want to call attention to the fact that nothing can be pulled out of the line now.[8] That is completely out of the question at the present moment.

[8] The following discussion refers to the tempo of the German retreat from Orel to winter positions along the Dnieper, the so-called 'Hagen' Line. Originally this was supposed to be a step retreat, from Orel to Karachaev, from Karachaev to the Desna, and from the Desna to the Dnieper, extending from the end of August well into the fall of 1943. In order to free troops for action in Italy, Hitler wanted to force Kluge to start this retreat much earlier and to withdraw at greater speed than had been originally planned. The German line was back on the Dnieper at the end of September. The German retreat has been characterized as methodical, the daily withdrawals from 5 August to 22 September from 1½ to 3½ miles.

HITLER: Just the same, it must be possible—

KLUGE: We can only withdraw troops when we reach the Hagen Line.

ZEITZLER: Let the 'Grossdeutschland' get to this point, then draw them out, keep them here for a while, and the 7th Panzer must leave soon—

KLUGE: We could not anticipate these over-all political developments. We couldn't guess that this would happen. Now a new decision must be made, first of all that Orel must be evacuated after we have moved out our own vital material.

HITLER: Absolutely.

KLUGE: But then, of course, we will be able to evacuate. But of course that doesn't mean that I can take out the whole civilian population and the stores and all those things. That simply can't be done in such a short period. That needs thorough organization. This is a thickly populated area, so that can't be accomplished at a breakneck speed. Then there is another question: this rear line, the so-called Hagen Line, is still under construction.

HITLER: Yes, unfortunately.

KLUGE: There is nothing that can be done about it. We have a huge number of construction battalions and God knows what all else. We have been having cloudbursts every day, of a style you couldn't even visualize here. All of the construction battalions had to keep the roads in shape; they were supposed to have been back in the Hagen Line long ago in order to finish it, but I needed them up front to straighten things out.

HITLER: Perhaps the rain will stop soon.

KLUGE: I certainly hope so. It was a little better today.

HITLER: But you have to admit, Marshal, that the moment your troops reach approximately that line, quite a number of your divisions can be moved out.

KLUGE: My Fuehrer, I want to call your attention to the fact that four divisions—

HITLER: —are very weak.

KLUGE: I have four divisions which are completely exhausted.

HITLER: I'll grant you that. But how many of the enemy's divisions are smashed?

KLUGE: Well, in spite of that. Now we come to the question of the so-called Karachaev position, my Fuehrer. If I move into that position, which isn't ready, and if I am attacked again with tanks and everything else, they will break through with the tanks, and then when they have broken through with their tanks, the moment has come. I am just mentioning that again because this is a good opportunity, because we might get into a very difficult situation. I would like to suggest again that it might be more practical to move all the way back behind the Desna River while we are at it. We must have the Karachaev position anyway as a skeleton, as it is now and as it will be after two more weeks of work, in order to give the troops support on the retreat. Therefore, my suggestion is that it would be more practical to move right behind the Desna now.

HITLER: Here you are safe and *here* you are not.

KLUGE: Bryansk—this part of the line is good, but this other piece is not fully constructed yet.

HITLER: That part is not better than this one. If you put these two pieces at Bryansk together, then they make up as much as—

KLUGE: But then I have to have time to construct them. I can't do that—

HITLER: You would have to construct the other one anyway.

KLUGE: Yes, I would here. But not over here at the Desna.

HITLER: Not here.

KLUGE: I have to build from here to here, and over there I wouldn't have to build anything.

HITLER: But that is practically the same length—

KLUGE: But this one is better because nothing can happen to me on this whole line.

HITLER: They won't attack here. They'll come down this way.

KLUGE: That's the decisive point. But then, my Fuehrer, I won't be able to draw back as early. First I have to construct the Hagen Line; I must have that in order, I can't just go back in a mad rush.

HITLER: Nobody said anything about a mad rush.

KLUGE: But at any rate not much faster than was planned.

HITLER: What was your timetable?

KLUGE: Timetable as follows: In about five days—

HITLER: Altogether, when will you be back on that line?

KLUGE: We had not intended to be back in there before the beginning of September.

HITLER: That's impossible, Marshal, completely impossible.

KLUGE: Naturally under these circumstances everything has changed a little. But it will take at least four weeks before the position is even usable.

ZEITZLER: Do it in two moves. Perhaps you can stay here until the line is ready.

KLUGE: That won't work for the following reasons: maybe for a short time, but not in the long run: the rail capacity to Orel is 50 trains, but the moment we lose Orel it decreases to 18 trains per day, which would be a very unpleasant situation.

ZEITZLER: You won't need very many trains if you are in this position.

KLUGE: No, that won't work. I don't even have facilities to unload them.

ZEITZLER: If your troops are here, this strip of rail line is of no value.

KLUGE: No, not any more. I just wanted to emphasize that if I give up Orel, I have to retreat in one move; but the important thing is that I have my positions prepared behind me.

ZEITZLER: If you can hold here for six or seven days, then you gain that much time and a few units here will be freed.

KLUGE: But the calculations must always be based on the situation in the rear. I must have at least a moderately strong position, or else they'll overrun me, and then I'll be in the hole again and won't be able to spare any troops.

ZEITZLER: Sir, on this line you will gain six or seven days.

KLUGE: You mean here? Oh no, the enemy will reach that in two or three days.

ZEITZLER: If you could hold this for six or seven days, then you could move the line down from here to here, so that in ten days you would be here.

KLUGE: You mean now?

ZEITZLER: Yes.

KLUGE: That would mean a headlong retreat in this whole area, which, in my opinion—

ZEITZLER: Perhaps the Army Group can make new calculations.

HITLER: Just the same, Marshal, we are not masters of our own decisions here; in war, decisions are frequently necessary—

KLUGE: My Fuehrer: If you order me to do it quickly—but then I would like to direct your attention to the fact that this plan is contradictory to that of the Hagen Line, which isn't finished.

HITLER: The other one isn't finished either, at least not at that point, and anyway, the Russians won't attack where the position is finished.

KLUGE: For instance, I could do the following, my Fuehrer: I could move back into this position, the construction of which is more advanced up here and also here, although over here practically nothing has been done. In that case I would have to allow for giving way a bit here, but then this has to be built.

HITLER: Certainly, that is supposed to be built, as a precaution; but I don't want a withdrawal at this point now, because that will have to be done anyway in the winter when the Russians attack. Model has built that up very solidly. It ought to be possible to build some sort of a position in that time. At the time of the advance we managed to build a position anywhere we had to stop, and to hold it. Those bastards over there can dig a position in two days, and we can't push them out of it.

KLUGE: My Fuehrer, actually the question is that of tanks. That is the main point. He batters so hard with his artillery and tanks that he gets through after all.

ZEITZLER: Sir, in my opinion, moving back into *this* line would free half of the divisions, which could then be pulled back here and you could have them dig for six days. Then that position would be ready.

KLUGE: No, that doesn't solve the problem. In my opinion, the earliest time for occupying the Hagen Line would be in—let's see, today is the 26th—in about four weeks, if we cut it fine maybe three or four weeks, but that's absolutely the earliest.

HITLER: Well, we just can't wait that long. We must free some troops before that. It's no use.

KLUGE: Sauckel won't be able to get his workers out before that.

HITLER: He has to. Look how fast the Russians can evacuate.

KLUGE: But my Fuehrer, that is an enormous crowd. He'll jam up all my bridges over the Desna.

HITLER: How many people are in here, anyway?

KLUGE: Several hundred thousand.

ZEITZLER: 250,000 men, I was told—

HITLER: What are 250,000 men? That's nothing at all.

KLUGE: My Fuehrer, I need my forces for fighting now. I can't use them for all kinds of other things.

HITLER: On the contrary, I would herd these people out of there immediately and put them to work on the position here.

KLUGE: We've already tried that. At the moment they are all harvesting. The rye has just been mowed. They have no idea of what is coming. If we move them back for construction work they'll all run away in the night. They'll run to the front just to mow their rye. All these are difficulties. Nothing has been organized.

HITLER: What is going to be done with the harvested rye? Is it going to be burned?

KLUGE: Certainly, we'll have to. Probably we will burn it, but I don't know whether we'll have time. We'll have to destroy it somehow. Especially the valuable cattle we have here. The famous Kaminsky[9] is here, the one who played a great role that other time.

HITLER: Where is he?

KLUGE: Around here, near Lokot, in this area; that's his empire.

HITLER: In my opinion, behind this position—

KLUGE: I have ordered that he is to be left alone, in order that these trecks, which have already started, can cross the Desna; and back here I have lots of guerrillas who are not finished off. On the contrary, they are making themselves felt again. They were suddenly reinforced by a huge parachute operation, here. And then there was this famous cutting of the rail line at four hundred points.

HITLER: All that may be perfectly true, but it doesn't alter the fact that this has to be done. I think that the Army Group 'South' is in a much worse position. Look at the kind of sectors it has. One of its divisions, the 335th, has a front of 45 kilometers.

KLUGE: But, my Fuehrer, I don't know how the impression originated that we didn't have long sectors too. That's where the 56th Division was, they had more than 50 kilometers; and the 34th had 48 kilometers. That calculation is not correct.

HITLER: That's true, you did have such sectors when we started out.

KLUGE: At the time we started out—

HITLER: On the whole, the Army Group 'Center' had an entirely different type of division sector.

KLUGE: Our sectors became narrower through the mass attack, but we still have 30 kilometers and more apiece. Our front is already thinned out to that extent.

HITLER: That's no comparison.

KLUGE: Up there in the sector of the 3rd Panzer it is very thin too.

HITLER: How is the situation here?

ZEITZLER: They haven't attacked here. The latest seems to

[9] Commander of some Russian formations fighting on the German side. The activities of these formations were mentioned in the Nuremberg *Trial of The Major War Criminals*.

be that they have pulled out their motorized corps here,
and have replaced them with rifle corps of the Guard.
They may be resting these corps in order to use them over
here. I'm a little worried about that place, because they
moved that Parachute Army up there too. I'm not sure
what he plans to do with that. Their railroad traffic is a
little heavier, so that I am of the opinion that they are
pulling troops out by rail. Or else they are bringing them
up there. So we have to watch that. They evidently had
too heavy casualties, so they've stopped trying to do that
with motorized units. They are pulling out here. I have
spoken to Manstein about this business, this as well as that.
He called up again today. Now that the 'Leibstandarte' has
left,[10] he wants to reconsider whether to attack at all. I
think it would be sensible to wait. This small matter
doesn't need to be cleaned up, since the pressure is not too
great.

HITLER: How soon can the 'Leibstandarte' leave?

ZEITZLER: The first train leaves tomorrow night. We are
counting on 12 trains per day. After four or five days, 20
trains. The whole movement, consisting of 120 trains, will
take from six to eight days.

HITLER: Only 120 trains?

ZEITZLER: Yes.

HITLER: Now, now, Zeitzler.

ZEITZLER: It might even be 130 trains.

HITLER: I'm afriad it will be 150.

ZEITZLER: It doesn't make much difference if there are ten
or fifteen more or less.

HITLER: What are they leaving behind? Are they going to
leave the Mark IV's here or are they going to take them
along?

ZEITZLER: Last night the order came through to leave
them behind, because they would get new ones. I counted
on that—but we should put pressure on the 'Leibstandarte'

[10] The 'Leibstandarte' Division in the process of being entrained for
Italy.

to leave them there. As far as I know Sepp,[11] he'll take them along unless we send someone down there to make sure. The best thing is for them to leave them.

HITLER: The two divisions that remain behind are weak anyway. It would be better to give them additional tanks, and one must see whether one can't give the Tigers to one of them. He[12] is going to get two Tiger companies anyway.

ZEITZLER: I agree that they shouldn't—

HITLER: That will be enough for the 'Leibstandarte.' How many Tigers is that—two companies?

ZEITZLER: He is going to get two more companies—22 Tigers.

HITLER: On top of that he's going to get 100 Panthers, his whole battalion. And then he must get replacements for his Mark IV's in the rear.

ZEITZLER: What should have gone there as replacements, I'll hold back, and he can have them too.

HITLER: Maybe assault guns too, so that he can leave his behind. That would strengthen the two remaining divisions. Then the next one to leave would be the 'Reich.' The 'Reich' can also leave part of its equipment to these or other units, and can get its 100 Panthers replaced in transit.

ZEITZLER: That way we are saving a lot of equipment.

HITLER: We are saving a lot of equipment, and the units out here are getting stronger. And then, Manstein has to get some more supplies for his divisions. For instance, the 16th Panzergrenadier Division must also get something.

ZEITZLER: When the other Panzer Divisions arrive, they can take over some of it——

KLUGE: Well, my Fuehrer, then we are confronted by a new situation.

ZEITZLER: Perhaps the Army Group can work out a plan for what is the earliest possibility, and what the risks involved would be.

[11] Sepp Dietrich, SS-Oberstgruppenfuehrer, commander of the SS Panzer Division 'Leibstandarte,' later of the 5th and 6th Panzer Armies.
[12] Evidently Dietrich.

KLUGE: We'll sit right down. I brought my G-3 along. We will go over it once more. But everything still depends on the construction of the Hagen Line. I don't want to slide back into a position that is practically nonexistent.

HITLER: This is how I really feel about it: If there weren't this pressing danger down here, I would have committed the two divisions you are getting right away, instead of the 113th.

KLUGE: Yes, my Fuehrer. Now there will be no forward commitment of these two divisions. There will be no attacks at all here; that would be useless; that would be senseless. That was all planned under the condition—

HITLER: Just secure the rail line so that it can be used.

KLUGE: According to the original plan, we would have had plenty of time to do this.

HITLER: Wouldn't it be possible to detach some units for the purpose of building up the position?

KLUGE: You mean take them away from Model? Though the others follow up every day—and we with the miserable remains of the 111th, 212th, 108th, with the 209th—

ZEITZLER: Those are the ones that were smashed up.

HITLER: All right then, draw out the broken divisions, fill them up, and build with *them*.

KLUGE: All right then, I'll have to free some units somehow. Unfortunately I also need troops to secure the roads along which these caravans are moving, or else they'll all be knocked off behind the Forest of Bryansk, because everything is swarming with guerrillas who have been reorganized.

HITLER: I too have to make difficult decisions, very difficult decisions.

KLUGE: I can well believe that.

HITLER: But there is nothing else to do.

KLUGE: But I absolutely cannot spare any units until this operation has been finished. We'll see how we can manage things afterwards.

HITLER: You must see to it that you finish it as soon as possible. I can tell you this much: 'Grossdeutschland' will be taken away in the near future, and secondly you will

have to give up a few units for that position down there.
You will have to give up a few Panzer—and a few Infantry Divisions—

KLUGE: Not Panzer! I have—

HITLER: Yes, we'll pull them out and they'll be refitted in
the West.

KLUGE: But I can't do anything without Panzer Divisions!

HITLER: But certainly you don't care about that 'junk.' You
can easily spare that.

KLUGE: What junk?

HITLER: You yourself said 'That's just junk.'

KLUGE: I did not say that!

HITLER: Yes, it slipped out. That's why we're going to take
them away from you.

KLUGE: No, my Fuehrer, I didn't mean that. I have so
little left, just a little bit. What I wanted to indicate was
that the situation is hardly tenable any more.

HITLER: Yes, you have no Panzers. That is why I say: they
can be taken away and refitted in the West. We can always
get them back again. Meanwhile they can be filled up. And
finally, the men have deserved it. It would be all wrong to
do it the other way. I can have these divisions reorganized
in the West, and the Western units can be moved up here.
The most important thing is to get the 9th and 10th SS
Divisions ready quickly.[13] Today I got an opinion how
the 'Goering' Division stands up in combat. The English
write that the very youngest, the 16-year olds, just out of
the Hitler Youth, have fought fanatically to the last man.
The English couldn't take any prisoners. Therefore I am
convinced that these few divisions composed of boys,
which are already trained, will fight fantastically well,
because they have a splendid idealistic spirit. I am completely convinced that they will fight fantastically well.

ZEITZLER: Well, the Fieldmarshal and I will sit down to it
later.

KLUGE: I'll have to think it over once more, my Fuehrer.

[13] SS Divisions 9 and 10 were organized in France during the winter
of 1942/3.

Now that I know what the over-all purpose is, I will act accordingly.

HITLER: As I said, the most important thing is that I get the SS Corps out. Manstein needs something down there as replacement. I don't know yet what I'm going to give him. Perhaps the 7th Panzer Division, which could be pulled down here if he could close this up over here. But he has to have replacements or else he won't be able to hold any of this business. And he needs a couple of infantry divisions. He can't hold this mess here. Of course, if the worst comes to the worst, we can't do anything except shorten the lines down here, too. But we have to realize that that would be a desperate situation. It's certainly not pleasant. These are very difficult decisions, decisions that bring us to a critical point. But I'm considering all the alternatives. Difficult to do anything up there at Leningrad, because of the Finns. I also considered whether we could give up this down there—

ZEITZLER: If we decide on something up there, we have to do something down there too.

HITLER: There wouldn't be much profit in this.

ZEITZLER: Yes, we would gain something. The enemy isn't doing anything big now.

HITLER: If the worst comes to the worst, we may even have to give *that* up.

ZEITZLER: That's easier to do than this——

HITLER: How many do you think we can get out of here? We have to be strong here or else they will start landing operations at Novorossisk again. First everybody says give it up, but then I hear Kleist,[14] or whoever else is down there, yelling: That's impossible. With such limited forces in this position, it is impossible to counteract and the enemy will only start attacking in this area. If that happens, we won't be able to bring any more ships in. We are still getting our ships through, but that would finish it.

[14] Generalfeldmarschall von Kleist commanded Army Group 'A,' which, after retreating from the Caucasus, held the southernmost part of the German Eastern front. Novorossisk, a port on the eastern side of the Kerch Straits, was still in German hands at this time.

What is already committed is all right, but I can't bring any more in.

ZEITZLER: We could try to form a small bridgehead. Then we could hold on there for a while.

HITLER: I'm afraid we can't hold it, but we can try. We'll have to think about that.

KLUGE: On our extreme northern wing we can fall back on our prepared positions at Velikie Luki, as I suggested. We can strengthen the line there, too.

ZEITZLER: That's been planned, sir, but that won't free any of your troops.

KLUGE: No, that wouldn't free any troops. We can't give up anything else, except that salient. Then we'll have to swallow Kirov and leave everything else the way it is, although I would have liked to improve things here a little, but unfortunately it isn't possible.

HITLER: We can retreat here, too.

KLUGE: Perhaps we could free a division here, but that is a complicated story, because the position there is already—

ZEITZLER: The positions there are particularly good.

KLUGE: The positions are good. They were built with terrific effort.

HITLER: But you'd rather have Kirov?

KLUGE: Yes, I would like to retake that. That is always a base for the enemy.

ZEITZLER: That would be more costly.

KLUGE: Under the present circumstances it is completely impossible.—

ZEITZLER: You can free something up there only after you have withdrawn here.

HITLER: Will I see you again?

KLUGE: No, I intend to return immediately. Heil, my Fuehrer.

[*Fieldmarshal von Kluge withdraws.*]

HITLER: ——If only the SS Corps were out of there already.

ZEITZLER: The 'Leibstandarte' leaves tomorrow at the earliest, at the rate of 12 trains per day.

HITLER: The SS Corps equals 20 Italian divisions.

ZEITZLER: He[15] must get 'Grossdeutschland' and the 7th
Panzer down there. If Kluge stays on this line for a week,
and moves half of the freed divisions over there, it ought
to work. If a division can dig itself in for six days in a
sector, it has got something. He is still mentally adjusted to
slow movements, and can't get away from this idea. Perhaps it will come to him. In my opinion everything would
be all right then——

*After Kluge's departure, the conference continues. Aside
from Hitler's regular staff, Himmler and Goering rejoin the
group, which is increased by the arrival of Doenitz,
Jeschonnek, and finally Rommel, who had just flown in
from Salonika. These parts of the transcript are very badly
damaged and some of the discussions are hardly coherent.
It appears that the main topics were further military details about the actions envisaged against the Badoglio government and plans for preventing dangerous repercussions
to these events in the Balkans. Hitler expresses the opinion
that Rommel should be placed at the head of the operations in Italy. At one point the report of the first interview between Badoglio and German Ambassador von
Mackensen arrives. This causes Hitler and Goering to
break into violent harangues against Badoglio.*

*No transcripts of further conferences on the Italian
crisis are preserved, but the Goebbels Diaries and Doenitz's reports reproduced in* Fuehrer Conferences on Matters dealing with the German Navy *(which are used in
A. Martienssen,* Hitler and His Admirals) *show that they
continued throughout the following days. These sources
give some insight into the general trend of the discussions.
The idea of including the Vatican in the anti-Badoglio
operation found immediate opposition, mainly from Ribbentrop and Goebbels, and was abandoned. The immediate
evacuation of Sicily was also opposed, especially by Doenitz, who objected vehemently. As a result, the latter operation took place much more gradually than had first been*

[15] Manstein.

envisaged. The chief problem was whether a sudden coup against the Badoglio government, restoring the Fascist party to power as Hitler intended, was feasible. The opinions of Hitler's political and military advisers seem to have been divided. Goebbels and Goering were in agreement with Hitler, while others, especially the military advisers like Jodl, Doenitz, and Rommel, opposed this improvised measure. They believed that Hitler underestimated the power of the Italian Crown and widely overestimated the popularity of Fascism. In their opinion it was advisable to tolerate the Badoglio government temporarily and to use the time thus gained for reinforcing the German troops in Italy. Their counsel prevailed, and this latter policy was put into effect. Also the Russian offensive toward Kharkov, which began on 3 August, may have made impossible such far-reaching withdrawals from the Eastern front as were originally planned.

III

AFTER TEHERAN

20 DECEMBER 1943

The starting time of this conference is not indicated in
the manuscript; it ended at
11.00 P.M.

Participants: HITLER,
BUECHS, BUHLE, FEGELEIN, JODL,
KEITEL, PUTTKAMER, VOSS,
AND ZEITZLER

*This whole transcript is very
badly damaged. The first part deals with a report by
Zeitzler and a general discussion on the situation at the
Eastern front. This entire section had to be omitted because it could not be reconstructed properly. The following
section is also greatly abbreviated because of its fragmentary condition.*

HITLER: I have studied most of these documents.[1] There
is no doubt that the attack in the West will come in the
spring. There's absolutely no doubt about it. I have the
feeling that they want to operate on very broad fronts ...

[1] Reference is probably to reports of the Teheran and Cairo meetings.
The communiqué summarizing the results of the Teheran conference
stated: 'As to the war, our military staff have joined in our round-table
discussions and we have consulted our plans for the destruction of the
German forces. We have reached complete agreement as to the scope
and timing of operations which will be undertaken from the east, west
and south.' In Cairo, on 4, 5, and 6 December Roosevelt and Churchill
had met the President of the Turkish Republic. The communiqué of
this conference emphasized that 'The closest unity existed between the
United States of America, Turkey and Great Britain in their attitude
toward the world situation,' and this was taken as an indication of
Turkey's imminent entry into the war on the Allied side, for which, as
we know now from Sherwood, *Roosevelt and Hopkins*, chapter xxx,

But judging from the proposed treaty with Turkey, it appears that they will go ahead with a second front. We must count on additional landings in Norway, as well as in the Balkans and on the Bay of Biscay. . . There's a distinct possibility that they will make a landing in Norway. . . Of course that would only be a diversion, but it could become unpleasant for us if the bastards hang on there and lure out our Air Force.——We must use a lot of submarines because we mustn't let them gain a foothold there. If the enemy does gain a foothold, it would be fatal for our whole Northern army. We wouldn't be able to get any more transports through to them. In the South we have found out what it means if the bastards sit on an island. That's the one thing. The other is the Bay of Biscay. We have to send a lot of submarines down there. We must operate with a lot of submarines down there, as well as with all the other stuff that has been prepared.

VOSS: Yes, that has been planned and will be done.

HITLER: ——The whole problem of the West has to be carefully considered. I am constantly thinking about new ways to improve the defense. Automatic flamethrowers, for instance, and oil cans that can be thrown in the sea, and then begin to burn.

ZEITZLER: Also the new mines which are detonated by the mine detector. I thought perhaps it would be better not to use them in the East, just the West. The first will probably be ready in January. If we use them in the East to begin with, the Russians will become acquainted with them. They would figure them out quickly. It would be better to put them all in the West. When the invasions come and they start to use the mine detectors, they won't expect the mines to explode.

HITLER: That will immediately shatter their confidence.

Churchill was pressing at Teheran, but in which Russia and the United States showed much less interest. Later on, the German secret service in Ankara acquired material which showed that the plan of a Balkan invasion had been abandoned and that there was no serious intention to force Turkey into war on the Allied side. See E. Kordt, *Wahn und Wirklichkeit*, p. 372.

VOSS: The Commander-in-Chief, Navy,[2] summoned all of his commanders the other day and called their attention to the danger in the West.

HITLER: There is no doubt but that they have made a decision. The attack in the West will begin in the middle of February or the beginning of March. I don't have the feeling that the English are approaching this attack with very much enthusiasm. There are too many cautious people over there who are saying even now, 'We had better not do it if this or that condition prevails.' There's another school of thought in England. Just as we once wanted to keep our small navy intact up to the end of the war,[3] these people want to keep their army intact because it is so small. That is clear. On top of that, the English production potential is falling extremely fast. One can see that day by day. They blame that on public opinion which doesn't believe that danger exists any more. Actually, however, their steel production is decreasing. If one produces a million tons of coal less per year, the steel supply will not increase. That is all interconnected. Do you suppose that is going to be made up by the Americans? They are doing the same thing we are. We were pledged to deliver this and that to our allies, but the fact is that even from the beginning we cut the deliveries to the bone. Somehow, everyone is his own best friend in time of war. Nobody is going to give the other person steel if he doesn't have enough for himself. In our case, we couldn't even fulfill these decreased quotas. We delivered somewhat less all the time. We were supposed to deliver 1 to 1.2 million tons of coal, but all we ever sent was 900,000 tons. If the Americans are supposed to deliver something of which they themselves are short, they will certainly deliver less and less all the time. Consequently the English are also holding back. But actually, they have done a lot. Just imagine, the English must have 50 per cent of their armed forces scattered all over the world. If one counts India, Africa, the Near East, and Australia, that means they have at least

[2] Doenitz.
[3] He means the First World War.

50 per cent of their forces out there, and 50 per cent at the most in England, and of course they want to maintain that ratio so as not to lose some possessions at the last minute. But the attack will come; there's no doubt about that any more ...

VOSS: The Grand Admiral[4] gave his commanders the order to defend their areas tenaciously, as if they were islands, not ceding an inch. . . . I believe that it is going to work. That worked in the Crimea and it is going to work down here too. He told them what is hanging in the balance.

HITLER: If they attack in the West, that attack will decide the war.

VOSS: Yes, he told that to all the commanders.

HITLER: If this attack is repulsed, the whole business is over. Then we can withdraw troops right away.

[*Jodl and Buechs mention air raids, particularly raids on the V-1 sites under construction.*]

HITLER: It's obvious that these launching sites[5] are getting on their nerves. If we heard of such objects which we knew could destroy Berlin, we would also become nervous and put pressure on our Air Force. They know all about everything. They say they are rockets. They have reported that one to two tons of explosives can be fired over in this manner. They've come to believe it themselves. They say that the Germans have originated this business, worked on this thing for a long time, and therefore have gained a certain experience. Therefore it should not be impossible that it might work, but they intend to take care of our launching sites.

[4] Doenitz. The passage probably refers to the defense of the French seaports.

[5] The fact that the Allies were already well-informed about V-1 construction can be seen from the statement on 28 December 1943 in the diary of Capt. Harry C. Butcher, *My Three Years with Eisenhower*, p. 462.

[A lengthy discussion follows, the subject of which is the distribution of anti-aircraft guns, as well as the expected attack on Norway.]

VOSS: I doubt if they will have the punch to get through there. After all, they have the example of this business in Italy, where they got completely bogged down.

HITLER: But we had certain advantages in Italy. First of all, we are defending. Secondly, we have a narrow strip, about 100 kilometers wide, with unequaled natural obstacles. We have divisional sectors as we had them in the First World War—in other words, not such huge battle areas. In the World War they were 9, 10, 11 kilometers. That's about the same down there, that's the good thing about Italy. In addition, the enemy has to bring everything up from a great distance. On the other hand, we have practically no Air Force down there.

We are hoping that our new planes will arrive before the enemy attacks. Every moment we delay that attack improves our situation. With each month, the likelihood increases that we will get a group of jet fighters. The decisive thing is to drop bombs on their heads the moment they land. That will force them to take cover. Even if there is only one plane in the air, they will have to take cover, which will waste hours and hours. In half a day we'll have started to move up our reserves. Even if we only pin them down on the beach for six or eight hours, you can imagine what that will mean for us. It means that they will be pinned down until our reserves arrive. Also, by then we would have an over-all picture. It would be nice to get an over-all picture at the first moment, to see which is the diversion and which is the main attack. I am very worried that they might use these 4000-kilogram blockbusters against the locks of our submarine pens.

PUTTKAMER: Brest and Lorient don't have any locks. Only St. Nazaire, La Pallice, and Bordeaux have them.

HITLER: The pressure must be enormous. If 3000 kilograms of high-powered explosives hit the water, it will push the whole works into the air. Yes, that is a great

worry. We have one advantage. They will come with
entirely inexperienced units.

BUHLE: If by January we really get all the units designated
for the West, nothing can happen there.

HITLER: Let's hope so.

BUHLE: But if everything is taken away from the West—
every time I have organized something, it is taken away
from me.

HITLER: Why do you tell me all this? I will not be blamed
for taking everything away from you. You have to talk to
Zeitzler about that. . . But I have terrible troubles too. I
see the situation in the East every day, and it is terrible.
With five or six divisions we might still force the decision,
or at least a great victory. But I have always been worried
about the West. I have never had the opinion that nothing
is going to happen there; rather, I think that the moment
will come when the English are forced to end the war in
some fashion. And the Americans have their presidential
election. If Roosevelt can't show any military successes,
and if he continues to get deeper and deeper into this
business, he may lose. If Roosevelt does lose, he will be
tried before an American court six months later. After
what that man has done he can leave office only after a
won war, with the national debt reduced by half. But as a
defeated presidential candidate, his successor, for motives
of self-preservation, will have to indict him. . . The successor must do it, because he has to solve the problems left
to him. In that nation, which has a liberal capitalist system—that's what they're fighting for—a national debt
which might by then amount to a couple of hundred billion
dollars can't be digested by the economy. They can always
contract new debts, but how can they pay them off? With
taxes? Then they will have to tax away 9/10 instead of
2/3. They can't do that any more. The thing is like a
deluge. They are holding it up a little with every possible
manipulation, but actually you can do that only with the
authority of the State, that means by force. We can do
that in Germany, but they can't do it. His successor will
have to do something about that. No matter who the

successor is, he will have nothing better to do than to prove that the whole mess is Roosevelt's fault. That is instinct of self-preservation. They will look for someone to blame, and he is to blame. That's obvious. One might say that it doesn't make any difference because he will be in again after four years—Well, four years is four years, in the course of these years the other hopes that the situation will change. At any rate, that man Roosevelt will do anything not to get beaten in this election. After all, his government is also pushing him on, because it has to, and if the man wants to stay in, he must show some kind of successes, and for that reason he will attack. The English are terribly clever. They want to give the supreme command to the Americans. They are being very clever about that, because if the Americans have the supreme command, the English will give precedence to the Americans, that's certain. If the whole thing fails, the Americans will be responsible. If it should fail under English command, they would be responsible. It is obvious that the English are not as confident about the whole business as Eisenhower is. Eisenhower has achieved one lucky landing, in both [sic] cases only with the help of traitors. He isn't going to find any traitors in our ranks. He'll catch hell here. There is a difference between landing in North Africa and being greeted by Mr. Giraud, or being opposed by Italians who mostly sit in their holes and don't fire a shot, and landing in the West where there is really going to be shooting. As long as our batteries can fire, they will fire, that's certain.

BUHLE: They'll have our batteries in their rear for days. They'll have to knock them out one by one.

HITLER: Well, I am firmly convinced that they are not qualified to solve this problem. They can't do it. If they had troops with two years' combat experience, one would say they might do it, but they are all new outfits.

KEITEL: Completely unaccustomed to war.

HITLER: Ours should not be called young. Ours have more men with combat experience among them. The others don't have that.

VOSS: Our men have been there for two years.

HITLER: I am of the opinion that the moment it starts it will be a relief. We saw that last year at Dieppe.[6] Actually that was a glorious action. I saw Dieppe that time. You remember how it was fortified then. Since then I have seen how the present fortifications look. I have only seen a small sector; compared to how it was before, it is a thousand times better. ——Can't we give a special allotment of flamethrowers to the West? Flamethrowers are the best thing for defense. That is a terrible weapon.

BUHLE: We have 1200 of them. And there are thousands of those Russian automatic electric ones in the West.

HITLER: But what about the direct ones? If it comes to the worst, we will have to make Speer[7] take emergency measures. He has workers to spare, because of the bombed factories. We could throw them in anywhere and let them produce flamethrowers. Flamethrowers are the most terrifying thing there is for defense. If someone with a rifle advances, then I can see him. Moreover he has to get close. But the defender is under cover. The attacker doesn't even know that the defender has a flamethrower. All he sees is the hole in which the defender has two little brackets, one for the machine gun and one for the flamethrower. The attacker approaches up to 20 meters, and suddenly the thing goes off. That's a very unpleasant feeling.

BUHLE: If during the months of January and February production goes according to schedule, there won't be a pillbox in the West without a flamethrower. We have 2000, then it will be 4000.

HITLER: But we have more pillboxes than that in the West. We already have about 7500 now. There will be 10,000.

BUHLE: I am now talking about portable flamethrowers, quite apart from those which are built in.

HITLER: That's the most terrifying thing there is. The attacking infantry won't have any stomach left for hand-to-hand fighting. As soon as they see that there are flame-

---

[6] The raid on Dieppe had taken place on 19 August 1942.
[7] Reichminister for Armaments and War Production.

throwers all over the place, they will lose all of their
courage. They'll lose their nerve. That's the most terrible
thing there is. There is another very unpleasant feeling to
hear something burning up ahead, it is almost worse than
actually getting hit. That really is a hell of a mess. When
we first started to use the flamethrower in the World War,
the mistake was to use it only here and there. If we had
saved up the flamethrowers for a mass attack during a big
offensive in the West, the effect would have been devastating. Because it is certainly one of the weapons which,
psychologically, have the most terrible effect. It is even
more effective in defense than in attack. When a man is
attacking, you can see him jumping around and you can
knock him off; but if he is down in a hole, one doesn't
know if he has a flamethrower or not. If the aperture is
very narrow, it is of course easier to aim a flamethrower
than a hand grenade. It is certainly easier to hit someone
at 30 meters with a flamethrower than to put a hand
grenade through a small aperture at that distance. Even
gun emplacements have to have flamethrowers. We have
to have flamethrowers all over the place. I even considered
using them against strafing planes, but that's not possible.
These are all possibilities. Buhle, remind me about this
tomorrow. We can call up Saur[8] about that right away.

BUHLE: I know that we have put a lot of pressure behind the
production of flamethrowers so that we have reached 1200
a month. It took a long time, but now we have reached the
point where we are getting 1200 a month.

HITLER: The elimination of factories gives us a certain
reserve of workers, which can always be added somewhere
for an extra. I don't know if the plants are working on two
or three shifts yet.

In case of a landing, we could also burn or blow up
barrels on the beach, so that they would have to wade
through fire. We can do that at certain places but not on
broad stretches. We can figure out the most diverse devil-
tries at different places. For example, one place is mined to

[8] Chief of the Department for Finished Combat Material in the Ministry for Armaments and War Production.

such an extent that absolutely no one can reach the shore.
At another place, oil barrels start burning; at a third place
the Russian flamethrowers—the one that squirts fire——
can be installed; at still another place we could concentrate
a terrific artillery barrage from the rear. One can think of
all kinds of things. After it is all over, they can get
together and swap their experiences during the landing——
The other day I was thinking if it wouldn't be possible to
infest the mine fields with other mines, as well as with
anti-personnel mines, to such an extent that even our own
men can't pass these mine fields, because they explode no
matter who steps on them. These mines should be cased in
plastic instead of metal.

BUHLE: The mine fields on the beaches are impassable even
for our own men. Even they can get through only by
means of the exactly marked lane, which can be seen only
from our side.

HITLER: (On the telephone) Saur, how many flamethrowers are you making now per month? — Yes, the exact
number. . . I need three times that many, and in two
months' time. You have to pour in workers as fast as
possible. In other words, during January and February I
want three times as much as you are making now. That is
the minimum demand. —Only 1200? I thought it was
2400. I wanted three times that number——Well hurry it
up. We need more and more. We need them very urgently.
——Thank you. Heil. Merry Christmas——

IV

THE RUSSIAN WINTER OFFENSIVE

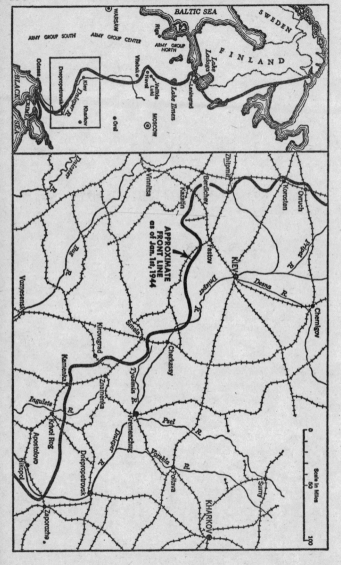

27 DECEMBER 1943

This conference lasted from
10.00 P.M. until 10.46 P.M.

Participants: HITLER,
BORGMANN, DARGES, SCHERFF,
AND ZEITZLER

During the winter of 1943/44
*tremendous changes took place on the Eastern front. At
the beginning of the winter the German front still extended
roughly from Leningrad in the north, over Gomel, Kiev,
and Dnepropetrovsk, to Melitopol on the Sea of Azov.
By the spring, the German armies had been thrown back
more than 100 miles to a line reaching from Narva in
the north over Pskov, the Pripet Marshes, the Carpathians,
to Rumania and Bessarabia. Although the Russians made
great strides by attacks in the fall and spring, their decisive
move was the great winter offensive. On 13 December,
they broke forward from the Nevel salient toward the
south, overwhelming the central sector of the German
front. On 24 December, they started their offensive from
positions west of Kiev, directed toward the south and en-
dangering the whole southern sector of the German line.
On 14 January, they commenced their attack against the
northern sector, which finally brought Leningrad out of
German reach.*

*The following conference of 27 December is important
because it takes place at the time when the first two
Russian winter offensives, those against the central and
southern sectors, were getting under way. This conference
is rather technical and detailed, and some of the problems
under discussion remain obscure for lack of further information. However, it seems worth while to publish this*

*record because it throws light on one of the most fateful
strategical decisions of the German leaders, namely that to
maintain the extremely exposed southern wing of the German front in the Dnieper bend in spite of the Russian
breakthrough before Kiev. This created a dangerously extended front with exposed lines of communications (for
details, see map opposite). This untenable bulge was
subsequently wiped out by the Russians in their spring
offensive, an action that constituted one of the most serious and costly German defeats. From the conference it
would seem that the maintenance of the position in the
Dnieper bend was Hitler's decision, and that he justified it
chiefly by the dangerous political repercussions which a
withdrawal in this area would have.*

*The conference begins with a brief and technical report
by Zeitzler on the situation in the central sector of the
Eastern front, where little had happened during the day.
Then he turns his attention to the southern sector:*

ZEITZLER: My Fuehrer, an estimate of the situation has
come from Manstein.[1] Perhaps I may present this situation on my 1:1,000,000 map because of the large area
involved. First, to answer these two questions. The one
concerned this position, and the other is about the bridgehead about which you inquired yesterday, my Fuehrer.
The Ilse Position is this one over here, this curve here.

HITLER: I didn't say anything about two small bridgeheads.

ZEITZLER: No, I didn't mean that. Only this one; but
they don't want to be squeezed there.

---

[1] After Manstein, commander of the Army Group 'South,' had vainly
attempted to force the Russians back in the southern part of the salient
beyond Kiev, the Russians started a counter-offensive on 24 December,
in exactly the same region. They succeeded in breaking into the German
line on a broad front, driving in the direction of Zhitomir and Kazatin.
This clearly endangered the connection with the entire southern wing
of the German front, which was still holding Krivoi Rog, Nikopol, and
the Crimea. Moreover, at the time of this conference, the Russians
launched a thrust at the most advanced eastern tip of this line, near
Zaporozhe, and succeeded in enlarging their bridgehead west of this
town. Under these circumstances Manstein recommended a withdrawal
of his whole Army Group. The various units mentioned were fighting in
the lower Dnieper bend.

HITLER: That's the Kamenka Position.

ZEITZLER: I have drawn them in over here. This is the Ilse Position and this is the Kamenka Position.

HITLER: You should say Kamenka Line, because it really isn't a position.

ZEITZLER: Some dugouts have been built.

HITLER: Even the forward part isn't a position, to say nothing of this here.

ZEITZLER: I have brought the specifications of the Kamenka Position. It's something at least, although it isn't much.

HITLER: How long is it?

ZEITZLER: This here is 160 kilometers, and that whole thing is 360, my Fuehrer. There are 21 units in here, and it saves us 200 kilometers. That is what I mentioned about ten days ago.

HITLER: Here is Nikopol.

[*Hitler reads Manstein's report.*]

HITLER: He hopes so, but he doesn't think so. He doesn't believe that seriously. 'They would exhaust themselves with frontal attacks.' It is by no means certain that they would exhaust themselves. Yes, I want to talk about that again tomorrow.

ZEITZLER: If I could show you that on the million map—I have drawn in the fronts here, and the traffic routes here. Along here, there is a double rail line with a daily average of 33 trains. The enemy is pretty close to that. In my opinion it's only a matter of days. In other words, this line will be gone the day after tomorrow. As for the other rail lines that are left, I have already worked this one down here very hard. Up to now we have been getting 4½ to 5 trains over this new bridge up near Trichata. I've increased it to 10 to 12 trains. The fact that we have stepped this up is therefore a kind of adjustment, in order to help us down here. But just the same, the loss of this other rail line will be felt severely. It can be partly made up by this single-tracked line, which carries 7 to 8 trains. But that one is also threatened, because there is not much distance between us and the Russians. This was the position when they started on the 24th; since then they have got half-way to the road. That leaves the line down here, it has a relatively low average so that we'll be really squeezed for railroads, if this key position falls. This is the border of Transnistria[2] already, so that we will have trouble with the roads too. Down here is the big direct Highway No. 4. If Highway 4 falls, we will really be squeezed ... I'm very worried about this.

HITLER: This business here doesn't mean that he[3] can hold that. It is the question of how many troops he gets in the next few days.

ZEITZLER: Yes, in the next few days. Then they may be able to slow down the enemy. Manstein says that he can't bring in anything from the west, because we don't have anything there, but the slowing-down can be achieved with the 4th Mountain Division, the small auxiliaries, and the 17th Panzer. Even so they won't be able to hold it firmly. Therefore we will have to look around for new forces. I think the only place to get them is from this salient here, for two reasons. First of all, it is the only way we can get them to the front; secondly, the salient is becoming untenable anyway. If the enemy gets this far, we'll have to make the withdrawal anyway and at present there is nothing with which to straighten it out. The 4th Mountain Division isn't there, and even the 17th Panzer isn't enough.

HITLER: If he didn't want to hold this here, why did he move the 4th Mountain Division away? Then it could have been brought there now.

ZEITZLER: My Fuehrer, in my opinion the 4th is needed here. We can't be strong enough at that point.

HITLER: But with the troops he has there now, he can't hold it any more. If we retreat here, then this too is lost.

ZEITZLER: The Crimea will be lost in the near future anyway. Of course, this way we'll lose it faster.

HITLER: We shouldn't have to lose it.

[2] Transnistria was under Rumanian administration, which meant that the German army did not have direct control over road and rail operation.
[3] He means Manstein.

ZEITZLER: In my opinion we can hold the Crimea only if we drive through a connecting link here.

HITLER: The movement of troops up to that point the other day—

ZEITZLER: It's hard to tell. Perhaps we smashed a few Russian Panzer corps so that the attack up there never came off. If we hadn't made that movement, if we hadn't shoved in here and had done the Fastov[4] thing instead, we might have stumbled into that attack and we wouldn't have been better off anyway.

HITLER: Well, it doesn't make any difference now. The worst thing was that the weather was so bad.

ZEITZLER: Even now the weather is so bad that the Air Force can hardly do anything.

HITLER: Where is the artillery division now, where does he have that?

ZEITZLER: That's en route from Zhitomir to Kazatin, where the 168th is also going, and where there are also parts of the 25th Panzer. They are all supposed to guard this Kazatin connection.

HITLER: We should find out how strong the enemy actually is up there. For a while it looked so dangerous up there, and now the enemy isn't doing anything.

ZEITZLER: My Fuehrer, I think that this down here is their winter offensive.

HITLER: That is quite true, but just the same, what completely new armies do they have here? They have just their old forces.

ZEITZLER: Well, they have rested these nine Panzer corps, they have been standing still for weeks.

HITLER: Yes, that's right, but they are still old forces. They don't have any new ones. There's one thing I don't understand; new tanks alone can't strengthen a Panzer corps. We always heard that they were having such heavy casualties among the crews, that some of them were burned in the tanks and killed by gunfire.

ZEITZLER: With them it's probably the same as with us.

[4] At Fastov, one of the decisive Russian break-throughs occurred in the offensive toward Zhitomir and Kazatin.

Actually we had very little trouble with our tank personnel. We always had enough crews.

HITLER: I'll think that over tonight.

ZEITZLER: Yes, I would be grateful if a decision were made about this, because every day counts now.

HITLER: Well anyway, this decision will stand.[5]

ZEITZLER: May I issue that order? That would help a little, anyway.

HITLER: Yes, you can issue that. That will free one division. But to give this whole area up, Zeitzler—we can talk big and say that this is lost anyway; but when the time comes when it really is lost, Mr. Manstein isn't going to take any responsibility. We'll have to take it.

ZEITZLER: That's obvious.

HITLER: It will mean anxious hours in which a big crisis will develop, thereby immediately affecting relations with Turkey. . . On 15 February the Allies want to put pressure on Turkey to enter the war. If there is a crisis in the Crimea then, it will make their propaganda for them. Mr. Manstein isn't going to take any responsibility for that; he'll just say that that is the politician's business.

ZEITZLER: Yes, and it will be difficult, because certainly little can be saved.

HITLER: We can't save anything. The consequences would be catastrophic. They would be catastrophic in Rumania. This is an important position. As long as we stand here and here, as long as we have the bridgeheads here, any airbases[6] here would be in a risky position.

ZEITZLER: Yes. Only if we don't do anything up there and let things run their course, the consequences will be the same, and in addition we'll have the whole problem of complications with the 1st Army.[7]

HITLER: Just wait and see. We've lived through a couple of those cases when everyone said that things were beyond

---

[5] This reference is not clear. It may refer to a decision made at the beginning of the conference, when Hitler had agreed to a small withdrawal further north.

[6] Hitler probably means airbases of the Allies in Turkey.

[7] Not clear. Perhaps he means the 1st Panzer Army, which formed part of the northern wing of Manstein's Army Group.

repair. Later it always turned out that things could be brought under control after all.

ZEITZLER: It's just that this is such a deadly place for us, so close.

HITLER: Yes, I see that. I haven't released the 4th Mountain Division for nothing. But it hasn't been proved that the Russians are using a completely new army; rather, they are just rested forces. There is no evidence for saying that the winter offensive has begun now; this is just a continuation of the battle now going on. There's no difference.

ZEITZLER: That's why I haven't referred to it as the winter offensive.

HITLER: They just don't want to give us time to reorganize. That's why they keep on attacking. That's all there is to it. You can see that they are bound to wear themselves out. They did it here. Gradually they fizzled out here.

ZEITZLER: Only there is the suspicion that they might have done that on purpose, so that they could keep on over here.

HITLER: No, I don't believe that.

ZEITZLER: Actually they made it pretty easy for us. They just stopped here.

HITLER: Because they couldn't advance further. After all, we don't have to suppose that they are like the mythological giant who became stronger every time he fell to the ground.

ZEITZLER: But they have kept it up for so many months.

HITLER: They must lose their breath sometime. I have read this report. In my eyes, the decisive thing is that actually the morale of the troops is poor. That's the decisive thing.

ZEITZLER: That's why I always submit those reports. I must always figure on those things.

HITLER: After all, I was the one who always called attention to that. I talked with the gentlemen of the Tank Forces; they say that the infantry isn't fighting at all. It differs greatly. Some divisions fight very well; nothing happens in their sectors. Whenever someone tells me that it is pointless to try and influence the moral of the infantry—Zeitzler, I want to tell you something. I am a man who has personally built up and led what is probably the greatest organization in the world,[8] who is still leading it today. During this time it has happened that I received reports from local districts to the effect that here the Social Democrats could not be beaten, or that there the Communists could not be beaten, that it was completely impossible to get rid of them. It always turned out to be the fault of the leader.

As a generalization it might be all right. If someone says to me that one can't exert a moral influence on the infantry, then I can only say: I once heard a major talk to his troops, and I felt then that speaking to the troops is pointless. I listened many times and didn't find any sense in it. But on the other hand, if an officer tells me that it is impossible to give the men any inspiration, then I would say: 'That only proves that your influence is worthless. Look at the neighboring company. They are completely in the hands of their leader. It was *your* lack of influence, and *you* will have to go!'

ZEITZLER: Yes, the troops are the mirror of their leaders.

HITLER: Always, absolutely.

ZEITZLER: I am sincerely convinced that in the case of poor units, the leaders are either dead, or they are poor leaders.

HITLER: If they're dead they have been replaced by a poor leader. That is quite clear. If the Russians lose their breath, and we can manage that with our present forces, we would tear our hair later if we retreat now. And that wouldn't mean that the business were ended——I can see the time coming when this will have great repercussions in that whole area down there. These are terrible decisions. If one talks about fighting through to victory, in my opinion that means today to bring the whole thing to a halt somewhere.

ZEITZLER: That's quite clear. It would be a victory for us just to stop the Russians, but we can't defeat them.

HITLER: We can't expect more at this moment. But we mustn't forget that last winter we were in a tragic situa-

---

[8] Hitler means the Nazi party.

tion. Just the same, by May we thought we were almost ready to attack, and in July we finally did attack.

ZEITZLER: It's just that the bow has been bent so fearfully. If we could just straighten that out a little and get some fresh troops, we could get going again.

HITLER: When the troops have dug themselves in and are in position, the psychological moment will come again. One must just take the leaders away from the worst divisions. One has to do that. I have read the report and I can only say that it shows clearly that some of the divisions are miserable. But if a leader says that nothing can be done about it, I can only say, 'It is you who can't do anything about it. You lack the strength to do something about it.' He may be telling the truth, but he only sees it from his perspective. His influence has failed completely.

I know this, too: during the four years of the First World War I came into contact with regimental commanders whose influence was laughable because nobody took them seriously. We had other regimental commanders who, no matter how bad the situation was, restored it in short order and steadied their troops. Essentially it depends on the man. In units which I know very well I can always tell if a group has a poor leader, because the group reflects that like a mirror.

Or I think back to my district group leaders. In every election I had districts of which I knew that, when the evening of the election came, there would be a victory there. Why? I couldn't just say: yes, that was Franconia, or that was Cologne—Cologne was Black-and-Red[9]—or East Prussia—what does that mean East Prussia? She was always completely reactionary, against us—or Mecklenburg, or Thuringia—Thuringia was always completely Red —but in one place I had Koch, in the other I had Sauckel, and then I had Ley.[10] I had the men.

[9] In Cologne, the Catholic Center party (Black) and the Socialists (Red) were the dominating parties before 1933.

[10] Erich Koch was District Leader (Gauleiter) of East Prussia, Sauckel of Thuringia, Streicher of Franconia, Ley of the Rhineland, Hildebrand of Mecklenburg, when Hitler came to power in 1933.

In those where I had no smart men, things went badly. I knew well enough that good districts meant good district leaders. Today it is the same thing. The other day I had a failure in Kassel.[11] That can be said quite frankly. Of course the man is going to be replaced. He will be replaced and put out of the way. He wasn't equal to his responsibility. You can't say that they've had it easy in Berlin and Hamburg; on the contrary, it was even harder in Hamburg. But there I have a guy with iron nerves, who doesn't let anything get him down,[12] whereas the man in Kassel just collapsed. He wasn't equal to his responsibility. Basically, the leader is the reflection of the condition of his troops, or the condition of the troops is the reflection of the state of the leader. This can also have catastrophic consequences. For instance, a good leader takes over and then he gets killed, the next takes over and is also killed; still another comes, and is also killed. Every case like this has its effect on the men. If an outfit likes its leader particularly, if a good leader is lost, it always has a worse effect than if a rotten one is lost. That's the old story. That can also happen. But one thing is quite sure; if a unit is continuously in poor shape, that is bound to be connected with the leader.

This isn't just talk, either. It really happened to us, didn't it, Zeitzler? We withdrew into a shortened line. Unfortunately we couldn't hold this shortened line. That is, we could have held it with a little greater nobility and a little less selfishness on the parts of the units. Quite a bit could have been saved. We have a classic example. The

[11] Kassel had undergone a severe air raid on the night of 22/3 October 1943. The ARP system of Kassel broke down completely, causing a disaster in the city. Goebbels in his *Diaries*, pp. 493, 497, 502, complains about the 'sorry role' which District Leader Weinrich played in this affair, and his failure to make 'suitable preparations.' He was later replaced by Karl Gerland.

[12] Karl Kaufman was district leader of Hamburg. According to Goebbels' *Diaries*, p. 419, he also 'lost his nerve somewhat' after the great raid on Hamburg.

whole catastrophe up there at Nevel[13] can only be ascribed to the petty egoism of the two Army Group commanders, who didn't want to tackle the problem, out of selfishness. Now we are forced to hold the longer line; it can be done, and it must be done.

I can see the consequences; they are world-wide consequences.

ZEITZLER: And also for the troops and for the whole position.

HITLER: It is terrible for the troops. If it is possible at all, we are duty-bound to defend this second Stalingrad. We can't just disregard that in cold blood, just because it has no direct bearing on Fieldmarshal von Manstein's army. We can't do that; we have to remember that all of those men will be lost.

Secondly [sic]: One could argue that it is necessary for long-range purposes. But perhaps we could achieve these long-range purposes by other means. But other things enter into it. Perhaps Turkey will enter the war. What Rumania will do depends on the State Leader.[14] If he loses his army here——you ought to see the letters he writes me.

ZEITZLER: No, my only worry is that the situation might become worse otherwise. That's my only reason.

HITLER: Well, we'll have to see. I've been wondering if it would be worth the risk to put the 16th[15] down there.

ZEITZLER: I was trying to make up my mind yesterday whether I should suggest considering sending the 16th down there.

[13] Nevel, where the sectors of Army Groups 'North' and 'Center' joined, had been captured by the Russians on 7 October 1943. From the Nevel salient, they had started, on 13 December, the attack that led to the partial encirclement of Vitebsk at the end of December. Vitebsk remained in German hands until the next summer.

[14] State Leader (Staatsführer), title of Marshal Antonescu, pro-Nazi dictator of Rumania. Seven Rumanian divisions were stationed in the Crimea. This would indicate that the previous discussion concerns the question of the abandonment of the Crimea.

[15] The 16th Panzer Division was then being transported to the Eastern Front. It seems that it was intended for the northern or central sector, but that they now consider sending it to the south.

HITLER: One thing is clear, Zeitzler: this decision is not as
hard as the decision about the Crimea. If we move back
there we'll lose the Crimea. We must consider very carefully if we shouldn't take the 16th after all. Then we would
have to put the 4th up here, and another one, and the
16th. That's three units, at least until the others are mobile.

ZEITZLER: At the moment the 16th can be spared, but
eventually things will get tough up there, and then this can
only be repaired by taking back this corner. I have a
feeling that this may become as tough as St. Petersburg
was.

HITLER: Not as bad as all that. If I move back somewhat
there and save a few divisions, it is still not as bad as down
here. This down here is worse, and will have the worst
repercussions. If I had to retreat somewhat up there to
spare a division—

ZEITZLER: No, not that so much, but if one would decide
on a thorough solution[16]—

HITLER: Well, that might become unpleasant because of
the Finns, but not as bad as it would become down there. I
would consider the loss of the Crimea the worst. That
would have the worst effects on Turkey. The Finns can't
make a separate peace. In the end they'll have to defend
themselves anyway. The 16th Panzer—I don't know, could
we look at the map of the Center again—could we leave
the Panther battalion up there and give them a few Mark
IV's instead?

ZEITZLER: I have a few minor remedies in mind. First an
assault gun battalion will arrive tomorrow in the area of the
General Government.[17] We can send that to Manstein.
Secondly I put also the Tiger reserve into the 503rd Tiger
Battalion, which is up here near Kirovograd. I told Manstein to take single Tigers out of his tank battalions and
send them all up there, and together with the 45 Tigers I

---

[16] Zeitzler probably alludes to his theory that since Hitler will not
allow a general withdrawal out of the Ukraine and the Crimea, a large
retreat in the northern sector is necessary.
[17] Poland.

am sending there, that will make a full Tiger battalion.——
If I hadn't kept the Tigers together and had scattered them
over the whole front, everybody would have gotten two or
three, and then they wouldn't have done any good. This
way we have a complete battalion.

HITLER: Well, up here he ought to be able to deal with the
situation with what he has.

ZEITZLER: My Fuehrer, I agree that it ought to work
pretty well. I'm only worried about the future.——I still
have a vague feeling that the heavy attacks will come in
the northwest, but I can't prove it.

HITLER: First of all they will try to crack Vitebsk in order
to get the highway and then the railroad junction.

ZEITZLER: The main attack will go into the northwest, and
then they'll start up there.

HITLER: Yes, you're certainly right about the northwest,
but I am not sure about an attack here.

ZEITZLER: Of course we have terribly few mobile units
there. We saw what happened to the 32d. That was supposed to be up there on 10 January. That would have been
a mobile unit. If it had only got there sooner.

HITLER: But if we had the 16th here, it wouldn't get
through either. One can't do anything here except gather
assault guns and load them up with infantry. Ordinary
Panzer divisions can't do anything in this terrain either.

ZEITZLER: At this moment it is so dangerous down there
that the 16th Panzer is naturally badly needed.

HITLER: Well, 'fighting through to victory'[18]—we shouldn't
get drunk on pretty phrases.

ZEITZLER: No, it will be a good thing if we can just hold
them up.

HITLER: We can't hope to 'fight through to victory.' The
most that we can attain down there is to stop that mess. If
we can achieve that, we will have accomplished a lot. We
can't expect more.

*The discussion continues on details about the equipment
available for the various units. They agree that the decision*

[18] Hitler seems to quote from Manstein's report; see also p. 146.

about the withdrawal can wait a few days. A number of other transcripts of conferences on this problem are preserved: A conference with Keitel, Jodl, and Zeitzler on the night of 28/9 December, a conference with Zeitzler on 29 December, and a conference with Fieldmarshal von Kuechler and Zeitzler on 30 December. In the conference of 28 December, which treats in great detail the quality and equipment of the forces then fighting in the southern sector of the Russian front, Hitler explains to Jodl and Keitel Manstein's suggestions for a withdrawal: he shows himself to be extremely irritated about Manstein, whom he reproaches for having miscalculated the situation. 'All that is said in Manstein's teletype is fantasy; I must even say, it is dreamland.' At another place Hitler remarks that 'I am worrying myself sick for having given permission for retreats in the past. It couldn't have been worse if they had remained in the forward position, on the contrary—.' While Jodl and Zeitzler show their agreement with Manstein's evaluation of the situation, Hitler remains doubtful and denies that a retreat could have the envisaged practical advantages of stabilizing the front. At the end of a very short conference with Zeitzler, on 29 December, which consists of a factual report by Zeitzler on the events of the day, Hitler states that he believes a great number of divisions could be spared by a withdrawal in the northern sector and that he prefers such a move to a retreat in the south. The discussion with Fieldmarshal von Kuechler on the next day contains the plans and preparations for the latter operation. Instead of the present line Leningrad-Lake Ilmen, they envisage as the final position after the withdrawal the line Narva-Lake Peipus, which they believe will mean a saving of at least eight divisions.

V

THE ATTEMPT ON HITLER'S LIFE, 20 JULY 1944

31 AUGUST 1944

This conference began at 3.35
P.M.; the closing time is not
indicated in the manuscript.

Participants: HITLER,
                KEITEL, KREBS, AND WESTPHAL

*In the conference preserved in this
transcript Hitler gave General Westphal, who had just
been appointed Chief of Staff of the Commander-in-Chief,
'West,' and General Krebs, who had been made Chief of
Staff of Army Group 'B' in the West, information about
the conspiracy of 20 July 1944. The record is interesting
because of the light it sheds on Hitler's attitude toward this
conspiracy. This transcript is very badly preserved. Since
sentences are frequently incomprehensible, and since the
transcript is broken into single fragments of which the
original sequence is by no means clear, parts concerned
with the same topic were placed together, but this arrangement is not necessarily correct.*

FRAGMENTS CONCERNING KLUGE:

HITLER: You know that Fieldmarshal Kluge committed
suicide.[1] There are strong reasons to suspect that, had he

---

[1] Kluge, who was Rundstedt's successor as Commander-in-Chief, West,
had taken some part in the conspiracy, but turned against it when he
heard that Hitler had not been killed. A. Dulles, *Germany's Underground*, p. 188, says: 'Kluge's eleventh-hour vacillation did not save
him. He was too deeply implicated. This he realized when General
Model, who had been appointed to succeed him, notified him of his dismissal in an abrupt telephone call, and told him to report to Hitler.
After a futile attempt to surrender to General Patton's army somewhere in the Falaise Gap—whether before or after his dismissal I do
not know—he boarded a plane at Paris, and on the flight to Metz took

not committed suicide, he would have been arrested anyway. The trial at the People's Court was interrupted yesterday.[2] I personally promoted him twice, gave him the
highest decorations, gave him a large estate so he could
have a permanent home, and gave him a large supplement
to his pay as Fieldmarshal. Therefore I am as bitterly
disappointed as I could possibly be. The manner of his
involvement may have been tragic. Perhaps he just slipped
into it; I don't know. Maybe he couldn't find his way out
again. He saw that a large group of officers had been
arrested, and he feared their testimony. His nephew, who
was deeply implicated, made statements in court that
caused President Freisler to interrupt the proceedings right
away, which was correct. Freisler wanted to question the
Fieldmarshal; but by that time he was no longer alive. I
don't want this to leak out. I don't want to disgrace the
German armed forces by having this business talked about.
If it ever came out that Fieldmarshal Kluge intended not
only to surrender the entire forces in the West but also
intended himself to go over to the enemy, it might not lead
to a complete demoralization of the German people, but it
would certainly foster contempt for the Army. For that
reason I want to keep silent about this. We only told the
generals that he committed suicide. He did commit suicide.
The first reports were wrong. First it was said that he had

[2] The proceedings at the People's Court (Volksgerichtshof), under its
presiding judge Freisler, against the conspirators were secret. Only reports about the trial of the first group of conspirators were published
in the press.

poison. Hitler ordered that the Field Marshal be buried without cere-
mony, and the few who knew the facts of his treason to the Fuehrer
were pledged to silence.'
But see also Liddell Hart, *The German Generals Talk*, p. 248, where,
on the basis of the testimony of Kluge's Chief of Staff Blumentritt, it is
stated that Kluge's prolonged absence was due to the fact that 'he had
gone up to the front, and there been trapped in a heavy artillery bom-
bardment. At the same time his wireless tender was destroyed by bombing, so that he could not communicate. He himself had to stay under
cover for several hours before he could get out and start on the long
drive back to his headquarters.' According to Blumentritt, Kluge's prolonged absence from his headquarters on that day was entirely accidental, but excited Hitler's suspicion.

had a brain hemorrhage. Actually he was waiting for an English patrol. They missed each other. He had sent his general staff officer away. The whole business didn't succeed. English and American patrols pushed forward, but evidently no contact was made. He also sent his son into the pocket. The English reported that they were in contact with a German general. The officer who probably arranged this contact is under arrest. Supposedly he was released from British captivity under some pretense, in order to make this contact, but now he is under arrest. The conspirators thought to bring about a change in fate by using this man to arrange a capitulation to the British and to have them join us in the war against Russia. An idiotic idea. . .

FRAGMENT CONCERNING ROMMEL:

HITLER: The 15th of August was the worst day of my life.[3] But for a coincidence, this plan would have been put into operation. All these things that were ordered by the Army Group headquarters can only be explained on that basis. Otherwise they would be inexplicable. I must say that there is something wrong with the staff of the 7th Army.[4] I think it would be a good idea, General Krebs, if you would take completely trustworthy men with you, and that you take all action necessary in order to clean up that staff. It is unfortunate that while Fieldmarshal Rommel is a very great and inspiring leader in victory, he

[3] The decisive day of the Falaise Gap battle. Hitler evidently considered this defeat, which decided the Normandy campaign, the result of Kluge's 'treason.' Hitler's belief that Kluge intentionally sabotaged the attack toward Mortain is also recorded by Warlimont. See Shulman, *Defeat in the West*, p. 152; see also Kluge's farewell letter to Hitler (ibid.) in which he justifies his conduct and explains that the reason for the failure of the attack toward Mortain and Avranches was the weakness of the German forces. At the end of this letter he asks Hitler 'to put an end to this frightfulness. There must be ways to attain this end and above all prevent the Reich from falling under the Bolshevist heel.'

[4] The 7th Army had been fighting in the Falaise Gap.

becomes a complete pessimist at the slightest difficulty.[5]
In North Africa, after the loss of El Alamein, he lost his
nerve completely, and he began to conceive ideas which
couldn't be carried out. He should have tried to hold the
line in front; that would have been the only way to save
everything. The superiority of the enemy was not counter-
balanced by Rommel's move into open space, but was just
made effective thereby. It might have been possible to
withstand an attack on this narrow front of 60 kilometers.
Once we were pressed out of there . . . then, according to
the lessons of desert warfare, the enemy had the opportunity to overtake us all the time. Then the enemy, instead
of Rommel, could maneuver. When I heard of this decision that night—it was really in the early morning—I
immediately countermanded the order. Due to an unfortunate chain of circumstances, the thing was held up here
and was submitted to me too late. . . He did the worst
thing a soldier could do in a case like that: he looked for
other than military solutions. He even prophesied our
immediate collapse in Italy. Up to now that hasn't happened. The events have proved him completely wrong, and
I was right in my decision to leave Fieldmarshal Kesselring
there, in whom I see a great political idealist as well as a
military optimist and I don't believe that military operations can be conducted without optimism. Within certain
limits I consider Rommel an extremely brave and also
clever leader. I do not consider him to have endurance.
That is also the opinion of all the other gentlemen.

KEITEL: Yes, that became more and more apparent.

[5] Rommel had been commander of Army Group 'B,' consisting of the
7th and 15th Armies, charged with the defense of the Channel Coast
under the Commander-in-Chief, West, von Rundstedt. He had a serious
clash with Hitler at the beginning of July when he had recommended
retreat from the coast and taking up of defensive positions along the
Seine. He had been wounded on 17 July and was hospitalized. At the
time of this conference Hitler did not know that Rommel had also been
involved in the conspiracy; when this became known, Rommel was
forced to commit suicide on 14 October.

FRAGMENT CONCERNING THE CONSPIRACY:

HITLER: All the things that happened in the 'Center,' things that are only coming to light now, the disgrace that there are German officers who are willing to speak on the enemy radio, the fact that German officers and generals are capitulating—all that can't be compared to what happened in the West.[6] That was the most unheard-of thing that ever happened. I think, Westphal, that you will get a staff that is almost uncorrupted. First of all, Fieldmarshal von Rundstedt is reliable and decent.[7] Then, Blumentritt is perfectly all right and his record is clear.[8] I think that he doesn't have the experience to lead a staff like that, and that he is very worried about what happened at that headquarters. But there's nothing against him.

In the section of the General Staff directed by Gerke, who is himself completely all right, not a single person who had anything to do with this conspiracy was found. On the other hand, in the other sections—Quartermaster General, Plans and Operations, Foreign Armies, et cetera——this disgraceful business was fostered from the chiefs on down. Everything that happened here was directed against me. If they had succeeded, it would have meant a catastrophe for Germany. The fact that it didn't succeed gives us the opportunity to free Germany of this cancer. But the damage it has done to our foreign policy, to our prestige with the Rumanians, the Bulgarians, the Turks, the Finns, and

[6] At the end of June and the beginning of July 1944, the Army Group 'Center' in Russia was badly smashed, and the Russians began to pour over the Polish Border of 1939. Some of the German generals captured in this offensive immediately joined the Free Germany Committee in Moscow and spoke over the Moscow radio. During the 20 July conspiracy, an abortive military coup against the Nazi Government was instituted by certain high German officers in France, including General von Stuelpnagel, military governor of France.

[7] Rundstedt had been replaced as Commander-in-Chief, West, on 2 July by Kluge, who, on 17 August, had been relieved by Model. Rundstedt was reinstalled as Commander-in-Chief, West, in September; Model remained in the West as commander of Army Group 'B.'

[8] Westphal was replacing Blumentritt, who, until then, had been Chief-of-Staff to Commander-in-Chief, West. Blumentritt received a new command.

all the other neutrals—that can't be underestimated. . . If I had had the 9th and 10th SS Panzer Divisions in the West, the whole thing probably wouldn't have happened. They were not sent there for what I think are criminal reasons, to bring about a revolution here. These people imagined that they could either go with the English against the Russians, or second, the Schulenburg school,[9] with the Russians against the English, or the third and craziest school of thought, playing one out against the other. Incredibly naive. . . It is like a Wild-West novel. If one looks at these people, Stieff[10] and the others, their level is really incredibly low. I dismissed a man like General Hoeppner[11] not only because he didn't carry out an order but also because he was of such a small caliber. Even Kluge was convinced that he would have to go. The events have shown how right I was. At the trial all the people in the courtroom could see what little men all those people were. The assistant judges asked how such men could have become officers. Well, how could they? I had to take what was available, and tried to make the best of that material.

FRAGMENT CONCERNING THE GENERAL SITUATION:

HITLER: The time hasn't come for a political decision. I guess I have proved plenty of times during my life that I am capable of achieving political success. I don't have to explain to anybody that I won't pass up such an opportunity. But it is childish and naive to expect that at a moment of grave military defeats the moment for favorable political dealings has come. Such moments come when you are

[9] Former German ambassador in Moscow, who had participated in the conspiracy and was executed.

[10] Generalmajor Stieff, Chief of the Plans and Operations Section, Army General Staff (OKH), had been among the first group of conspirators to be judged by the People's Court and hanged.

[11] Generaloberst Hoeppner, who on 20 July acted for the conspirators as Chief of the Replacement Army, had been brought to trial before the People's Court and had been hanged. In the summer of 1942 he had been dismissed from the army after being court-martialed for advocating a retreat in violation of Hitler's orders.

having successes. I have proved that I did everything to
come to some understanding with the English. In 1940,
after the French campaign, I extended my hand to the
English, abandoned all my claims. I didn't want anything
from them. Even on 1 September 1939, I repeated an
offer, which I had already made through Ribbentrop in
1936, that is, the suggestion of an alliance under which
Germany would guarantee the British Empire. . . All of
these proposals were opposed first by Churchill, and then
by the whole circle of hatred around Vansittart, who
wanted the war and now can't back out of it. They rush
toward their own destruction, but the time will come when
the tension between the Allies will become so great that
the break will occur just the same. All of the coalitions
have disintegrated in history sooner or later. The only
thing is to wait for the right moment, no matter how hard
it is. Since the year 1941 it has been my task not to lose
my nerve, under any circumstances; instead, whenever
there is a collapse, my task has been to find a way out and
a remedy, in order to restore the situation. I really think
one can't imagine a worse crisis than the one we had in the
East this year. When Fieldmarshal Model came, the Army
Group 'Center' was nothing but a hole.[12] I think it's
pretty obvious that this war is no pleasure for me. For five
years I have been separated from the rest of the world. I
haven't been to the theater, I haven't heard a concert, and
I haven't seen a movie. I live only for the purpose of
leading this fight, because I know that if there is not an
iron will behind it, this battle cannot be won. I accuse the
General Staff of weakening combat officers who joined its
ranks, instead of exuding this iron will, and of spreading
pessimism when General Staff officers went to the
front . . .

If necessary we'll fight on the Rhine. It doesn't make
any difference. Under all circumstances we will continue
this battle until, as Frederick the Great said, one of our

---

[12] Generalfeldmarschall Model had succeeded in restoring the front of
Army Group 'Center' after it had been smashed by the Russians (see
above, note 6). He was then transferred to the West.

damned enemies gets too tired to fight any more. We'll fight until we get a peace which secures the life of the German nation for the next 50 or 100 years and which, above all, does not besmirch our honor a second time, as happened in the year 1918. . . Things could have turned out differently. If my life had been ended, I think that I can say that for me personally it would only have been a release from worry, sleepless nights, and a great nervous suffering. It is only a fraction of a second, and then one is freed from everything, and has one's quiet and eternal peace. Just the same, I am grateful to destiny for letting me live because I believe . . .

VI

THE BEGINNING OF THE END

The three following transcripts all stem from the last months of Hitler's regime. In the five months that had passed since the date of the last conference, the German battle lines had been pushed back to the German frontiers in the East and West. The circle of participants differs greatly from that of the earlier meetings and reflects the changed circumstances of the atmosphere of unreality and self-deception current at Hitler's 'court' at the end of his reign, which has been described in books like H.R. Trevor-Roper's The Last Days of Hitler. *Characteristic of this atmosphere is the length of discussions devoted to extremely trivial matters in this, the critical period, just preceding the complete collapse of the German Armed Forces.*

27 JANUARY 1945

This conference lasted from
4.20 P.M. until 6.50 P.M

Participants: HITLER,
 ASSMANN, BELOW, BRAUCHITSCH,
 BUECHS, BUHLE, BURGDORF,
 FEGELEIN, FREYTAG-LORINGHOVEN,
 GOEHLER, GOERING, GUDERIAN,
 GUENSCHE, HEWEL, JODL, JOHN VON
 FREYEND, KEITEL, KOLLER, PUTT-
 KAMER, SCHERFF, SCHUSTER, VOSS,
 WAIZENEGGER, WINTER, AND ZANDER

*The meeting begins with a
weather report by Dr. Schuster, then Guderian reports on
the military situation on the Eastern front, first in the
South [Hungary], then in the Center (Silesia), then in
the area of Army Group 'Vistula,' and finally in the
North (East Prussia). Hitler makes some suggestions for
accelerating withdrawal to shorter lines in Hungary. There
is a brief discussion on the value of Vlassov's division (a
Russian division which fought on the German side),
about which Hitler speaks very contemptuously, regretting
that its members wear German uniforms. 'Mr. von Seeckt
sold German steel-helmets to the Chinese. In such things
we have no sense of honor at all. Every wretch is put into
a German uniform. I have always been opposed to it.'
When it is said that the Vlassov divisions are reliable on
the Eastern front because, if they run over to the Russians,
the Russians kill them, Hitler says: 'We do precisely the
same with those who have collaborated in the West. The*

165

Allies have already now difficulties in finding a mayor.' A
short discussion on the status of German arms production
follows. Then Jodl reports on the situation in the West,
particularly in the Alsace, where Hitler insists on the
establishment of an improved defense line through coun-
terattacks. Jodl then states that questions of command in
the West were to be discussed.

HITLER: Oh, yes, I wanted to talk to you about that,
Goering. These people here today seem to think that
Student[1] has really become very tired.

GOERING: Well, he doesn't have to remain there. They
don't know him, they don't know his terribly slow manner
of speech. The don't understand that. That's what everyone
thinks who speaks with him. But in my opinion he is, with
the exception of Model, still one of our staunchest and
most steady men, one who will hold tight when it gets
tough again. He is unbelievably slow. They think he's nuts
because they don't know him. I'll take him with pleasure.

HITLER: He was like that also during the operations in
Italy.[2]

GOERING: He spoke just as slowly then. They all thought
he was dumb. I'll gladly take him because I know—and
these gentlemen will be my witnesses—that he will be
called back at the time of a crisis. I'll take him back
gratefully because I know that he can inject the old spirit

[1] The question is whether to relieve Student and replace him with
Blaskowitz. At this time Student was in command of Army Group 'H'
in the Netherlands and Lower Rhine area, of which the 25th Army
under General Christiansen formed a part. Generaloberst Blaskowitz
was in command of Army Group 'G' in the Saar and Upper Rhine,
which consisted of the 11th and 19th Armies; chief of the 19th Army
was SS-Obergruppenfuehrer Hausser, who had been severely wounded
in August 1944. The bridgehead mentioned is the one the 19th Army
still held west of the Rhine, south of Colmar, and which was then under
French attack. Himmler's special interest in this situation derives from
the fact that Hausser was an SS man; moreover Himmler, who had
just taken over command of the Army Group 'Vistula,' which was
fighting in the northern sector of the Eastern front between the Oder
and the Vistula, had in December '44 been in command of Army Group
Upper Rhine (Oberbefehlshaber Oberrhein).
[2] Student had been in charge of Operation 'Eiche,' which rescued
Mussolini in 1943.

into his Parachute Army. He says: 'The—Fuehrer—told—
me—!' I know him and the others don't. I don't blame
them, though, because they have no other way of judging
him. The other day somebody asked me if I had a dope
there. I said: 'No, he's no dope. He always spoke that
slowly.' And now he was knocked on the head, and so they
all think that's why, but it was always that way. But for all
that, no matter what he undertakes, he says: 'The best
thing is to jump right on the enemy.'

HITLER: He has done the most terrific things.

GOERING: I'll gladly take him so that his reputation won't
suffer. I know you'll want him back at the time of a crisis.
He is a tenacious guy. He may not be a genius in other
respects, but he is staunch and straightforward and he
knows that his troops must hang on. But I'll take him back
gladly and then we can see how the line is held after he's
gone.

HITLER: I would be sorry about a thing like that. I'm not
sure what to do. Is Blaskowitz tenacious like that?

GOERING: No, he's much more pliable. Student's little toe
is worth more than all of Blaskowitz.

HITLER: That's just the question.

GOERING: Well, I'll be glad to take him because I know
that when there comes a crisis you'll be enraged and call
him back. I am looking forward to that day.

HITLER: I am not looking forward to that day.

GOERING: No, but you'll take him back. Why should I
expose such a superior man to all this jabber? You know
him; he always spoke that slowly.

HITLER: The time I explained that business in the West, he
developed the same slowness, but in the end he accomplished it just the same. The same thing applied to the
liberation of the Duce.

GOERING: He did his work well in Italy on the whole, too.

HITLER: He cleaned up the situation in Italy completely.[3]

GOERING: If he had remained there, that bridgehead business wouldn't have happened. But I need him urgently; I

[3] This reference and Goering's following remark about a bridgehead
are not clear in the light of the present state of our knowledge.

want him to put some backbone into the Parachute Army and to reorganize the divisions. Then you will always have someone at your disposal when things get tough. He won't wiggle and wobble. It may be that he might speak still more slowly, that is possible, but he would also retreat all the more slowly.

HITLER: He reminds me of Fehrs, my new servant from Holstein. Everytime I tell him to do something, he takes minutes to think it over. He is a completely dull oaf, but does his work splendidly. It's just that he is terribly slow.

GOERING: And then Student is a man who thinks up the cleverest things. You can't deny that he thinks up things by himself.

HITLER: It has been suggested that we send Blaskowitz up there and give this to Hausser, or the other way around.

JODL: That Hausser be sent up.

GOERING: But Hausser has worked himself into the situation here.

JODL: There are more SS units here.

HITLER: I wanted to say that this will be a complete improvisation. If I want to carry it out, I would like to have Hausser here.

FEGELEIN: Especially because he is constantly subjected to the influence of the Reichsfuehrer, even though the Reichsfuehrer cannot give commands any longer in that area. He still pushes him—[4]

HITLER: To undertake it. The Reichsfuehrer has set his heart on this business. He says: 'My Fuehrer, if we have this here, then the enemy is deprived of an important supply line, we have a marvelous position, and I can guarantee that nothing will happen in Breisach.' In the end the whole bridgehead depends on it, because, useful as light ferry traffic back and forth may be, a bridge is much better.

JODL: At any rate, the difficulties of the split in command

---

[4] It would appear from this discussion that an operation to defend and enlarge the German bridgehead west of the Rhine in the Alsace was planned. If so, this operation did not come off; on the contrary, the German pocket was eliminated by 3 February.

are becoming apparent already. Hausser has massed everything he possibly could collect and thrown it in down
there, so that at the moment you don't even know how to
get the fast units away. Therefore it is really necessary to
put all that under a single command, because if so many
high staffs are around there, it only causes difficulties. On
top of that, he doesn't have a Quartermaster Staff. I would
suggest that we leave Hausser here and give him the 1st
Army in addition. I consider that the right thing to do.

HITLER: Hausser is a wise-guy. He gives the impression of
a weasel.

JODL: An extremely sarcastic, witty man. At least that's
what he was.

HITLER: He has the face of a fox.

GUDERIAN: He has a very sharp wit.

KEITEL: Very quick on the trigger.

HITLER: With his crafty little eyes. Only I'm not sure if he
hasn't been affected by the serious wound he recently
received.

FEGELEIN: No, he was not affected. It has been checked.
The Reichsfuehrer said that he didn't trust the story. He
says that if Hausser suffers from after-effects and does
something down there that isn't right because his mind is
affected, it would be most unpleasant for him. The Reichsfuehrer is so clever that he would never have suggested
this appointment if he wasn't entirely sure it would be all
right, because he would get the blame. The Reichsfuehrer
is very sensitive about these things.

HITLER: We all are.

FEGELEIN: But the Reichsfuehrer is always being criticized.

HITLER: When something goes wrong.

GOERING: I just want to ask that the relief of Student is
not made to look as if he were a failure; because he hasn't
failed on a single point: never, I want to emphasize that.
Rather, he carried out his task to perfection, although
nothing spectacular was going on there. He was in charge
of the flooding there, et cetera. I want to make it look as

if I need him desperately for the Parachute Army and have made an application.

FEGELEIN: Besides, Hausser has the philosophy that a soldier of 65 years can do nothing better than to die bravely in the front line.

HITLER: But I don't want that.

FEGELEIN: Well, he exaggerates.

HITLER: That's no kind of philosophy.

GUDERIAN: I know him very well. That isn't necessarily true. He is a man who enjoys life.

FEGELEIN: At any rate he never spares himself. He walks through artillery fire and when his adjutants take cover he asks them why they are so sensitive.

HITLER: I would take cover. I only had one general who didn't take cover. But he couldn't hear.

JODL: Just the same, I would suggest this. It is a little weak here. Christiansen is not exactly a born Army commander.

GOERING: I'll grant you that.

JODL: Not many good leaders are up there.

HITLER: All right, then.

JODL: I really think it would be the best thing to do. That way the Reichsfuehrer will get his staff in the East, too.

GUDERIAN: That is especially important, because the Reichsfuehrer's present staff is a miserable improvisation, with which he can't achieve a thing. His communications system isn't functioning—it is very poor. It isn't going to work this way. Something has to be sent out there right away.

KEITEL: Suited to his personality.

HITLER: Well, then it'll be done that way. Hausser stays here, Blaskowitz there.[5]

FEGELEIN: My Fuehrer, I have another quick decision for you to make. I just checked, and there are 6,000 men out there in the 'Leibstandartes' barracks, destined for the I Panzer Corps. As things stand now that will take some time, and so I would like to request that at least 4,000 to

[5] Hitler's decision was to replace Student with Blaskowitz and to give Hausser Blaskowitz's Army Group. Student became Commander-in-Chief of Parachute Troops in Berlin.

5,000 of them, under the best officers, be put behind Schoerner.[6] In the next two weeks it doesn't matter whether they are in the barracks or on the roads.

HITLER: No, we won't do that because they have to be trained. When the 'Leibstandarte' goes into the line, they will have to move up.

FEGELEIN: They are trained.

HITLER: Afterwards I can't put my hands on them. This corps won't have much time to wait. Take those cavalry men, there are 1,500 of them. You can always attach a few Volkssturn men.

FEGELEIN: Shall I summon the commander?

HITLER: As you wish. I don't need to talk to him.

FEGELEIN: Well, then, those 'Leibstandarte' men may not be taken away.

HITLER: No.

VON BELOW: Then there is the ammunition allowance.

HITLER: Yes, that business about ammunition allowance. He says that he cannot carry on defensive fire with 8 or 5 rounds per heavy field howitzer.

JODL: That is the calculation of the Quartermaster General, and he has added that it will get even worse.

HITLER: But he can't fight a defensive battle at a critical point with that.

JODL: I suppose that that has all been included in the calculations.

HITLER: It may work if somebody has a long front with quiet sectors, but if somebody has the bad luck to—

JODL: That figure includes every gun on the whole Western front.

HITLER: That's just what I mean. If somebody has the bad luck to be in a sector where he is constantly attacked, he isn't going to make out with his 5 rounds; because for a single day's defensive fire he needs 500 to 600 rounds. In the First World War, in the big defensive battle, we fired 500 to 600 rounds from a small battery.

[6] Schoerner, commander of Army Group 'South' (later 'A') on the Eastern front, was then fighting along the upper Vistula and in Slovakia.

GUDERIAN: This calculation is meant for the entire front.

HITLER: That's just what I mean. It is better for the people with large sectors.

JODL: The order applies to the whole Western front anyway.

HITLER: Now he is doubly unfortunate. All the others have divisions, while he has a hodge-podge without any artillery there along the Rhine. For that reason his allotment is very low, because he only has artillery where there is firing and where there is a desperate need for it. Except for that, he doesn't have any artillery; he does have some Russian guns, et cetera, they won't fire anyway. Say that for argument's sake he has 100 field howitzers, which are placed where there is constant heavy fighting. If he can fire 500 rounds per day with 100 howitzers, that isn't going to amount to anything in a major battle. One has to consider that if he gets a larger sector this will have to be evened out.

JODL: No, that is calculated for the entire Western front.

HITLER: During the First World War, in normal times, in 1915 and 1916, we really had an ammunition allowance that was hair-raising.

GUDERIAN: 1 to 2 rounds per gun per day.

HITLER: Sometimes the regiment begged all day for permission to give retaliation fire. Toward evening they usually allowed us six rounds, four with time fuses and two with contact fuses. That was the entire artillery support for an infantry regiment. Mostly it came when the enemy had stopped, so then the enemy always started up again. We got mad as hell and wished that we hadn't even bothered with the six rounds. But I must admit that when a major attack was to be made, there was unlimited ammunition available. At those times we fired as much as the gun barrels would take.

GUDERIAN: That is not the case at the present time.

HITLER: Under normal circumstances, we were terribly restricted. But when an attack was planned or begun, we really pumped it out. I know that on the 9th day of May the battery of our Major Parseval fired almost 5000 rounds. They fired as hard as they could all day long, which means over 1000 rounds per gun.

JODL: In Italy everything was quiet—snow and fog. The last remains of the 29th Panzer Grenadier Division have been pulled out of the line, and the last parts of the 4th Parachute Division have been put in. The 1st and 4th Parachute Divisions are now united as the I Parachute Corps.

HITLER: I don't know—Do you think that deep down inside, the English are enthusiastic about all the Russian developments?

JODL: No, certainly not. Their plans were entirely different. We may only discover the full details later.

GOERING: They certainly didn't plan that we hold them off while the Russians conquer all of Germany. If this goes on we will get a telegram in a few days. They had not counted on our defending ourselves step for step and holding them off in the West like mad men while the Russians drive deeper and deeper into Germany, and practically have all of Germany now.

HITLER: In that respect it is possible that the National Committee, that traitor's organization,[7] still has some significance. If the Russians really proclaim a national government, the people in England will really start to be scared.

JODL: They have always regarded the Russians with suspicion.

HITLER: I have ordered that a report be played into their hands to the effect that the Russians are organizing 200,-000 of our men, led by German officers and completely infected with Communism, who will then be marched into Germany. I have demanded that this report be played into English hands. I told the Foreign Minister to do that. That will make them feel as if someone had stuck a needle into them.

GOERING: They entered the war to prevent us from going

---

[7] Refers to the Free Germany Committee, composed of German officers, in Moscow; see note 9 on p. 62.

into the East, but not to have the East come to the Atlantic.

HITLER: That is evident. It is something abnormal. English newspapers are already asking bitterly: 'What is the point of the war anyway?'

GOERING: I read a report in the *Braune Blätter* to the effect that they can support the Russians with their Air Force; they can reach the Russian lines now with their heavy bombers, although it is a long flight. But the report comes from an absurd source.

HITLER: They can't support them tactically. Even we don't know where the Russians are and where our troops are. How can they know it?——I have still an unpleasant job today. I have to hypnotize Quisling today, or I'll have him come at 3 o'clock tomorrow. Below, try to find out if that is possible. I would like to speak briefly to the Foreign Minister afterwards to see whether it is possible to receive Quisling tomorrow at 3 o'clock, or whether it can be arranged for him to wait until the end of the war. That is a terrible story. He is completely crazy. Those people have driven him out of his mind.[8]

> [*Jodl resumes his report on the fighting in Yugoslavia. Hitler inserts a few remarks about a new giant tank the enemy is reported to possess, and suggests the construction of a new shell to counter it. Assman follows with a report on naval developments, which were limited to minor coastal operations, and Buechs reports on air operations over Germany.*]

BURGDORF: I have here some excerpts from edicts of Frederick the Great and Frederick William I. I can have them sent up for you to read.

HITLER: Everyone thinks that I am so brutal—it would be a good idea if all those proper people would read them.

---

[8] Below reports later that Quisling's visit could be postponed till tomorrow; 'one day more or less doesn't matter.' Hitler remarks that Quisling will be only too glad to be able to stay on in Germany.

But it always the same. These things should be given to our officer corps as required reading. They have absorbed only the spirit of Schlieffen, and not the spirit of Moltke, Frederick the Great, Frederick William I, Bluecher, et cetera. That was a good spirit too. The 73-year-old Courbière had it too.[9]

GOERING: That proves that age has nothing to do with it.

HITLER: No, on the contrary, when they get old they get stubborn as mules. I've experienced that.

BURGDORF: Schoerner has taken strong action in matters under your jurisdiction, my Fuehrer, such as dismissals, et cetera. But I am not in favor of countermanding his orders, because then we would never get anywhere. He also writes that he will have this commandant here hanged unless he restores some order. (*A document is submitted.*) This matter about the officers, which I have presented here, has been taken up by the Reichsmarshal again. The Reichsmarshal takes the view that it would be better to let the people keep their rank and simply use them in lower positions for which they are suited.

GOERING: For instance, I have a commanding general as company commander in a parachute regiment. Up to now, demotion has been part of the punishment when someone committed a crime. If somebody has been discharged with full honors, and if he is now conscripted again, he only gets a small job because he can't fulfill a larger task any longer, we can't draft him as a staff sergeant. That is a demotion. I don't see why anyone would want to become an officer under those circumstances. Even an honorable record wouldn't protect a man any more.

HITLER: Only it becomes very difficult if you have a general command a company under a battalion commander who might be a first lieutenant.

GOERING: In this case it works quite well. Only he should not be demoted.

BURGDORF: If I may explain the development as it occurs

[9] Courbière, one of Prussia's military heroes, defended the fortress of Graudenz against Napoleon I in the war of 1806-7. At the time of this conference, Graudenz was being threatened by the Russians.

frequently in the army: at this time we have several
thousand officers who have never had combat service, or
at least not since the end of the First World War. Since
that time they have either had office jobs or administrative
jobs, or else they were used as railroad-station commanders or commanders of rail-line patrols at a time when the
fronts were far away and these areas had to be protected.
Now these people are surplus. Reichsminister Goebbels[10]
has made the justified demand that in a time when everyone back to those born in 1886 gets drafted, these people
should not be let out because they cannot be used as
officers. If we dismiss these men from active service it
might mean that younger men who are still fully capable
for military service would be released while older ones are
being drafted. The fact that we are keeping them on active
service hasn't been criticized at all by the Reichsmarshal.
It is clear that they have to stay in. The question is, how
can these people be used?

GOERING: These people did their duty as officers in the
First World War and were honorably discharged.

BURGDORF: But they haven't been trained for combat at
all. We have an officer's training regiment in Wildflecken.
The people there are divided into three parts: those who
are to be dismissed because they are not capable of service
any more and who would be of more use in the economy—
that is carefully checked—and then those who can be
employed in some useful capacity in the units, and finally
those who have systematically dodged throughout the
whole war. We have found people who were in fifteen
different positions in one year, which means that they were
always sent away to some other place.

GOERING: All right, if you have a slacker, court-martial
him and take his commission away. But I am of the
opinion that it is impossible in any profession anywhere—

[10] The discussion is concerned with a problem that arose from the fact
that on 14 October 1944, a German Volkssturm had been set up, which
included every man between the ages of 16 and 60 capable of bearing
arms. The organization, training, and the equipping of the Volkssturm
was entrusted to Himmler, but Goebbels exerted a supervisory function
in his capacity of Trustee of Total Mobilization.

that a man who has served with honor and against whom nothing can be said be deprived of his rank just because he has to be used in a subordinate position.

HITLER: We think that impossible, but not the English.

GOERING: He must remain an officer.

BURGDORF: A retired officer has to start from scratch. Hewel told me about a colonel who re-entered the service and was shot down as an air gunner.

GOERING: You'd better find out why he was retired.

BURGDORF: Hewel thought that he was all right.

HITLER: In England, the rank is connected with the job.

GOERING: I checked on it. If a man is a captain and expects to be a major in ten years, and the next day he is given a job that calls for a major, he is immediately promoted to major, and if he is moved off to a captain's position, he becomes a captain again. However, he is still in line for his majority after ten years, and when that time is up, he becomes a major regardless of what temporary rank he is holding at that time. That only counts if someone has been promoted out of order.

HITLER: All right, I want an exact description of how it is done in England. Who can provide that?

FEGELEIN: General Christian knows all about it. I spoke to him about it. He was in America.

BURGDORF: It would also have to be decided whether to form units consisting entirely of officers. In an officers' unit a lieutenant colonel might be a squad leader and a captain a platoon leader, so that ranks would just be nonsense. However, I would like to warn against that because I have seen these men. The last remnants of respect for the officer corps can be destroyed if an entire battalion of officers should run away. Because these people I saw will run away.

GOERING: That's right. But are you going to get men to become officers if they know that they can be demoted at any time without having done anything wrong?

BURGDORF: The moment the Fuehrer adopted the policy of promoting men according to their ability instead of their seniority, the logical thing would have been to demote those people who did not have the ability for the rank they were holding.

KEITEL: But these men are a completely different type of person. If they had been told that, they wouldn't have joined up. They would have chosen another profession.

BURGDORF: In this war there is not a single officer who has not been promoted three grades during the course of the war.

GOERING: Naturally they were promoted. If an officer was discharged for age or because of temporary illness—illness does not concern us—

HITLER: I believe the whole question boils down to the following, Goering. This whole bureaucratic structure is going to be cleaned out now because it has been over-staffed to the point where it compares to the civilian bureaucracy like a dinosaur to a rabbit. That is connected with the fact that at the beginning of the war the Army naturally drafted all people with previous service or any sort of a record. They drafted them on the basis of their previous ranks.

Then they were promoted some more. These people have grown old and can serve as leaders only in a very limited way. They are officers from the First World War who hold general's ratings and are not capable of leading a battalion any more. The situation which now arises is that I draft all men out of the whole nation who are even slightly or in part capable of military service, no matter what kind of jobs they might have had in civilian life, while on the other hand I dismiss men who are just sitting in unnecessary positions and send them home. Because I can't use them: I can't give the general a division or a regiment because he couldn't handle it. I can't give the colonel a battalion because he simply can't handle it. He has been promoted automatically but he can't even lead a company. That is the problem. That has nothing to do with their pension rights. But at the same time I am calling up the Volkssturm and drafting God knows what kind of people into the Armed forces under the lowered age limit, I go and send home people who are perfectly fit for service, just because they are doing jobs which obviously don't even have to be done, which they aren't even filling because those jobs are superfluous, because they are squatting in a bureaucracy which we want to air out. In other words I am sending home people who are fit for military service and drafting others who are not soldiers and who are only partially fit for military service.

GOERING: Right. That shouldn't happen. That man should be put into a job in which he could be of use, but keep his rank.

HITLER: Yes, but I can't use him in his rank.

GOERING: Not in a position corresponding to his rank. But he did his duty in the First World War and became an active officer.

HITLER: I admit all that. But, for instance, if a man like that is a colonel now—to give him a regiment would be the murder of 3000 men.

GOERING: No, a man like that shouldn't get a regiment.

HITLER: He may not even be in a position to lead a squad. That's what makes it difficult.

GOERING: In a case like that he can pull guard. I have given that choice to some of my generals. I said I couldn't give them anything else.

HITLER: Did the generals accept that?

GOERING: Yes, some did, some didn't.

HITLER: And the latter?

GOERING: I am going to detail them under more stringent orders now. Up to now I haven't actually assigned them, I left it to their own initiative.

HITLER: What are you going to have them do now?

GOERING: If nothing else is available, they will pull guard.

HITLER: As general?

GOERING As general.

HITLER: Do you think that will better serve the purpose?

GOERING: This particular general fought bravely as a battalion commander in the First World War, was discharged as a colonel, and was then drafted again because he was needed.

HITLER: In the First World War, a battalion commander was not discharged as a colonel.

GOERING: As a lieutenant colonel.

HITLER: My regimental commander was a major, was retired as lieutenant colonel, and I finally made him a colonel. People weren't promoted at all in the First World War. That was the worst promotion system that ever existed.

GOERING: Some were promoted. But this one was retired as a lieutenant colonel, was drafted as a lieutenant colonel because he was needed in some bureaucratic affair, and was promoted from there. In the officer corps, demotion has always been considered the most disgraceful thing that could happen to anybody—there's no doubt about that. It simply won't be understood.

HITLER: I'm also of the opinion that it has to be done in a basically different way. As a matter of principle, we have to do it so that the rank and the job are identical.

GOERING: That's right. I agree with you completely. I have plugged for that for three years.

HITLER: That is the English principle. If a man leads a division, he is a division general, if he leads a regiment he is a colonel, and if he leads a battalion he is a major. If he has led a regiment temporarily, he is later returned to his former rank.

GOERING: Only a complete bastard would stand a demotion. If he weren't one, he would shoot himself.

HITLER: But that wouldn't be a demotion.

GOERING: If a man was a colonel and is drafted again as a sergeant, that's a demotion—

HITLER: His pay won't be changed.

GOERING: I would throw the pay in their face and say: 'You are robbing me of my honor. You know that up to now this has been considered as the worst humiliation for an officer.'

HITLER: But in reality it isn't so. That's just the way you people look at it. It was even considered as a humiliation when I promoted a man like lightning. The officers corps regarded it as a humiliation when I promoted a Major Remer to colonel right away.[11]

GOERING: He didn't, anyway.

BURGDORF: If I, as a general, should have to do a major's work, I would rather do it in a major's uniform, because otherwise I would be constantly humiliated in public and everyone would know it.

GOERING: You say that because you won't be in a situation like that. If you would do so in such a situation, it would be a shining example.

BURGDORF: I trust that I can still be used in my present rank.

GOERING: Everything would have to be changed. As things are now, it would be regarded as a demotion without court martial.

HITLER: That's not a demotion. A man like that won't be demoted, he'll just be put into a rank he can fill, which he outgrew without being in the position to fill the higher rank. According to you, it would be a demotion if I take the chairman of the board of some factory and draft him as a common soldier.

GOERING: No, he is not an active officer, he has not chosen the officer's profession.

HITLER: But he has chosen a profession and must be able to do the work. If he can't do that, it's not a demotion.

GOERING: But if a chairman of a board can't do his job, he is discharged.

HITLER: He can't be chairman of the board any more, so he becomes only something like shop steward.

GOERING: Or somewhere else perhaps a traveling salesman.

FEGELEIN: It was always done that way with the party's political leaders.

HITLER: As a matter of principle I believe the English system is healthier in that it states: One who leads a division is a division general, one who doesn't isn't, and if a

[11] Hitler had promoted Major Remer to the rank of colonel for his part in putting down the revolt of 20 July 1944.

division general one day leads a regiment, he is a regimental commander again.

KEITEL: In the Reichswehr we used to be of the opinion that generals should never have to lead battalions and regiments, and therefore we did away with the rank insignia of the old army because it was unsuitable. We just decided that we would not wear insignia, just stars, so that in those days a general could also lead a battalion. We couldn't have done it any other way.

GOERING: One of my generals led a squad.

HITLER: And what kind of insignia did they wear?

KEITEL: In the Reichswehr, only stars.

FEGELEIN: Hausser was discharged as a Brigadier-General, and was a Standartenfuehrer in the SS.[12]

HITLER: There's an example right there. I just want to say how many people were discharged from the army as generals, went into the Waffen-SS, and took subordinate ranking positions there.

GOERING: They weren't forced to do that.

HITLER: What do you mean 'forced?' We are in a great emergency today. The point is that I have to imagine myself in the position of a company commander. The company commander is a lieutenant who is capable of leading the company; he has a colonel who is completely incapable of leading a company because he hasn't done it for twenty-five years. This man leads a platoon, perhaps not even that, but he is wearing a colonel's uniform. What kind of a mess are we going to get then? Does the company commander salute his colonel?

GOERING: It is a fundamental change that would overthrow and crush everything that has existed up to now; an idea that would have been inconceivable up to now. I just want to call attention to that.

HITLER: In the rest of the world it's that way already anyway.

GOERING: No, not in the rest of the world. It has never been that way in England. That's why I made the sugges-

---

[12] The SS 'Standarte' corresponded to a regiment, so that Hausser assumed the functions of a Colonel in the SS.

tion that one should differentiate between the rank and the job.

KEITEL: Up to now there hasn't been any trouble about this in the Volkssturm.

GOERING: No, not there. You said something about the Reichswehr. You mean to tell me that in the Reichswehr a policy was introduced whereby someone who was a general but led a battalion was only a major?

KEITEL: Yes, he didn't wear a general's uniform; he was called battalion commander, not major, lieutenant-colonel, or general.

GOERING: How long did that last?

KEITEL: That was carried through in the Reichswehr. Then it disappeared again because it was said: 'How can we do such a thing? That's crazy.' I was the one who said that we didn't have any ranks any more, no lieutenant, captain, major, lieutenant-colonel; instead we had platoon leader, company commander, battlion commander, regimental commander.

GOERING: When was a general, for instance, a platoon leader?

KEITEL: I ought to know. I was Chief of Organization in the General Staff of the Army.

GOERING: Which years are you talking about?

KEITEL: The years from 1925 to 1930. The mobilization regulations, which applied to the entire armed forces, were officially introduced and accepted. There was no more rank, only the table-of-organization rank connected with the job.

GOERING: That's what I have been requesting for two years. But it never happened that a general, who really had a general's rank, was suddenly made a corporal.

JODL: I would suggest saying Lieutenant-Colonel X be drafted as platoon leader.

HITLER: He won't be demoted. That's a definition that was suddenly thrown in here. But his grade as such will remain in abeyance.

GOERING: If a man was a general and he is drafted as a

corporal, that is a demotion according to our concepts up to now.

HITLER: I can't draft him as a general.

GOERING: If he is drafted as a platoon leader or squad leader, that's something else.

KEITEL: At that time we were in an emergency situation, and with the gigantic officer corps after the First World War, we couldn't have done it in any other way.

JODL: These extreme cases probably won't even occur.

BURGDORF: If somebody is made a squad leader, he must have lost his entire quality of leadership.

GOERING: How far are you going to grade down the commissions? You yourself spoke about sergeants' and corporals' ranks.

BURGDORF: There are so many captains and majors with whom I am stuck.

GOERING: You spoke about generals. But even with colonels it's not a very happy situation.

BURGDORF: I'll always be able to use a colonel as an officer. But the mass of those people have never been soldiers at all.

GOERING: Right. I agree with your definition entirely, if we use the job designations.

HITLER: But they still can't run around in generals' uniforms. Because what kind of a company are you going to get if the company commander wears the uniform of a lieutenant and his platoon leader runs around in a general's uniform, to take an extreme case? I don't know which would be the greater humiliation.

On the other hand, I can't give a general a unit that would suit his rank if he can't manage it. How can I give a general a young volunteer division if, as a result, it will be ruined? In the First World War he might have been a bad company commander of whom everyone knew that in normal peacetime he would never have been capable of leading a company. He would have had to attend courses, just like today. We are promoting lots of people and we know that under normal circumstances in peacetime they couldn't do the job.

JODL: Can't we just say: 'Colonel X will be drafted as a Volkssturm company commander' even if he's sent somewhere else?

BURGDORF: That way he would be judged by other standards.

HITLER: In the SA and the SS I had people who advanced only with great effort. That is impossible in the Army. Just imagine how a company would look in practice. It is led by a capable lieutenant who has come from the ranks, who can and must lead it, and under him he has a couple of lieutenant-colonels or generals wearing their uniforms. In my opinion, the rank must remain in abeyance during this period. There is no other way.

GOERING: You mean that out of the service he keeps his old rank, but during the time of service his rank is in abeyance?

HITLER: One thing has to be avoided, and that is that people who are fit for service but can't do a certain job any more do not fight at all, while others, who are only good for limited service, have to do the fighting. Today I have to consider the psychological effect on the entire German people, not just on the officers. After all, that isn't a humiliation.

GOERING: But all that has to be made clear.

JODL: They should not feel that they are being demoted without cause.

BURGDORF: They'll be given six weeks' training to show the stuff they are made of. I have seen these people, and, Herr Reichsmarshal, you would immediately say: 'Those guys have to take their uniforms off entirely.' I just don't have the personnel necessary to give detailed legal justifications for thousands of demotions.

GOERING: In a case like that I would just say: 'Out of the Armed Forces and into the Volkssturm with them.'

BURGDORF: The Volkssturm is for old men. This way we would fill it up with men who might be only 46 years old, fully fit for service, who gold-bricked successfully and were in the West.

GOERING: Well, you can demote people like that.

HITLER: People like that can't command troops either. They've never had jobs like that. I can't even trust them with the smallest units.

GOERING: Then you'll have to take quite a number of people out of the line outfits, too.

BURGDORF: You can see that pretty quickly in a combat outfit.

FEGELEIN: The Reichsfuehrer has done the same thing. He just told the 19th Army: 'I am of this opinion,' and that finished the matter.

HITLER: After all, the military profession is a fighting profession. That has to be the goal.

GOERING: It just has to be settled on principle, because it is a completely different way of looking at it.

HITLER: It isn't a demotion at all. Instead, the original rank is in abeyance during the combat period. If the man is capable, he will soon be back in his old rank. He has it much easier than other people. But some sort of a solution must be found. One thing has to be avoided and that is that a military housecleaning takes place which results only in cleaning people out of the military bureaucracy and putting them into civilian idleness. I can't even use them in the labor program, because we have a certain labor surplus. But even disregarding that, the public rightly says: 'That man is fit for military service, that other one is not, and yet the latter one is drafted.'

BURGDORF: The transfer of a mortar platoon to the Reichsfuehrer in the Black Forest did wonders for the Officers Training Regiment. But it did make a bad impression down there, in the Black Forest, when a lieutenant-colonel and three lieutenants were dragging around a mortar.

HITLER: In my eyes that's much more degrading than the other alternative. The other alternative consists in giving a person a job that is commensurate with his abilities and with which I can trust him. In the other case I let him run around in his old uniform and do work which a private or non-com can do.

GOERING: That way one has to draw the consequences right away by freezing promotions, et cetera.

BURGDORF: Only the line officers should be promoted.

GOERING: Then nobody will stay on the staffs.

BURGDORF: We still have positions which men like to be in.

KEITEL: We have jobs which really have to be done by people who have combat experience. We can't do anything with morons.

BURGDORF: It is much worse to pull out the people who are fit for service.

KEITEL: Will you please read my order concerning the pulling out of men who are fit for service? The situation is gradually becoming unbearable.

GOERING: I can't force anyone to stay on a staff if he says: 'I can't be promoted on the staff, I have to prove myself as a troop commander, you can't expect me to stay here; today I can still command a company, but after you've kept me here a year I won't be able to command a squad anymore, and that won't be my fault either.' That's what they will say.

BURGDORF: We promote them. We are taking over paymasters as company commanders and battalion commanders as soon as they can do the job.

HITLER: I consider it a much poorer idea today to organize so-called officers' battalions. If they fail, it will make a very bad impression. The news will spread among the other units, and then they'll be considered as punishment battalions.[13] I think it would be better to absorb those people. Because this other thing would be a complete defamation.

GUDERIAN: In that mortar battalion that was mentioned earlier, there is a lieutenant-colonel who was my G-4 in Poland, France, and Russia. He was decorated, I myself gave him the Iron Cross First Class. This man was denounced by one of his compatriots from the Upper

---

[13] In the German Army, malefactors were often sentenced to duty in the so-called 'Strafbataillone,' units that were constantly placed in the most exposed parts of the front.

Danube for supposingly having made some remarks in the period before the *Anschluss,* remarks which he never made. Thereupon he was removed from his position, and was put in this mortar battalion in Wildflecken, and now, as a decent and splendid lieutenant-colonel, who in this case was an exceptionally capable and especially splendid man, he is lugging around trench mortars. He has written me the most terrible and heartbreaking letters. He says: 'I have been disgraced without any cause, without any proper investigation and check-up, just because of a dirty gossip who denounced me. I don't know how to help myself.' As far as I know he has not been cleared yet.

HITLER: The cases we are discussing arise from the fact that we have to dismantle five-sixths of our administration. It is not a question of defamation. The administration has to be dismantled, and this five-sixths cannot be let out of the Army just because they cannot be given a command commensurate to their rank.

GUDERIAN: Then they must be used in a different capacity. If a colonel can only be used as a battalion or company commander, then he will do that and will take off his epaulettes for the period of this service.

HITLER: Well, that's the whole point.

GOERING: But he won't become a non-com.

GUDERIAN: No, he will remain a colonel or a general, with full pay and allowances.

GOERING: Let's leave the pay out of this.

FEGELEIN: The Escort[14] includes many Hauptsturmfuehrer who serve as non-commissioned officers in the 'Leibstandarte.' There has never been any trouble about that.

GOERING: The Waffen-SS is an active unit. The others are not active. The people who serve in them are doing reserve duty. A man can be governor of a province and still be a private first class. That's not comparable. Not a single person is going to stay in a headquarters because he feels that that might endanger his rank

[14] The SS 'Leibstandarte' Division provided Hitler's personal bodyguard, the 'Escort.'

HITLER: First of all, under no circumstances can I let these
people go home. That would mean that the same time I
draft partially unfit men almost 56 years old, I discharge
45-year-old men, although heretofore they've always been
soldiers. That's impossible. Secondly, it is also impossible
for me to hand units over to people who are just not
capable of leading them.

GOERING: And thirdly, I can't tell people who were
capable of leading units before I took them for staff work,
that they won't get units again because they worked on a
staff.

HITLER: If they are capable of leading units, they will get
them.

GOERING: No, they were capable.

HITLER: Then they will be soon again. They'll just have to
learn it again. That's no disgrace. I had to learn to be
Reich Chancellor, too. I was party leader, and as such my
own boss, and as Reich Chancellor I was subordinate to
the Reich President. For a while I was Councillor in
Brunswick.[15]

GOERING: But not in active service.

HITLER: Don't you say that. I did a lot for that country.

BURGDORF: We will put them all through courses and
school them further. Besides, we have a standing request
with the higher headquarters to give us those men for two
months and they'll get them back. Then they won't forget
it all.

HITLER: I can take a born combat leader into any staff
today, but when I return him I can't demand that he start
right in again as if nothing had happened. That's impossible, because they have to learn so much. Anybody who is
leading out there these days can tell you that. But in a few
months he will certainly prove his ability for leadership
again. If he really is a born combat leader, he will get the
job equivalent to his rank right back. That's clear, that's

[15] In 1932, the government of Brunswick, which was controlled by the
National Socialists, gave Hitler an official post through which he automatically acquired German citizenship, this being a prerequisite for his
candidacy for the office of Reich President.

not too difficult. If you take the born combat leader today, in a very short time he will be back in his original rank.

FEGELEIN: Those 10,000 officers and non-commissioned officers, the Englishmen and Americans in Sagan,[16] are moving off in two hours, in a convoy. In addition, 1,500 men who were in the vicinity somewhere in the General Government[17] are marching on foot toward Sagan. Since there was no transportation, they were told they could stay and wait for the Russians. They declined that and offered to fight for us—

HEWEL: They want rifles.

JODL: If we could succeed in getting Englishmen and Americans to fight against the Russians, that would cause a sensation.

HEWEL: It hasn't been confirmed yet, though.

HITLER: Maybe one of them said something like that and then it was generalized right away. I'm extremely suspicious about that.

FEGELEIN: Good. If it is possible we may do it then.

HITLER: But not just because one of them said so.

FEGELEIN: Those 1,500 marched on foot. They wouldn't get on trucks because they were afraid that they were going to be driven to the Russians. That's why they marched, because they saw that the Russians drove into a German civilian convoy. That made such an impression on them that they started off on foot.

HEWEL: It would be perfectly all right to let them get a couple of English officers.

JODL: But they might be aircraft specialists.

[16] In a previous, unpublished part of this conference, Hitler had given strict orders to do everything to move the prisoners of war from the prison camp at Sagan so that the approaching Russians could not liberate them.

[17] That is, occupied Poland.

MARCH 1945

Exact date and starting time of
this conference is not indicated in the manuscript; the
conference ended at 7.45 P.M.

articipants: HITLER,
BURGDORF, FEGELEIN, GUDERIAN,
JODL, KEITEL, AND PUTTKAMER

*The transcript of this discussion
is preserved only in fragmentary form. The surviving fragment is published in its entirety.*

ITLER: But what he has up front are not divisions.[1]
They're just rubbish. Just the same, he has to make something out of that rubbish. He has merely a bunch of staffs
here. That's what I consider the great danger—that we
have all these staffs here, and that they maneuver themselves into a position like that which existed in the 19th
Army from the beginning, namely a position that isn't
based on a firm foundation.

ODL: That's why I've asked for the map. This defense line
isn't as bad as all that, since it has first the West Wall and
then the Rhine.

IITLER: Unfortunately, this part of the West Wall is as
weak as it could be, since the bunkers up front are of no
value at all.

KEITEL: The commanding general has been there from the

[1] The following remarks are concerned with the German military situ-
ation in the Upper Rhine area, where the 19th Army was then stationed.
Bach-Zelewski and Reinefarth had been fighting, as commanders of the
XIV and XVIII SS Corps respectively, in the Mulhouse-Strasbourg area
until January 1945, when they had gone to the Eastern front with
Himmler.

beginning. The Fifth Defense Command[2] is in charge
down there. The LXIV Corps is here. In my opinion this
Corps should be re-staffed. Then we would get commanding generals down there who know how to improvise in
their sectors. They can work that out with the Commanding General of the Fifth Defense Command.

HITLER: You mean if they can do it.

KEITEL: I'm convinced of it. The Reichsfuehrer has taken
them away. He took along Bach, who had been up here.
Both men who were given commands at that time were
improvisors. One was Bach and the other was Reinefarth.

HITLER: If I had Bach-Zelewski here I would be entirely at
ease. He would scrape up prisoners, convicts and everything. By the way, where is Bach-Zelewski now?

KEITEL: The Reichsfuehrer took him along.

HITLER: If I had Skorzeny down there, I'd be satisfied
too.[3]

GUDERIAN: Bach-Zelewski had the X SS Corps for a
while. I think that was changed. For a while his health was
not too good.

KEITEL: The Reichsfuehrer took both of these people along
with him.

GUDERIAN: The Reichsfuehrer is also Commander-in-
Chief of the Replacement Army.[4] That's a big advantage.

GOERING: Bach-Zelewski has the Older Corps.

KEITEL: At that time he committed General Pfeffer here.
He had the sector that bordered on Switzerland. There was
an SS Corps here, and another here. Bach-Zelewski did all
that. He's the one who was stationed near Strasbourg.

BURGDORF: He now has the X SS Corps.

[2] The German Reich was divided into a number of Defense Command Districts, which were in charge of the drafting and training of
reserves. With the war reaching German territory, they began to play
a more active role and to become involved in the actual conduct of the
war.
[3] Skorzeny was then in charge of a school for the training of sabo-
teurs.
[4] That means he headed the various Defense Command Districts.

GUDERIAN: That's stationed east of the Oder in the region of Dramburg.

HITLER: There are old tanks which can't be driven any more. Anyone else would throw them away. . . He digs them in at any crossroad.

FEGELEIN: Obergruppenfuehrer von dem Bach is on the Oder front.

KEITEL: I think that if it would set your mind at rest you should take the two men whom the Reichsfuehrer personally selected. That's proof that they are the right men.

FEGELEIN: Reinefarth and Bach are the men.

HITLER: I want Feuchtinger again to be given some job, to organize something.[5] We can't allow ourselves the luxury of keeping such people in jail. That applies to Hanneken too. It doesn't make any difference to me. That business can be straightened out later. Right now every man counts. It doesn't matter a damn to me if he took a little bit too much furniture or not. If I give Feuchtinger any kind of trash—he always managed to make a division out of a pile of rubbish. When it was later said that he couldn't lead, that was, of course, prejudice, because in spite of all prophesies he managed to make something out of piles of rubbish. Here on the Upper Rhine front something has to be made out of rubbish piles——the troops just aren't there. The commands are given in vain. He can give orders to his two corps every day, and both of the corps can give them to their divisions, and the divisions can send the orders on down; but there is nothing there.

JODL: In that case it would be best to give that army to a powerful Army commander, because you can't make something out of nothing. Even if you put an SS leader in there, he will just muster up what is left from among the SS troops. He won't make something out of nothing either.

[5] Generalleutnant, commander of the 21st Panzer Division which fought in France in the summer of 1944 and after the German retreat became involved in the Alsace battles. Feuchtinger as well as the later-mentioned Generalmajor von Hanneken, former director of the Department of Industry in the Economics Ministry and deputy for the iron and steel industry, seem to have been in prison awaiting a court martial for corruption.

They just happen to be there. And the Army officers don't have anything.

HITLER: No, it isn't that way. We have the Army people who have just as much as the others. Some Army people can make something out of nothing and others don't make anything of much. I had one Army man who claimed that to defend Zaporozhe he had to have at least . . . men. And yet there were 80,000 men in Zaporozhe. But he didn't see that. It was the same thing in Dnepropetrovsk.[6]

JODL: There won't be any more of that now.

HITLER: Oh yes, we still have that today. We haven't changed them. They are still alive and we still have to use them. It's just that there are two different types of talents. In my eyes, Manstein has a tremendous talent for operations. There's no doubt about that. I am the last one to deny that. And if I had today an army of, say, 20 divisions at full strength and in peacetime condition, I couldn't think of a better commander for them than Manstein. He knows how to handle them and will do it. He would move like lightning, but always under the condition that he has first-class units, gas, and plenty of ammunition. But if something breaks down in his outfit, he doesn't get things done. If I got hold of another army today, I'm not at all sure that I wouldn't employ Manstein. Because he is certainly one of our most competent officers. But there are just two separate talents. You saw that yourselves. The great commanders of the First World War did not manage to raise even one single army by themselves. Leaders arose out of nothing. They then raised the army of liberation and for a time saved Germany.[7] After that they were given a kick

[6] See above p. 152 for Hitler's dissatisfaction with Manstein's handling of the defense of Zaporozhe and Dnepropetrovsk. Manstein had been relieved of his position as commander of the Army Group 'South' in Russia after the collapse of the German line in the Ukraine during the Russian spring offensive of 1944.

[7] Hitler alludes to the formation of Free Corps after the First World War. Pfeffer, Petersdorff, Primken, and Kirchheim were leaders of various Free Corps. Pfeffer subsequently became leader of Hitler's SA, but was removed when he became too independent, and replaced by Roehm. The O(rganization) C(onsul), a secret organization of Free Corps men, specialized in the assassination of German democratic ministers in the Weimar period.

in the pants and thrown out, except in the Navy. The Navy was decent enough to take in all those outlawed 'OC' people. But the Army kicked them out, disgraced them and humiliated them. They were very different men. Some were only organizers—I know them all—who never fought at all. For instance Petersdorff and Pfeffer were never at the front. Pfeffer is a born organizer. I would let him organize something, and when that is finished, let him go.

GUDERIAN: Primken just raised money in the Rhineland and hired the unemployed who were around. Then he brought the Free Corps to the front.

HITLER: Unquestionably, Pfeffer raised a Free Corps and then used it for extortion against his government. I would have knocked ideas like that out of Pfeffer's head. I would have strung him up afterwards, but the Free Corps was there.

GUDERIAN: People like Petersdorff were extremely questionable in combat.

HITLER: The Free Corps 'Petersdorff' fought but Pfeffer didn't. Pfeffer spared his Free Corps. . .

GUDERIAN: That was an active Jaeger battalion.

HITLER: Anyway, those people managed to do it. I consider Kirchheim as suited for a job like that even today. Under me those people did not become great leaders either, because their capabilities were so limited. Neither do I claim that Feuchtinger would be capable of leading an army. But he organized a division, out of an ash heap. Why shouldn't I use his talents? I don't have anything to do with Feuchtinger. I'm not a shareholder in a corporation. I've seen Feuchtinger three or four times in my life, once or twice at the Nuremberg party congress. Once he rushed the people at me so hard they almost knocked me down. During the war I saw him two or three times.

KEITEL: He demanded 257,000 marks from the government for a three-room apartment. That's an achievement in itself.

HITLER: I'd let him make that good with organization work. We can still grab him afterwards.

BURGDORF: I can't do anything in Feuchtinger's case.

Feuchtinger and Hanneken are under the jurisdiction of the Supreme Military Court.

KEITEL: In that case the Fuehrer must give the order to have them released from arrest.

HITLER: Both of them have to make that good now. Everything will depend on that. If they don't make good, they'll be chained as galley slaves. Hanneken used to be the man who did most of the screaming about the steel distribution. Thereupon the Reichsmarshal took a very clever step and told him to distribute the steel himself. That's how Hanneken suddenly rose to power. These people are useful only in jobs like that.

JODL: The Commander-in-Chief, West,[8] is waiting for a decision on whether he can consolidate the flanks.

HITLER: That can only mean that he wants to take off and go back over the Rhine. I would retire only to the West Wall...

---

[8] Because the exact date of this conference is not known, the precise meaning of the following exchange is not easy to establish. Since the Remagen bridge was taken on 7 March, but since there is no mention of American troops having passed the Rhine, the conference must be placed in the first week of March. At the end of February, Bradley had started attacks against the central sector of the German Western front; his First Army was advancing toward Cologne, which was reached on 5 March, and toward Remagen; his Third Army was advancing along the northern bank of the Moselle. Thus the decision Rundstedt is asking for is permission to withdraw all the German forces, which were fighting north of the Moselle, over the Rhine. Jodl's remark concerning 'the Maas sector' as 'the last finger-hold' probably refers to the Lower Rhine area where in the northern sector of their front the Germans were still holding a bridgehead, though under strong pressure and nearly encircled by Canadian and American troops of Montgomery's Army group, which had started to attack some weeks earlier than Bradley's. Hitler's later remark ('Above all, we have to cure him of the idea of retreating here') probably refers to this same sector; Hitler seems to fear that an abandonment of this bridgehead would free Montgomery's troops for action in the southern sector. This southern sector, namely the area between Rhine and Moselle, was then still in German hands, and Hitler reproaches Rundstedt for having expected an attack there and for having left too many reserves in this southern sector, instead of making them available for countering Bradley's attack further north. In general see Eisenhower, *Crusade in Europe*, pp. 372-82, Montgomery of Alamein, *Normandy to the Baltic*, pp. 183-96, and, for Hitler's insistence on leaving German troops in the northern sector west of the Rhine, Shulman, *Defeat in the West*, pp. 268-72.

JODL: The Mass sector, which he still holds, is his last finger-hold.

HITLER: That doesn't make any difference. Here is the West Wall. That's behind our line.

JODL: But now the enemy has come through and has rolled up our front here. The report came in just before I came to the conference.

HITLER: That's not so certain, either. That could be two or three tanks.

JODL: But at present we still have a line of communication over to here.

HITLER: That isn't anything.

JODL: This is a barricade position. This is the West Wall proper.

HITLER: At any rate, I want him to hang on to the West Wall as long as it is humanly possible. Above all, we have to cure him of the idea of retreating here. Because at the same moment the enemy will have the entire 6th English Army[9] and all the American troops free, and he'll throw them all in over here. These people just don't have any vision. That would just mean moving the catastrophe from one place to the other. The moment I move out of here, the enemy will have that whole army free. He can't promise me that the enemy will stay here instead of going over here.

There's no doubt that the building-up of reserves at the most dangerous point here was not done with the energy that might have been possible. That wasn't so much Model's fault—he is concerned only with his own sector—that was the fault of the Commander-in-Chief, West.[10] The C-in-C West should have tried from the beginning to get a division like the 6th, for instance, out of there. The 11th should have been put in up here, and not all the way down there. He should have committed the Panzer Training Division in here. No reserves were formed down there. All

[9] He means the 2nd British Army.

[10] At this time the Commander-in-Chief West, was Rundstedt. He was replaced by Kesselring on 18 March. Model still commanded Army Group 'B', which held the central part of the Western front.

this wasn't done with foresight, I must say. If you're fair, Jodl, you must admit that.

JODL: He considered the dangers down there too acute. He was wrong at Saarbruecken and he was wrong in the Weissenburg gap. He was right on the Moselle.

HITLER: I want to tell you something: even if he had been right at Weissenburg, what could have happened to us there? ... We would have been pushed back to the West Wall again.

JODL: No, the main reason is really this: He would have had his reserves up there long ago if the 6th Panzer Army had not needed his small supply of gas for its movement.[11]

HITLER: Can't we chase a couple of officers down there? We have to get a couple of officers down there—even if they only have one leg or one arm—officers who are good men, whom we can send down there so that we get a clear picture. Burgdorf, we must have some officers here whom we could send out there—no matter how badly wounded they are, even if they only have one arm; they will still be perfectly suited for a job like that. They could then find out what is really happening. Because I don't trust reports at all. Reports are given to throw dust into our eyes. Everything is explained and afterwards it turns out that nothing happened. Suddenly he[12] is sitting on the Kaiserstuhl[13] or some other mountain, and then everybody says: 'My Fuehrer, the story was quite different. Things were not as they had been reported.'

BURGDORF: Yes, and then I wanted to make that suggestion about the Supreme Command Upper Rhine.

JODL: At the present time Obstfelder is there.[14]

---

[11] The 6th Panzer Army under Sepp Dietrich, which had participated in the Ardennes offensive of December 1944, had suddenly been sent to Hungary at the end of January 1945, for the purpose of protecting Vienna. This denuded the Western Command of reserves and fuel.

[12] 'He' means the enemy.

[13] Mountain in Southern Baden, east of the Rhine.

[14] On 3 March, Generaloberst von Obstfelder became Acting Commander of the 19th Army in the Upper Rhine area, succeeding Foertsch, who became Acting Commander of the First Army in the Saar area.

BURGDORF: The Commander-in-Chief, West, brought him
there via command channels. Foertsch was down there. He
was taken away because he was supposedly needed on the
Saar.

HITLER: The man who has this here can only improvise.
The organization of units in the rear is done by the
Commander of the Replacement Army anyway. These
units are committed to action only when something is
happening. But the actual organization is carried through
by the Commander of the Replacement Army.

JODL: Yes, by the Commander of the Replacement Army.

HITLER: That is none of his business anyway.

JODL: Yes, that's right. He is only concerned with the
commitment of these forces in case of major offensive.

HITLER: Then they have to be committed. But he has the
responsibility of building up a front by all possible means
of improvisation, by picking up everything there is in
Germany; by mustering everything there is, as far as I'm
concerned, even women. That's all the same to me. So
many women who want to shoot are volunteering now,
that I am of the opinion that we ought to take them
immediately. They are braver anyway. If we put them into
the second line, the men won't run away at least. Here
behind the Rhine nobody can go over to the enemy. That's
the beauty of it. From here they can only take off to the
rear. . . Those boys over on the enemy side have to be
made so restless that they won't get any rest at all any
more.

JODL: I don't know what a man like that is supposed to do
here. Even to improvise he has to have something; something must be given to him. He doesn't have any jurisdiction over the countryside. Otherwise he'll get into terrific
fights with the District Leaders right away.

HITLER: Just let me tell you something: unquestionably I
have splendid officers, but I am convinced—to cite an
example: Captain von Petersdorff, who happens to be a
tramp, and Captain Pfeffer, who was also a tramp, organized a Free Corps without having any jurisdiction. Manstein could never do that. Manstein can operate with

divisions as long as they are in good shape. If I had an Army here consisting of 10 to 20 first-rate divisions, I would give it to Manstein. If the divisions are busted up, I have to take them away from him in a hurry; he can't handle such a situation. . . That has to be a person who works completely independent of any routine. He makes himself felt, he moves around, and he gets things from all conceivable sources.

JODL: He'll get something from the District Leaders. But there is a simple solution: All I have to do is appoint somebody who doesn't care about anything. Then he'll just steal his recruits, et cetera, from the Replacement Army.

HITLER: What do you mean 'steal'? He will take men who otherwise won't be taken at all. We just saw it recently, when the first crisis occurred. It was possible to build up something like a defense front here in a very short time. It won't work if somebody comes and says: 'I demand a division, this division needs so-and-so much artillery, Class A battalions, consisting of three batteries, et cetera.' Then it doesn't work. He has to take *everything*. There is so much rattling around that isn't even being spit at. If I should offer a normal division commander the sort of thing Himmler got together that time, he would spit and say: 'Are you crazy? Keep your garbage.' But in a situation like that one has to take it.

23 MARCH 1945

Although this conference is
the evening conference for
the date given above, it actually took place from 2.26
A.M. to 3.43 A.M. 24 March
1945.

Participants: HITLER,
BELOW, BORGMANN, BRUDER-
MUELLER, BURGDORF, GOEHLER,
GUENSCHE, HEWEL, JOHANNMEIER,
DE MAIZIÈRE, SUENDERMANN, AND
ZANDER

*This is the last transcript that is
preserved. In the East, the front line then stretched along
the Oder from Stettin to Frankfurt a.d. O. Behind the
Russian line, the cities of Koenigsberg, Danzig, and
Breslau were encircled but still holding out. In the
Southeast the Russian armies had advanced from Budapest
halfway to Vienna. In the West, the Allies had reached the
Rhine at all points, and had crossed it at Remagen, where
a large bridgehead had been formed. On the morning of
the conference, Patton had succeeded in crossing the Rhine
near Oppenheim, between Mainz and Worms. During the
conference, the news of Montgomery's attack near Wesel
arrived.*

*The conference begins with a report by Brudermueller
on the situation in the West, particularly the battles near
the Remagen bridgehead and Ludwigshafen. Then de
Maizière reports on the situation in the East, in Hungary,*

in Silesia, and along the Oder. Below reports on air operations.

HITLER: I really consider the second bridgehead, the bridgehead at Oppenheim, as the greatest danger.

BURGDORF: Because the enemy managed to bring up his bridge equipment so fast.

HITLER: A pontoon bridge.

HEWEL: The Rhine isn't even so very wide there.

HITLER: A good 250 meters. On a river barrier, only one man has to be asleep and a terrible misfortune can happen. Actually, the upper bridgehead is probably the salvation of some of the units down here. If it hadn't happened, and if the enemy in the south had pushed over the Rhine with all his strength, nobody would have gotten out. The moment one lets oneself be pushed out of a fortified position, it's all over. The leadership acted miserably in this case. They drummed into the troops, from the top down, that they could fight better in open country than in here.

BURGDORF: Reichsminister Dr. Goebbels[1] requests permission to build up the East-West Avenue of Berlin into a runway. It would be necessary to cut down all of the lamp posts on the sides and to clear away 20 meters more of the Tiergarten on each side. He thinks that it would have the advantage that the East-West Avenue could be widened at a later time.

HITLER: Yes, he can do that. But I don't think that it is necessary; 50 meters' width should be enough.

ZANDER: I still have the last three radiograms from Hanke.[2]

[1] Goebbels, in his function as District Leader (Gauleiter) of Berlin, was responsible for the defense of that city. The East-West Avenue runs through Berlin's main park, the Tiergarten, in the middle of which stands a large monument commemorating the victory over France in 1871, the Victory Column (Siegessaeule). It was not removed nor was it destroyed during the battle of Berlin. The trees of the Tiergarten were cut down and used for fuel in the winter of 1945/6.

[2] District Leader of Lower Silesia, in charge of the defense of the beleaguered city of Breslau, which was being supplied by air.

[*They are submitted.*]

HITLER: I want all of the last radiograms.

ZANDER: They are in the emergency quarters of the Party Chancellery. I'll have to ask for them.

HITLER: Ask for them right away. A telegram came in which he wrote that the enemy is now using the heaviest weapons, against which they don't have any countermeans. Thereupon, the heavy infantry howitzers were requisitioned. These howitzers have been messed around with as usual in such cases. The Army Group was supposed to furnish them. However, I ordered that they be sent directly from the central depot here, and I made sure that they have heavy infantry howitzers here. Buhle acted surprised. In fact they had to be furnished by the Replacement Army. The Army Group has no heavy infantry howitzers. It took them an eternity. Then it was said that they wouldn't fit into the planes, then that they could be fitted in if they were dismantled, then suddenly it wasn't possible to land them. Actually, they are just afraid to land. Now they are explaining that if they fly in howitzers, they can't fly in ammunition. Actually, it is only six planes, six cargo gliders. All the rest are available for ammunition. But Hanke is a tanker; he doesn't know a damn thing about this. If they really want weapons to be sure to shoot the enemy out of certain blocks, there are much better things; but one can't fly them in. There is no more effective weapon that can be flown in, than the heavy infantry howitzer. On the other hand, if they can only bring in 18 rounds of ammunition, it is a hell of a mess. You can't do anything with 18 rounds, although a heavy infantry howitzer can knock a house all the way down to the cellar with one round.

BURGDORF: Can I give Reichsminister Goebbels the go-ahead on this thing?

HITLER: Yes, but I don't understand why it has to be made wider. They aren't going to land with 'Goliaths.' It's 52 meters wide.

VON BELOW: If the JU-52's are going to have to land in the dark, those street lamps will cause trouble.

HITLER: All right, the street lamps. But to chop down 20 to 30 meters of the Tiergarten on the right and left—

VON BELOW: That's hardly necessary.

HITLER: They don't need more than 50 meters' width. It wouldn't help anyway, because it couldn't be paved on the right and left. That's completely useless.

JOHANNMEIER: There's just the sidewalk and then the slope.

VON BELOW: I don't consider the cutting of 20 meters necessary either, but the removal of the street lamps—

HITLER: He can remove the street lamps.

BURGDORF: Then I can pass that on.

HITLER: It just occurred to me that ME 162's and ME 262's could take off on the East-West Avenue.

VON BELOW: Yes, it is long enough.

HEWEL: But not with the Victory Column in the middle.

BURGDORF: That would have to be removed.

HITLER: It's almost 3 kilometers to the Victory Column. That's long enough.

BURGDORF: Lankeit has been commanding the 12th Division up to now. He'll be free now. I just wanted to suggest whether we couldn't put him into the 'Hoch-und Deutschmeister' Division. He did very well with the 12th Division. He is from Upper Bavaria.

HITLER: The 12th Division in the West?

BURGDORF: Yes. Before that he was in the East and knows the situation there. And then again the question: what do you intend to do about Guderian's furlough in these days?

HITLER: Once and for all, I want the opinion of the doctor about Wenck,[3] and I want him to commit himself definitely. I'll make him vouch for it with his head: 'by that time Wenck will either be well or not.' Period. They talk

[3] General Wenck was then supposed to become the commander of the 11th Army, which was being formed in central Germany; after its annihilation, he was placed at the head of the 12th Army, on which Hitler to the very end based his hopes for liberation.

and talk, and say that on such-and-such a day he can leave the hospital. Now they don't even seem to know whether he must be operated on.

BURGDORF: The doctor told us that Wenck should stay until 15 April, although he is already getting impatient.

VON BELOW: My Fuehrer, when you are not at Obersalzberg,[4] can they save their smoke screen down there? At the present time they are sending up an artificial fog every time aircraft is reported, and that is very hard on the smoke chemicals.

HITLER: Yes, but then everything is gone, of course; we have to realize that. That's one of the last hideouts we have. Nothing is going to happen to the bunker, and it doesn't matter about my house, but the whole plant will be gone. If Zossen[5] up here is smashed up one day, where will we go then? A heavy raid on Zossen and it will be gone. Probably a large part of it is gone now.

BURGDORF: It's perfectly usable. All of the houses are still there, and enough of the barracks. But if the barracks are ever smashed, the last possibility will be gone.

HITLER: I saw that one picture. It was a 1-meter-thick concrete wall. They used army concrete there. Because a bomb like that shouldn't even have pushed it in, since it was above ground.

BURGDORF: Since I was a guest there, I don't want to call attention to the building of the Air Fleet 'Reich'; but if I had had an inkling that such an object existed in the vicinity of Berlin, I would have said it was a scandal. Because both of the General Staffs as well as yourself, my Fuehrer, would fit in there. Out there in Wannsee they have a bunker with 3.5 meter iron concrete on top, and with our stories, one under the ground and three above the ground. That's the old Air Raid Protection School. I just saw it by accident.

HITLER: Up to now that has been kept from me entirely.

VON BELOW: That's the bunker of the Air Fleet 'Reich.' It

---

[4] Hitler's famed retreat near Berchtesgaden in Bavaria.
[5] A town in the vicinity of Berlin near which the headquarters of the Army General Staff (OKH) was located.

used to be the Air Raid Protection School, and about two years ago the Air Fleet 'Reich' built the bunker.

HITLER: This is the way it is: actually nothing is safe, that's obvious. But against bombs up to 1,000 kilograms the bunkers right here in the Chancellery are safe, on the whole. That means that one part can always be quartered here. After all, I can throw some more things out of here. Certainly, that could be done. One part can be quartered here. Zossen out there is not safe; and not because it could not be safe as such, but because it was built by the Army and not by a construction firm. If the OT[6] and a real construction firm had built it, 1-meter-thick walls would be strong enough so that the underground part at least could not be penetrated so easily. But I saw that a bomb went in sideways and crashed right through 1 meter underground. And then I also saw the armor: the outside armor is two layers at the most. That's a joke of course. You don't call that a concrete structure. Speer's earlier constructions are not quite perfect either, that must be recognized. Even the buildings here in the Chancellery are very massive only because of the huge buildings that stand on top of them and that provide a tremendous cover. But it's still not entirely safe. The Army constructions out in Zossen are complete swindles. We might as well admit that. The people who built them deceived themselves. If a real bomb barrage hits them, all the houses at Zossen will be swept away, all the buildings there—first of all everything aboveground, of course, but also the two bunkers under the ground. They are weak too. Now the question is: Can the whole unit function if all the constructions aboveground are gone?

BURGDORF: Yes, they can work underground.

HITLER: Will that be enough for the whole organization?

BURGDORF: Yes, for the immediate command organization, which is already there.

DE MAIZIÈRE: Already large sections work down below as long as their aboveground quarters are not repaired.

___

[6] 'Organization Todt.'

For instance, General Krebs, the chief of the operations section, works mostly below. In other words, the organization that is there now can work even if the buildings aboveground are destroyed.

HITLER: We certainly hope to figure on that. Because the enemy is certainly going to get reports about what has been destroyed. And I fear that there, as in the case of the Reich Chancellery, they had the brilliant idea of using foreign workers for cleaning up. So the enemy's intelligence will get reports of what was damaged two weeks earlier.

VON BELOW: I will find out about that.

HITLER: Then the attack will be repeated, that's certain; and when the attack is repeated, one day we will have to count on their blowing up these objectives, although I am assuming that the second floor of the underground bunker— the ceiling of the first floor is only 1 meter thick, that's nothing at all, and I don't even know, since it isn't indicated in the drawing, if the ceilings have supports—

JOHANNMEIER: They have supports. You can even see parts of them. I lived down there myself once for four weeks.

BURGDORF: You can see them running along the ceiling when you come in, just as in this room.

HITLER: Frontal supports?

JOHANNMEIER: Yes.

HITLER: Normally you could take it for granted that a 1,000-kilogram bomb couldn't penetrate 1 meter, but these really blast. They penetrate 50 to 60 centimeters and then break through the whole works right away, so that the upper story is gone after one bomb like that.

BRUDERMUELLER: The first two battalions of those 6,-000 parachutists have left the combat area today and are to be loaded in the area of Bolzano.[7] However, the Brenner track is still out of order due to air raids. For that

---

[7] Where and to whom these reserves are to be sent is not clear, but they were evidently in a combat area south of the Alps.

reason we are figuring on three days to the area of Bolzano. The empty convoys which are driving down will be used as far as possible, but there are very few because at the moment there is very little shooting. The main part will have to march to the Bolzano area on foot.

HITLER: Then they won't make Bolzano in three days. From there to Bolzano is a trip of three weeks, 20 days or 14 days, 10 days at the minimum.

BURGDORF: Even from Trento to Bolzano is a day's march.

BRUDERMUELLER: A time estimate is very hard to make at the moment, because very few empty convoys are driving back since at this time they don't have much to bring down to the front because there isn't much shooting and for that reason they need comparatively few supplies.

BURGDORF: Can't they at least go by rail part of the way? They can always get off and get on again. There's nothing to reload. It's just the men with small arms.

HITLER: The point is to have the 7000 men who are to be combined with these 6000 men in readiness, so that they can be joined together immediately after arrival. The 6000 men must be instructed in transit about what they need to know, so that when they arrive they can be formed into divisions immediately. Then they are fit to be used for defense purposes in any case. Then we'll have to see where we will put them. We don't have to decide that now. These are two units that can get here. The other two units—I don't know yet. They must be units from home. That will still have to be improvised.

BRUDERMUELLER: He is going to get the cadre of the Danube Division.

HITLER: With that alone it won't work.

BRUDERMUELLER: Of course he can use it to build up other, used-up divisions.

BURGDORF: In my opinion the 11th, 9th, and 7th Defense Commands haven't raised anything yet, at least they haven't been as cleaned out as the other Defense Commands. Something should be feasible along those lines.

HITLER: Take that up with Juettner[8] right away. That must be done under all circumstances.

BURGDORF: Yes, I shall say again that the Defense Commands 11, 9, and 7 will have to make a contribution now, somehow or other.

HITLER: We just don't know what is floating around. I just heard for the first time, to my amazement, that a Ukrainian SS-Division has suddenly appeared. I didn't know a thing about this Ukrainian SS-Division.[9]

GOEHLER: It has existed for a long time.

HITLER: But no reference was ever made to it in our discussions. Or do you remember one?

GOEHLER: No, I don't remember.

HITLER: I don't know. It may have been reported to me a long, long time ago. How strong is the Ukrainian Division?

GOEHLER: I'll find out again.

HITLER: Either the outfit is trustworthy or it's not trustworthy. I can't organize units in Germany today because I don't have any weapons. It's just insanity for me to give weapons to a Ukrainian Division which isn't quite trustworthy. I'd rather take their weapons away and raise a new German division. Because I suppose they are splendidly armed, better armed than most of the German divisions we are raising today.

BURGDORF: It's the same thing with the 20th, the Latvian Division. That also fell right apart down there.

DE MAIZIÈRE: The Latvian one is fighting up in Courland at present, and quite well, too. That one down there was the Esthonian.

BURGDORF: Yes, the Esthonian one was gone right away. We must imagine their psychology. It is expecting a little too much of those people.

HITLER: What are they supposed to be still fighting for, anyway? They are away from home.

[8] SS Obergruppenfuehrer, permanent deputy to Himmler in his function as Commander of the Replacement Army.
[9] Pro-Nazis of non-German nationality had been organized into a number of SS-Divisions. Vlassov was a Russian general who, after his capture, had declared for the German cause and had raised and led an army of anti-communist Russian troops; see p. 165.

BURGDORF: If even we have hordes of timid people, it is expecting a little too much of those people.

HITLER: We have to find out exactly what foreign units are still there. For instance, the Vlassov Division is either good for something or it is not. There are just these two possibilities. If it's any good it must be considered a regular division, and if it's no good it would be idiocy to equip a division of 10,000 or 11,000 men while I can't raise German divisions because I don't have any weapons. I'd rather just raise a German division and give it all of those weapons.

BURGDORF: The Indian Legion.

HITLER: The Indian Legion is a joke. There are Indians who can't kill a louse, who'd rather let themselves be eaten up. They won't kill an Englishman either. I consider it nonsense purposely to put them opposite the English. Why should the Indians be braver in our service than they were under Bose[10] in India? They used Indian units under Bose's leadership in Burma for the purpose of freeing India from the British. They ran away like a bunch of sheep. Why should they be braver here? I think that if we used the Indians to turn prayer-mills or for something of that sort, they would be the most indefatigable soldiers in the world. But to use them for a real death-struggle is ridiculous. How strong are the Indians? But it's all nonsense. If you have a surplus of weapons, you can afford a joke like that for propaganda purposes, but if you don't have a surplus of weapons, such jokes for propaganda purposes are entirely irresponsible. What is this Galician Division anyway? Is that the same thing as the Ukrainian Division?

BORGMANN: I can't say.

HITLER: There's always a Galician Division floating around. Is that the same as the Ukrainian Division? Because if that is made up of Austrain Ruthenians, the only thing to do is to take their weapons away immediately.

[10] Subhas Chandra Bose was head of a Nazi-backed Free India movement. In 1942 he went to Burma, where he organized an Indian army to support the planned Japanese invasion of India.

The Austrian Ruthenians were pacifists. They were lambs, not wolves. They were miserable, even in the Austrian army. This is just self-delusion. Is this Ukranian Division the same thing as the so-called Galician Division?

GOEHLER: No, the Galician is the 30th, the Ukrainian is the 14th. The 30th is being rested, I believe in Slovakia.

HITLER: Where did it fight?

GOEHLER: The 30th, the Galician, was originally committed in the Tarnow sector, and hasn't been committed since.

DE MAIZIÈRE: The division was committed in the area of the 1st Panzer Army during the battles around Lwow. At that time it was attached to, I believe, the XIII Corps and suffered the encirclement, and only some parts of the division came back. As far as I know, it hasn't been used since.

HITLER: And they've been resting ever since? Do they have weapons?

GOEHLER: I'll have to check on that.

HITLER: We can't afford a joke like this while I don't have enough weapons to equip other divisions. That's ridiculous.

GOEHLER: The Ukrainian Division has a table-of-organization strength of 11,000, and an actual strength of 14,000.

HITLER: Why more actual strength than T/O strength?

GOEHLER: Probably they got more volunteers than the T/O allowed them.

HITLER: And the equipment?

GOEHLER: They gave a large part of their equipment to the 18th SS.

HITLER: But if they are ready for combat now, they must have weapons again. I don't want to insist that you can't do anything with these foreigners. Something could be done with them, but it takes time. If you have them for six or ten years, and if you govern their home territories, as the old Hapsburg monarchy did, then they will become good soldiers of course. But if you get the men, and their homelands are on the other side—why should they fight at all? They are susceptible to every piece of propaganda. I assume that there are still very strong German elements among them.

[*Sturmbannfuehrer Goehler submits a report.*]

GOEHLER: They have the following weapons: 2100 pistols, 610 submachine guns, 9000 rifles, 70 rifles with telescopic sights, 65 automatic rifles M-43, 434 light machine guns, 96 heavy machine guns, 58 light mortars, 4 heavy mortars—

HITLER: You could equip two divisions with that.

GOEHLER: 22 flamethrowers, 1 medium AT gun, 11 75mm AT guns, 17 light infantry howitzers, 3 heavy infantry howitzers M-33, 93 mm AA guns, 37 light field howitzers, 6 heavy field howitzers.

HITLER: I must know what this division is worth. I want to speak to the Reichsfuehrer right away tomorrow. He's in Berlin anyhow. We have to investigate exactly what we can expect of a unit like that. If one can't expect anything, there is no sense to it. We can't afford the luxury of keeping units like that.

GOEHLER: The Indian Legion has a strength of 2,300 men.

HITLER: We would be doing them the greatest favor if we told them that they don't have to fight any more.

GOEHLER: They have 1,468 rifles, 550 pistols, 420 submachine guns, 200 light machine guns—

HITLER: Just imagine, they have more weapons than men. Some of their people must carry two weapons.

GOEHLER: —24 heavy machine guns, 20 medium mortars, 4 light field howitzers, 6 light infantry howitzers, 6 AT guns, it doesn't say what kind, 700 horses, 81 vehicles, 61 passenger cars, 5 motorcycles, 12 prime movers of which 11 are ready for use.

HITLER: What is the Indian Legion supposed to be doing?

GOEHLER: I can't say. They've also been resting for quite a long time.

HITLER: But they've never been in battle.

GOEHLER: No.

HITLER: A unit which is in a rest area should, in my opinion, be a unit that has seen heavy fighting and is being refreshed. These outfits of yours are always refreshing themselves and never fighting.

BRUDERMUELLER: Army Group 'H' reported at 3 o'clock that the enemy has moved up for attack 1 1/2 kilometers south of Wesel and near Mehrum.[11] The strength and the nature of this attack has not been reported yet. That attack was to be expected. Since 17.00 o'clock there has been heavy artillery fire on our main battle line as well as on rear areas.

HITLER: Since 1 o'clock.

BRUDERMUELLER: No, the report reached Supreme Command West at 3 o'clock. It's 3.30 now.

HITLER: There are parachutists here?

BRUDERMUELLER: Yes, it was expected here. The Commander-in-Chief West reported this evening already that he expected the attack near Wesel, since there had been very heavy artillery fire there since 17.00 o'clock, and since there was also unusually great activity by combat observation aircraft.

HITLER: There are parachutists here?

BRUDERMUELLER: The 108th Division is here; it is comparatively strong.

HITLER: They have something like 8000 men.

BRUDERMUELLER: It has been filled up again. The battalions are almost at full strength.

[*Report is submitted.*]

Altogether, counting the attached batteries, they have artillery to the amount of 22 batteries in that sector, including 6 heavy batteries. . .

BORGMANN: General Thomale[12] and General Buhle report that at the present time no unit is available to be sent

[11] This announcement indicates the beginning of Montgomery's huge attack at Wesel, which had been planned as the principal Allied thrust into Germany east of the Rhine and which culminated in the surrender of all German forces in northern Germany, Holland, Schleswig-Holstein, and Denmark by Admiral Friedeburg on 5 May at Lueneburg.

[12] Generalmajor Thomale, Inspector General of Panzer Troops. For Buhle, see list of participants.

to Oppenheim. There are only 5 tank destroyers in the camp at Senne, which will be ready today or tomorrow. They could be put into battle in the next few days. In the following days two more will be added so that the unit can be raised to 7. Everything else is committed at the moment, and at this time nothing else is ready.

HITLER: They're at the Senne Camp?

BORGMANN: Yes.

HITLER: Actually they were meant for the upper bridgehead.

BORGMANN: Yes, for Remagen, for the 512th battalion.

HITLER: When do they leave?

BORGMANN: They'll be ready today or tomorrow. They can probably move out tomorrow night.

HITLER: Then we'll take that up again tomorrow. If we only knew which of the 16 or 17 Tigers they brought back can be repaired, and when. That would be very important.

BORGMANN: I'll make another inquiry so that General Thomale can give a clear picture about those 16 by tomorrow noon, or afternoon.

BRUDERMUELLER: I have already informed General Thomale that everything must be done to repair them quickly, even if spare parts have to be sent by air. I told him that if necessary an engineering officer from here who knows something about that must be sent. He also reported that he has relieved the battalion commander, the adjutant, and the signal officer, because his officers down there reported that these were duds. Tomorrow morning he is sending the best man he has over there in a car.

HITLER: I did not get the impression that the battalion commander was particularly heroic.

JOHANNMEIER: He was in the 'Adlerhorst'[13] once.

BURGDORF: If on the basis of our information I should tell the Inspector General how to compose his battalions, there would be a row immediately. That's impossible. They all reserve the right to decide what to do with their specialist battalions.

---

[13] Hitler's Western headquarters near Bad Nauheim.

HITLER: He didn't make a very enthusiastic impression that time. Or did you think so?

JOHANNMEIER: No, he didn't make a very good impression. He talked a great deal, but I didn't think there was very much behind it. And that time General Thomale was very enthusiastic about him.

HITLER: I don't know.

JOHANNMEIER: He was very badly wounded. I think he was wounded eight times. I'm sure he couldn't manage physically.

HITLER: I admit that, but that isn't necessarily proof.

BURGDORF: Just in the Tank Forces we have many young and vigorous people, because they all came from active units. We have very good replacements, much better than in the infantry.

A telegram came from District Leader Forster.[14] It concerns the withdrawal of the 450 Security Police specialists. Altogether, there are 12,000 men up there.

HITLER: They claim that they can't get along without them, but we'll have to turn them down if it would be wrong for psychological reasons.

BURGDORF: Shall I answer that they are to stay there?

HITLER: Get in touch with Kaltenbrunner right away.[15] Kaltenbrunner said that he can hardly spare them. But he says that if it's psychologically necessary for the defense, they will have to stay in Danzig.

VON BELOW: May I ask about the aircraft again? The '335' is supposed to be assembled from the parts that were prepared.

HITLER: Yes.

VON BELOW: In regard to the production, Speer suggests that the ME-109 be stopped completely, so that all those people who have been busy with its preparations can be freed for this other thing.

HITLER: Yes.

---

[14] District Leader (Gauleiter) of Danzig-West Prussia, at this time in charge of the defense of the city of Danzig.

[15] SS-Obergruppenfuehrer, Chief of the Security Police (SD).

VON BELOW: And the '190' production will be stopped within the next four months.

HITLER: Yes. The '190' is better than the '109'?

VON BELOW: Yes, it is better. It has a better engine now and as a combat plane it is more useful than the '109.' After production is discontinued, it would be replaced by the '152.' That isn't supposed to be used as an interceptor at all.

HITLER: Yes, only I think that the constantly increasing Mosquito attacks, which don't bother us because we are in a deep cellar but which are very disagreeable for the population, can only be stopped by planes with far superior speed and a greater safety factor, so that they can land even if one motor goes dead. There's no doubt that a twin-engined plane is better than a single-engined plane. That's the case with this machine, so I would give it priority over the anti-tank plane.

VON BELOW: The anti-tank plane isn't supposed to be used as an interceptor over Germany at all, but only as an attack plane at the front.

HITLER: But then we need another plane as long as we're not sure of the '262.' I think that the what-do-you-call-it is better.

VON BELOW: Then I would suggest if it wouldn't be possible for you to have a discussion with all the people concerned with the ME-262. I would suggest that sometime, perhaps at the beginning of next week, you summon the Reichsmarshal, General Koller, Kammhuber, General Peltz, who is in charge of the combat units, Speer, Saur, Degenkolb, Messerschmitt, and Dorsch. There are several questions which you alone can decide.

HITLER: I've been saying the whole time just what what's-his-name said today: There is too much of a discrepancy between what we are supposedly producing and what is actually being committed in battle. That isn't happening in any other country in the world, and formerly it didn't happen here.

APPENDIX

APPENDIX

Hitler's Speech to his Generals,
28 December 1944

              In addition to the stenographic records of the daily military conferences, the material found at Berchtesgaden contains the record of two of Hitler's speeches which were delivered in December 1944. These speeches were addressed to the top military leaders, the commanders of army corps and divisions, together with their chiefs of staffs, for the purpose of briefing them for the impending offensive operations in the West. The meetings at which they were delivered were extremely secret. According to the report of one of the participants, the officers were assembled at Rundstedt's headquarters and 'told to attend a special briefing.' 'We were,' he continues, 'all stripped of our weapons and briefcases, loaded into buses and then driven about the countryside for about half an hour. Finally we were led into a large room which was surrounded with SS guards who watched our every move. Then Hitler arrived accompanied by Fieldmarshal Keitel and General Jodl. Hitler looked sick and broken, and began to read from a long, prepared manuscript. The speech lasted for two hours ...' However, the statement that Hitler spoke from a manuscript is contradicted by the official stenographers, who say that he spoke without using a manuscript. In any case, the stenographic recordings preserved among the minutes of the daily military conferences appear to be the only known surviving records of the speeches, and even these records are not complete.

    According to the stenographers, Hitler made three speeches—on 11, 12, and 28 December. Of the speech on 11 December nothing has been preserved. Of the one on the 12th only the first part has survived, and even this is in fragmentary form. The surviving fragments are not concerned with the military situation but rather are given over to an extended historical survey in which the Second World War is interpreted as a continuation of the wars of unification, for the purpose of securing for the German nation the living space which is its due, and in which 1939 is characterized as the most favorable moment for the beginning of this necessary war. Although these ideas are developed at perhaps greater length in this speech than anywhere else, Hitler has expressed them frequently elsewhere in briefer form.

The speech of 28 December has been preserved almost in its entirety and is here published in full.

The surprise offensive toward the Ardennes, The Battle of the Bulge, has passed its climax, and Hitler is briefing the assembled officers for a second offensive, somewhat farther to the south, from the region of Saarbruecken toward Lorraine and Lower Alsace. This offensive, which began on 1 January 1945, pushed the Allied forces out of German territory and advanced, with heavy fighting taking place near Bitche, for more than ten miles beyond the frontier; but it never reached even its first objective, the Saverne Gap. It has hardly been regarded as a major operation, and the great anticipatory importance Hitler attaches to it in his speech comes as something of a surprise. From the point of view of military history the speech has great interest because it contains Hitler's evaluation of The Battle of the Bulge.

The character of this document is, of course, very different from that of other documents published in this volume. It does not show us Hitler expressing unvarnished opinions to the regular attendants of his daily conferences. Rather it is a propaganda speech, designed to bolster up the morale of the officers who were to participate in the coming offensive. It is filled with incorrect statements, and it may be doubted whether Hitler himself believed in what he was saying. It may be added that his sentences, relatively clear and well constructed in the beginning, become more and more involved and even obscure as he nears the end.

GENTLEMEN: I have asked you to come here before an operation on the successful conclusion of which further blows in the West will depend. First, I want briefly to place this particular operation in its true significance. I want to relate it to the over-all situation that confronts us and to the problems which we face and which must be solved. Whether they develop in a happy or an unhappy fashion, solved they shall be, ending either in our favor or in our destruction.

The German situation can be characterized in a few sentences. As in the First World War, so in this war the question is not whether Germany will be graciously permitted by her enemies, in the event of their victory, some kind of existence, but whether Germany has the will to remain in existence or whether it will be destroyed. Unlike earlier wars of the seventeenth or eighteenth century, this war will decide neither a question of political organization nor a question of the adherence of a people or a tribe or a former federal state to the German Reich. What in the last analysis will be decided is the survival of the very essence (*Substanz*) of our German people, not survival of the German Reich but survival of the very essence of the German people. A victory of our enemies must 'bolshevize' Europe. What 'bolshevization' means for Germany everybody must and will realize. In contrast with earlier times, it is not now a question of a change in the form of our government. Changes in the form of government have taken place in the lives of peoples on innumerable occasions. They come and go. Here the survival of the very essence is involved. Essences are either preserved or they are removed. Preservation is our goal. The destruction of the essence under certain circumstances destroys the race forever.

Struggles such as are going on now have the character of clashes of philosophies of life (*Weltanschauungen*) and they frequently last a very long time. Therefore they are not comparable to the struggles of the time of Frederick the Great. Then the issue was whether, within the framework of the gradually crumbling and disintegrating Empire, a new great German power would emerge and whether this power would, so to speak, achieve recognition as a great European power. Today Germany no longer needs to prove herself a great European power—her importance as such is clear to everyone. The German Reich is now fighting an ideological war for its very existence. The winning of this war will, once and for all, stabilize this great power, which quantitatively and qualitatively is already in existence. The loss of this war will destroy the German people and break it up. Parts of Germany will be evacuated.

A few weeks ago you heard Churchill say in the English Parliament[1] that the whole of East Prussia and parts of Pomerania and Silesia would be given to Poland, who in turn would give something else to Russia. Seven or ten or eleven million Germans would have to be transferred. Churchill hopes in any case to eliminate by air attack six or seven millions, so that the population transfer (*Aussiedelung*) would offer no great difficulties. This is today the sober statement of a leading statesman in a public body. In earlier times you would have regarded this as a propaganda argument, as a propaganda lie. Here it is said quite officially, though it by no means corresponds to what will actually happen, because, in the case of a German collapse, England would be unable to offer serious resistance to bolshevism anywhere.

That is pure theory. In these days when Mr. Churchill leaves Athens in humiliating failure,[2] and is unable to oppose bolshevism even on a small scale, he wants to give the

---

[1] Hitler refers to Churchill's speech in the House of Commons on 15 December in which he had discussed the Polish-Soviet frontier and had said that Poland would 'gain in the North all of East Prussia south and west of Koenigsberg, including Danzig' and 'would stretch broadly along the Baltic on a front of 200 miles. The Poles are free, so far as Russia and Great Britain are concerned, to extend their territories at the expense of Germany in the West.' He had added that this change of frontiers would be accompanied by 'the total expulsion of Germans from the areas to be acquired by Poland in the West and North; for expulsion is the method which, so far as we have been able to see, will be most satisfactory and lasting.'

[2] After a visit of four days Churchill had left Athens without the conferences he had held there seeming to have led to an end of the severe fighting between the opposing Greek parties. The chief result of Churchill's visit—namely the establishment of Archbishop Damaskinos as Regent—was announced only after Churchill's return to London.

impression that he is able to halt the advance of bolshevism at any frontier in Europe. That is ridiculous fantasy. America can't do it. England can't do it. The only country whose fate will be decided in this war is Germany. She will be saved or, in the event of the loss of the war, she will perish.

I hasten to add, gentlemen, that from these statements of mine you are not to draw the conclusion that even remotely I envisage the loss of this war. In my life I have never learned to know the word 'capitulation,' and I am a self-made man. For me the situation in which we are today is nothing new. I have been in very different and much worse situations. I mention this only because I want you to understand why I pursue my aim with such fanaticism and why nothing can wear me down. As much as I may be tormented with worries and even physically shaken by them, nothing will make the slightest change in my decision to fight on till at last the scales tip to our side.

The objection that, with respect to such issues, we must think in sober military terms can best be refuted by taking a quick look at the great events of history. In the time after the battle of Cannae, everyone would, by sober military calculations, have been forced to the conclusion that Rome was lost. But, though abandoned by all her friends, betrayed by all her allies, the last army at her disposal lost, and the enemy at the gates, Rome was saved by the steadfastness of the Senate—not the Roman people, but the Senate, which means their leadership. We have a similar example in our own German history, not of the same world-wide significance, but tremendously important for the whole course of German history, for the later foundation of the German Reich was determined by this hero, was made possible by his historical achievement. I refer to the Seven Years War. As early as the third year countless military and political officials were convinced that the war could never be won. According to human calculations it should have been lost: 3,700,000 Prussians were pitched against about 52,000,000 Europeans. In spite of that, however, this war was won. Even in struggles of a world-wide nature the spirit is one of the decisive factors. It enables men to discover new ways out (*Ausweg*) and to mobilize new potentials. Above all, in such situations it is decisive to know that the enemy is made up of men of flesh and blood, of men who have nerves, and of men who do not fight for their very existence in the same sense that we do. That means that the enemy does not know, as we do, that this is a fight for existence. If the English should now lose this war, this would not be decisive for them, in view of the losses they have already suffered. America would lose neither its political form nor its racial essence. But Germany fights for her very existence. That the German people are aware of this you all realize. You need to look only at today's German youth and to compare them with the youth of the First World War. You need to look only at the German cities and to compare their attitude with that of the German people in the year 1918. Today the entire German people remain unshaken and will remain unshaken. In 1918 the German people capitulated without necessity. Now they realize the dangers of the situation and are aware of the problem with which we are confronted. That is what I wanted to say as a brief introduction before I discuss the purely military issues.

What is the military situation? Whoever studies the great world-historical struggles which are known to us will very frequently find situations of a similar character, perhaps even situations much worse than the one with which we are confronted today. For we should not forget that even today we are defending a territory—German territory and Allied territory—which is essentially larger than Germany has ever been, and that we have at our disposal an armed force which even today unquestionably is the strongest on the earth. If anyone wants to get the over-all situation into correct perspective, he should visualize the following: he should take by itself one of the world powers which are opposing us, Russia, England, or America. There can be no doubt that singly we could dispose of each of these states with ease. That not only is proof of the strength of the German people, but also of the strength of the German military force, which, of course, in the final analysis grows out of the strength of the German people, which cannot be imagined to exist in a vacuum.

In a military sense it is decisive that in the West we are

moving from a sterile defensive to the offensive. The offensive alone will enable us to give once more to this war in the West a successful turn. To the extent to which the enemy succeeds in mobilizing resources, defensive warfare would get us into a hopeless position within a calculable period of time. The offensive would not cost such sacrifice in blood as people generally assume—at least less in the future than at present. The view that under all circumstances an offensive would be more costly in blood than a defensive is wrong. We ourselves have had that experience. The battles that were most bloody and costly were in all cases our defensive battles. If we take into account the losses of the enemy and our own losses and if we include the numbers of war prisoners, offensive battles have always been favorable to us. The same is true of the present offensive. If I imagine the total number of the divisions the enemy has thrown in here, and if I calculate his entire losses in prisoners alone (losses in prisoners are the same thing as losses in killed; the men are eliminated), and if I add his losses in blood to his losses in material, then if I compare them with our losses, there can be no doubt that even the brief offensive we have just undertaken has resulted in an immediate easing of the situation on the entire front. Although, unfortunately, the offensive has not resulted in the decisive success which might have been expected, yet a tremendous easing of the situation has occurred. The enemy has had to abandon all his plans for attack. He has been obliged to re-group all his forces. He has had to throw in again units that were fatigued. His operational plans have been completely upset. He is enormously criticized at home. It is a bad psychological moment for him. Already he has had to admit that there is no chance of the war being decided before August, perhaps not before the end of next year. That means a transformation of the entire situation such as nobody would have believed possible a fortnight ago. That is the net result of a battle in which a great part of our divisions has not even been committed. A considerable part of our Panzer divisions still follows in the rear or has been in combat for only a few days. I am convinced that the defensive would in the long run be unbearable for us. For the losses in blood of an enemy offensive will steadily decrease; commitments of material will increase. The enemy will not continue these monotonous assaults with men, for the criticism at home will on the one hand be decisive, and on the other, of course, the gradually improving flow of ammunitions and war material will have its decisive effect. To the same extent to which he repairs the harbors and solves his transportation problem he can accelerate the moving up of supplies as long as the stock piles suffice. He will become accustomed to the tactics that were actually employed at Aachen,[3] namely concentrated artillery fire on a position, destruction of single pill boxes by fire from tanks, and then occupation of a completely pulverized area by relatively weak infantry forces. In the long run his losses in manpower will be fewer than ours. During this time he will demolish our rail system—slowly but surely—and will make transportation gradually impossible for us. We do not force him to use his bomber squadrons over the battle front but open to them the German homeland; and in turn that will react upon the front because of decreases in delivery of ammunition, of gasoline, of weapons, of tools, of motor cars, et cetera, and that will have unfavorable effects upon the troops. In other words, the result of a continuation of the present or former tactics which were forced upon us by circumstances, because we were unable to attack earlier, might result in extremely heavy losses in blood while the losses of the enemy would probably decrease considerably.

Consequently, if possible, we shall abandon these tactics the moment we believe that we have forces enough for offensive action. That is possible. The result of the present first act of our offensive in the West has already been that the Americans have all told been forced to move up something like 50 per cent of the forces from their other fronts,

[3] Aachen had surrendered on 21 October after a siege of 13 days. Captain Butcher, *My Three Years with Eisenhower*, p. 692, writes: 'The 1st Division's capture of Aachen, General Huebner said, was methodical, and relatively inexpensive in lives. A great deal of artillery was used and the city was "cleaned up" house by house and block by block. He said his division had lost only 150 men killed and some 1,200 wounded in taking the city.'

that their other offensive formations, located north and south
of our break-through point, have been greatly weakened, that
the first English divisions are arriving, that the enemy is
already moving up a great part of his Panzer forces. I believe
that eight or nine Panzer divisions, of a total of fifteen, have
been in action. That means that he has had to concentrate his
forces there. In the sector in which we are now starting to
attack, lines have become extraordinarily thin. He has pulled
out division after division and now we must hurry in order to
be able to annihilate a still larger number of divisions—
perhaps the enemy has left there only three or perhaps
four—if we have luck it may be five, but hardly six.[4]

I want to emphasize right away that the aims of all these
offensives, which will be delivered blow by blow (already I
am preparing a third blow), is first the elimination of all
American units south of the penetration point[5] by annihilat-
ing them piece by piece, division by division. Then we shall
see how we can establish a direct connection between this
operation and the penetration point. The task of our forces
at the penetration point is to tie down as many enemy forces
as possible. The penetration point is at a spot vital for them.
The crossing of the Meuse would be immensely dangerous
for both the Americans and the English. An advance toward
Antwerp would be catastrophic for them. The advance did
not succeed, but we did succeed in one thing, namely in
forcing them to concentrate all essential and available forces
in order to localize the danger. This is our first positive gain.

[4] On the question of the strength of the American division in the Saar
and Lorraine, the following statement by Colonel Lingner, who took
part in this offensive as commander of an SS Division, is interesting:
'When the break-through in the Ardennes had been stopped by the
Allies, it was realized that several Allied divisions had been sent north
to aid the Americans in their defense. It was therefore decided to launch
an attack against what we felt was sure to be a weak position. This offensive was only given very limited objectives and I believe it was
undertaken on the theory that an attack was the best means of defense.
We apparently miscalculated Allied strength in the Saar, for we were
very surprised by the number of divisions still opposing us. As a result
the operation only achieved very limited success.' (Quoted by Shulman,
Defeat in the West, p. 257.)
[5] Hitler means the bulge created by the German Ardennes offensive.

Now our task is to destroy the forces south of the penetration point, first by means of a number of single blows.

Thus the task set for this new offensive does not go beyond what is possible and can be achieved with our available forces. We are committing eight divisions. With the exception of one division which comes from Finland, seven are of course worn out from fighting, though parts of a few are rested; but the enemy who opposes us (if we have luck with five divisions, possibly only with four, possibly only with three) is not fresh either. He too is worn out, with the exception of one division which is stationed directly along the Rhine, and of which we shall have to see how it will prove itself, and with the exception of the 12th American Panzer Division, of which it is not certain whether it will be committed at all, and which in any case is a new unit which has not yet been in combat. But the rest of the units on the enemy side are also worn out. We shall find a situation which we could not wish to be better.

If this operation succeeds it will lead to the destruction of a part of that group of divisions which confronts us south of the break-through point. The next operation will then follow immediately. It will be connected with a further push. I hope that in this way we shall first smash these American units in the South. Then we shall continue the attack and shall try to connect it with the real long-term operation itself.

Thus this second attack has an entirely clear objective—the destruction of the enemy forces. No questions of prestige are involved. It is not a question of gaining space. The exclusive aim is to destroy and eliminate the enemy forces wherever we find them. It is not even the task of this operation to liberate all Alsace. That would be wonderful. It would have an immense effect on the German people, a decisive effect on the world, immense psychological importance, a very depressing effect on the French people. But that is not what matters. As I said before, what matters is the destruction of the man power of the enemy.

However, even in this operation, it will be necessary to pay attention to speed. That means, in my opinion, that we should take what can be taken quickly, like lightning, without being deflected from our proper target. Sometimes you can not catch up in weeks with what you failed to do, or missed doing, in three or four hours. A reconnaissance unit, or a small motorized unit, or an assault gun brigade, or a Panzer Battalion is sometimes able to cover in three or four hours 20 to 40 decisive kilometers which afterwards could not be gained in six weeks of battle.

Unfortunately that is what we experienced in our first operation. This stood under a number of lucky as well as unlucky stars. A lucky omen, we succeeded for the first time in keeping an operation secret—I may say for the first time since the fall of 1939, since we entered the war. A few bad things happened even here. One officer carrying a written order went up to the front and was snapped. Whether the enemy found the order and made use of this intelligence, or whether they did not believe it, cannot be established now. At any rate the order reached the enemy. However, thank heaven, it had no effect. At least no reports have come in from any quarter that the enemy was put on guard. That was a lucky omen.

The best omen of all was the development of the weather, which had been forecast by a young weather prophet who actually proved to have been right. This weather development gave us the possibility of camouflaging, though this had seemed hardly possible, the final assembly of the troops during the last two or three days, so that the enemy gained no insight. The same weather prophet, who again forecast the present weather with absolute certainty, has again proved to be right. Then there was the complete failure of the enemy air reconnaissance, partly because of the weather but partly also because of a certain existing conceitedness. Those people did not think it necessary to look around. They did not believe it at all likely that we could again take the initiative. Perhaps they were even influenced by the conviction that I am already dead or that, at any rate, I suffer from cancer and cannot any longer live and drink, so that they consider this danger also eliminated. They have lived exclusively in the thought of their own offensive.

A third factor has also to be added, namely the conviction

that we could not possses the necessary forces. Gentlemen, here I want to tell you something immediately. Certainly our forces are not unlimited. It was an extremely bold venture to mobilize the forces for this offensive and for the coming blows, a venture which, of course, involved very grave risks. Hence if you read today that things are not going well in the south of the Eastern front, in Hungary,[6] you must know that as a matter of course we cannot be equally strong everywhere. We have lost so many allies. Unfortunately, because of the treachery of our dear allies, we are forced to retire gradually to a narrower ring of barriers. Yet despite all this it has been possible on the whole to hold the Eastern front. We shall stop the enemy advance in the South too. We shall close it off. Nevertheless it has been possible to organize numerous new divisions and to arm them, to reactivate old divisions and to rearm them, to reactivate Panzer divisions, to accumulate gasoline, and above all to get the air force into shape so that, weather permitting, it can be committed to a number of daylight flights and can come forward with new models which are able to make daylight attacks in the enemy's rear, and against which he has at present nothing to oppose. In other words, we have been able to reassemble enough in the way of artillery, mortars, tanks, and infantry divisions to restore the balance of forces in the West. That in itself is a miracle. It demanded continuous pushing and months of work and plugging, even with regard to the smallest detail. I am by no means satisfied yet. Every day shows that there is something which is not yet ready, which has not yet arrived. Just today I received the sad news that the needed 21-cm-mortars, which I have kept after like the devil, probably still won't come. I still hope they will. It is a continuous struggle for weapons and men, for supplies and fuel, and God knows what. Of course this cannot go on forever. This offensive really must lead to a success.

If we succeed in cleaning up, at least half way, the situation in the West—and that must be our unalterable goal—

[6] The Russian armies had just encircled Budapest and broken into the heart of the city. Bitter house-to-house fighting continued there till 13 February.

then we should be able to rectify the situation with respect to iron ore, because we need not only the Saar territory but most of all we need the Minette.[7] This is a prerequisite. The more critical our situation in the rest of Europe, the more important is this iron-ore region. We cannot continue this war for any length of time, we cannot continue to exist as a nation, without having bases of certain raw material at our disposal. That also is crucial. I hope this objective also will be reached in the course of these operations.

The enemy did not think that possible. He was firmly convinced that we were at the end of our rope. That was a further, third, reason why initially we succeeded in our offensive.

Then difficulties arose. First of all, the terribly bad roads. Then the repairing of bridges took longer than anticipated. Here for the first time it became clear what it means to lose ten hours. To a Panzer division ten lost hours can mean, under certain circumstances, the loss of an entire operation. If you don't succeed in getting through in ten hours, you may not be able, under certain circumstances, to make that up in eight days. Speed, therefore, here means everything. That is one point.

The second was: because of the delays caused by bad roads, because of the destruction of certain bridges which could not be quickly repaired, we did not begin our offensive with the mobility that would have been desirable, but were heavily burdened with equipment and most of all with vehicles. Exactly why all these vehicles were taken along I do not know. It has even been claimed that the vehicles were taken along in order that everyone could carry with him what he could grab. I do not know about that, but it is certain that we were encumbered with vehicles. In that respect we must learn from the Russians.

One primary fact was demonstrated at once. In this attack infantry divisions generally advanced quite as fast as Panzer divisions, and indeed sometimes faster, although these infantry divisions were advancing on foot. That reminds me of the

[7] The high quality iron ore mined in Lorraine.

year 1940 when, for instance, a division like the First
Mountain Division, about which I had seriously worried
whether it could catch up at all, suddenly whizzed along like
a weasel. All of a sudden it reached the Aisne, nearly as
quickly as our Panzer units. Quite a number of infantry
divisions have given very good accounts of themselves, some
of them young divisions, though they were really impeded in
their own progress by the road jam caused by the Panzer
units. They would have advanced faster if the roads had not
been clogged by the Panzer units. One thing is clear, namely,
that Panzer units which are fully motorized—I always hear it
said that they are 75 to 80 per cent or 65 per cent motorized; that is usually too much because then everything is on
the road and there are eight or ten men to a truck whereas
formerly there were thirty—I say Panzer units can cover 100
kilometers per day, even 150, given free terrain. But I cannot
remember that there has been one offensive when even for
two or three days we have covered more than 50 or 60
kilometers. Generally at the end the pace has hardly exceed-
ed that of the infantry units. The Panzer units made only
short hops. They quickly took possession of something, but
the advance units of the infantry division then had to close
up. As soon as a Panzer division cannot roll excessive motorization becomes a burden. The vehicles cannot get off the
roads and if, because of the danger from the air, they have
to move at intervals, the final result is that some of the forces
will not be in their places. Either the artillery, or the infantry, or the grenadiers won't get to the front. Actually the
battle out front has been fought out by quite small spearheads. That happened in the fighting of the Army Group
Model,[8] also of the 'Leibstandarte.' In the last analysis only
the spearheads did the fighting. Only the spearheads of the
12th SS Panzer division were in the battle, but a gigantic
network of roads toward the rear was completely clogged and
blocked. You could not get ahead and you could not get
back. Finally not even the fuel was brought up. The vehicles
hardly moved. They actually let the motors idle. They let

[8] Model, Commander of Army Group 'B,' was in charge of the Ardennes offensive.

them keep running during the night in order to prevent damage from freezing, et cetera. The men kept warm that way too. An immense amount of gasoline is needed. Everywhere the roads were bad. You had to drive in first gear . . .

We can really learn from the Russians. When today I get a report about a Russian road which leads to a front section where there are 36 infantry divisions and Panzer units, so many armored regiments, and so and so many other units, and when this report says that last night 1000 vehicles were on the road, tonight 800, and then 1200 and 300 vehicles, this report causes an alarm that runs through the whole Eastern front, for it is understood to mean that an attack is imminent. Our Panzer divisions have 2,500, 3,000, 4,000, 4,500 trucks, and then they report that they are mobile only 60, 75, or 80 per cent. Quite by chance I found out about two Mountain Divisions, of which one had 1,800, the other 1,400 trucks. Those are Mountain Divisions. Of course, they will get plucked if they have not plucked themselves already. This development would not be so bad if we could afford all that and if we could operate in large open terrain. But at a time when you are hemmed in and crammed onto a few roads, this motorization can even be a misfortune. That is one of the reasons why the right wing first got entirely stuck—bad roads, obstacles because of bridges which could not be repaired in a short time, then thirdly the difficulty of coping with the masses of vehicles, then again the difficulty of the fuel supply, which, unlike in earlier offensives, could not be brought up by the Air Force, and then finally of course the threatened clearing of the weather. We have to realize that the Air Force did a pretty good job. It has thrown itself into the offensive and has done everything that it could do considering the number of planes which can be committed and the kind of planes at our disposal. Nevertheless, in good weather it is impossible for us to give such protection in the air that no enemy planes can get in. In the case of such crammed roads, the roads then become mass graves for vehicles of all kinds. Nevertheless, we had immense luck, for when the good weather came the disentanglement was in general already getting under way.

As I said before, those were the unlucky moments among the lucky ones. Nevertheless, for a moment, the situation seemed to justify the hope that we could hold out. At the beginning I did not at all believe that the enemy would thin out his fronts to such an extent. Now that the thinning out has taken place it is time to draw the consequences at other parts of the front, and they must be drawn quickly. Here I must take up a very decisive consideration, namely the objections that can be raised to a continuation of this operation. The first objection is the old one, the forces are not yet strong enough. Here I can only say that you have to take advantage of a unique situation even at the risk of being not yet quite strong enough. We have committed very strong units. If circumstances had been somewhat more favorable, weaker units certainly would have achieved a greater success than the strong units in default of lucky circumstances. Thus yardsticks of strength are relative. The enemy, too, is not up to his full strength. He too has weaknesses.

Another argument always put forward is that a greater period of rest should be allowed. Gentlemen, speed is everything today. If we permit the enemy to regain his wits, then, in my opinion, we shall have lost half the chance we possessed. The year 1918 should be a warning to us. In 1918 the intervals between the various attacks were much too long. Reasons have been given why, but there can be no doubt that if the second offensive at Chemin des Dames had followed the first one sooner, the outcome would have been very different.[9] Connection with the wing of the first great assault group would have certainly been established via Compiègne, and a decisive turn might have occurred. Perhaps we might have reached the sea. Rest periods, therefore, are not always desirable.

Gentlemen, there is something else I want to emphasize. I have been in this business for eleven years, and during these eleven years, I have never heard anybody report that everything was completely ready. On the contrary, during these

[9] The German attack starting from Chemin des Dames toward Soissons and Château Thierry took place in May 1918, two months after the offensive toward Amiens.

eleven years a report usually arrived saying that the Navy requested urgently a delay for such and such a length of time because this and that should still be done and would be ready at such and such a date. Then when the Navy was ready, the Army had its say: 'It would be a great pity if we should do that now, because the Army is just about to introduce this and that thing and would like to wait for it.' When the Army was ready then the Air Force came forward and said: 'It is quite impossible to do that. Until the new model is introduced it is impossible to attack or to expose oneself to such a danger.' When finally the Air Force was ready the Navy came back and declared: 'The present submarine has not proved itself. A new type must be introduced and a new type cannot be ready before the year so and so.' We have never been ready. That has been true for every offensive. The most tragic example perhaps was the fall of 1939.[10] I wanted to attack in the West immediately but I was told that we were not ready. Afterwards I was asked: 'Why did we not attack? You had only to give the order.' I then had to admit that a mistake had been made. We should have declared simply: 'We attack in the West on 15 November at the latest. That is final, no objection permitted.' Then we would have started action. I am convinced that we should have beaten France to a pulp that winter and would have been completely free in the West.

You are never entirely ready. That is plain. In our situation it is not even possible. The big problem is that when in theory you are ready, the things that were ready are no longer at your disposal but have been used somewhere else. Today we are not in a position to put divisions on ice. Everyone is watched with the eyes of Argus. If there is quiet, or no large-scale battle in the East for two weeks, then the commander of the Army Group in the West comes and says: 'There are unused Panzer units in the East, why do we not get them?' If there is quiet momentarily in the West, then the

[10] Throughout the whole of November 1939, a struggle was waged between Hitler and the General Staff on the question whether the attack on France should begin immediately or should be postponed till next year. For details see Shulman, *Defeat in the West*, pp. 36-8, and Liddell Hart, *The German Generals Talk*, pp. 108-10.

same commander, if in the East, would declare immediately: 'There is complete quiet in the West; we should get at least 4 to 6 Panzer divisions over here to the East.' As soon as I have a division free anywhere, other sections are already eyeing it. For myself I am really glad the divisions are in existence at all. Now I am following the example of some clever army or army-group commanders. They never pull out any divisions but leave them all in, even if the divisional sectors at their front get very narrow; and then they declare: 'I have no divisions at free disposal, they are all committed.' Then it is up to me to unfreeze a division; otherwise I would never get one.

Therefore, I have to state that we do not have unlimited time at our disposal. Events march on. If I don't act quickly at one point, then somewhere else a situation may arise by which I am forced to send something away. Time is of value only if you make use of it.

Then a further worry is the problem of ammunition. I am convinced that we can afford the ammunition needed for this offensive, because experience shows that an offensive eats up less ammunition than a defensive. Furthermore the following consideration should be emphasized. It is generally believed that we are unable to equal our enemies' supply of ammunition. According to the reports of our troops, our reserve of ammunition in the West was . . . of that of the Allies. In the East our expenditure of ammunition is nearly 100 per cent greater than that of the Russians. Although you may sometimes hear it said that the Russians send over gigantic quantities of ammunition, the fact is that the German expenditure of ammunition is exactly 100 per cent higher than the Russian, and I do not count the ammunition we leave behind on retreats. That beats everything. So far as ammunition is concerned, we can afford this offensive. The real problem is transportation.

The fuel actually needed for this operation is available. That we shall get it there, there is no doubt. The general transportation situation is more difficult. Improvement in the transportation situation will depend on the extent to which each commander of a unit, each troop leader, examines conscientiously what he needs to take along and what is not absolutely essential. Everything that is taken along and is not absolutely necessary is not only a burden for the troops but a burden for the supply forces, a burden for the entire fuel situation, and that means a burden for the coming operation. I consider it important to ask oneself rigorously again and again: 'Is there anything that I do not absolutely need?' The character and the honor of a Panzer division—whether an army or an SS division makes no difference—is not demeaned if its battalions march for once on foot. If they cannot close up because of a road jam, then they are compelled to march on foot anyway. They have to get up to the front under all circumstances. If this operation were headed for the Sahara or for Central Asia, I would say that I understood that you do not want to part with your vehicles, but this operation, which in any case will not extend for more than 50 to 60 kilometers, can be carried out on foot. The infantry has to do that anyway and has never known otherwise. The infantry accepts this as its God-appointed fate and its honorable duty, but Panzer units regard it as a kind of disgrace if suddenly some must for a while march on foot.

I believe this to be a decisive factor for the success of this operation. On the whole the plan of the operation is clear. I am in full agreement with the measures that have been taken. I particularly hope that we shall succeed in moving the right wing forward rapidly in order to open the way to Saverne and then to push into the plains of the Rhine and liquidate the American divisions. The destruction of these American divisions must be our goal. I further hope that by then the fuel situation will permit a re-grouping for a fresh assault and a further blow, as a result of which I confidently expect that additional American divisions will be destroyed by the growing forces on our side. For the number of our forces will by then have increased somewhat. I can support this next attack with . . . additional divisions, one of them a very good one from Finland. Unless the enterprise is cursed with bad luck from the beginning, it should, in my opinion, succeed.

I do not need to explain to you a second time how much

depends upon it. It will largely determine the success of the first operation. By carrying out the two operations, A and B, and by succeeding in them, the threat to our left flank will disappear automatically. We shall then immediately fight the third battle and smash the Americans completely. I am firmly convinced that we can then turn toward the left.

Our firm aim must be to clean up the situation in the West by offensive action. We must be fanatical in this aim. Perhaps there are some who will secretly object, saying, 'All right, but will it succeed?' Gentlemen, the same objection was raised in the year 1939. I was told in writing and vocally that the thing could not be done, that it was impossible. Even in the winter of 1940 I was told, 'That cannot be done. Why do we not stay within the West Wall? We have built the West Wall, why do we not let the enemy run against it and then perhaps attack him as a follow-up? But let him come first; we can perhaps advance afterwards. We hold these wonderful positions, why should we run unnecessary risks?' What would have happened to us if we had not attacked them? You have exactly the same situation today. Our relative strength is not less today than it was in 1939 or 1940. On the contrary, if, in two blows, we succeed in destroying both American groups, the balance will have shifted clearly and absolutely in our favor. After all I rely on the German soldier being aware of what he is fighting for.

Only one thing is not in our favor this time and that is the air situation. But that is why we are now forced, despite all hazards, to take advantage of the bad winter weather. The air situation forces us to action. I cannot wait till we have more favorable weather. I would prefer to delay matters somehow until spring. Perhaps I could then organize another 10, 15, or 20 divisions, and we could then attack in spring. But, first of all, the enemy also will bring over 15 or 20 new divisions. Secondly, I do not know whether in the spring I shall be any more master of the air than I am now, but if I am then no more master of the air than now, the weather will give a decisive advantage to the enemy, whereas now there are at least several weeks during which carpet bombing of troop concentrations cannot take place. That means a lot.

How important it is to get an early decision you will realize from the following. The enemy has full knowledge of the flying bombs. He has already reconstructed them entirely. We know that. He has put them into production. Unquestionably, exactly as we are causing continuous disturbances to the English industrial regions through these flying bombs, so the enemy will be able almost to demolish the Ruhr area by the mass shooting of flying bombs. There is no protection against them. We cannot even fend them off with fighter planes. I do not want to talk about the rockets. There is no remedy against them at all. Everything, therefore, speaks in favor of cleaning up this situation before the enemy begins to use super-weapons of this kind.

The German people have breathed more freely during recent days. We must prevent this relief from being followed by lethargy—lethargy is the wrong word, I mean resignation. They have breathed again. The mere idea that we are on the offensive has had a cheering effect on the German people, and when this offensive is continued, when we have our first really great successes—and we shall have them—for our situation is not different from that of the Russians from 1941 to 1942, when, despite their most unfavorable situation, they maneuvered us slowly back by single offensive blows along the extended front on which we had passed over to the defensive. If the German people see such a development taking place here, you can be sure that they will make all sacrifices which are humanly possible. We shall obtain whatever we ask of them. Nothing will deter the nation—whether I order a new textile collection, or some other collection, or whether I call for men. The youth will come forward enthusiastically. The German people as a whole will react in a thoroughly positive manner. I must say the nation behaves as decently as could possibly be expected. There are no better people than our Germans. Individual bad incidents are just the exception that confirms the rule.

Finally, I wish to appeal to you to support this operation with all your fire, with all your zest, and with all your energy. This also is a decisive operation. Its success will automatically result in the success of the next operation. The success of the second operation will automatically bring about the collapse of the threat on the left to our offensive. We shall actually have knocked away one half of the enemy's Western front. Then we shall see what happens. I do not believe that in the long run he will be able to resist 45 German divisions which will then be ready. We shall yet master fate.

Since the date could be fixed for New Year's night I wish to say that I am grateful to all those who have done the gigantic work of preparation for this operation and who have also taken upon themselves the great risk of being responsible for it. I consider it a particularly good omen that this was possible. In German history New Year's night has always been of good military omen.[11] The enemy will consider New Year's night an unpleasant disturbance, because he does not celebrate Christmas but New Year's. We cannot introduce the New Year in any better way than by such a blow. When on New Year's day the news spreads in Germany that the German offensive has been resumed at a new spot and that it is meeting with success, the German people will conclude that the old year was miserable at the end but that the new year has had a good beginning. That will be a good omen for the future. Gentlemen, I want to wish each of you, individually, good luck.

Gentlemen, there is one thing more. A prerequisite for the success of this operation is secrecy. Anyone who does not need to know about it should not know about it. Whoever does need to know about it should hear only what he needs to know. Whoever does need to know about it should not hear about it earlier than he needs to know. That is imperative. And nobody should be ordered up to the front who knows something about it and might be caught. That also is imperative.

---

[11] Hitler alludes to the 1st of January 1814, when Prussian troops began the final campaign against Napoleon by passing the Rhine.

FIELDMARSHAL VON RUNDSTEDT: My Fuehrer, in the name of all the assembled commanders I wish to give you the firm assurance on the part of leadership and troops that everything, absolutely everything, will be done to make this offensive a success. We ourselves know where in our first offensive we have made mistakes. We shall learn from them.

Page numbers refer to the accounts of conferences given in this text. Other conferences are briefly summarized below. The conferences were called 'morning situation' (*Morgenlage*) and 'evening situation' (*Abendlage*). The first conference, concerned with the situation existing in the morning, frequently took place in the early afternoon; the second, for the discussion of military developments during the day, sometimes late at night. During the last months of the war, expressions like 'noon situation' (*Mittagslage*) and 'afternoon situation' (*Nachmittagslage*) occur; this might indicate that the schedule was changed or that, in this critical period, the number of conferences was increased.

Date			Preservation and Contents of Transcript
1942	1 Dec.	Evening.	See p. 41.
	12 Dec.	Morning.	See p. 48.
1943	1 Feb.	Morning.	See p. 57.
	4 March	Evening.	Long, badly preserved transcript. Reports from all fronts. Discussion particularly concerned with reports by Rommel and Kesselring on North African situation and mention of possibilities of Allied invasion in the Eastern Mediterranean.
	5 March	Morning.	See p. 64.
	21 March	Morning.	Badly charred fragments. Trend of discussion no longer comprehensible.
	? March	Evening.	Very poor condition. Refers to situation on Eastern front and to Italian weaknesses, of which a recent strike in Turin is regarded as a characteristic indication.
	19 May	Conference with Keitel	Preserved in part. Deals with possibility of Italian collapse and with the military importance of the Balkans, which Hitler considers more crucial than Italy, chiefly for economic reasons. Detailed discussion about sending military reinforcements to the Balkans.
	20 May	Conference with Neurath.	See p. 71.
	? May	Morning.	Long but very badly preserved transcript. Contains a report by Zeitzler on situation on Eastern front, by Warlimont on the Balkans, and by Christian on air activity. Hitler remarks: 'I shall finish off definitely these small states, God help me.'
	25 July	Morning.	See p. 83.
	25 July	Evening.	See p. 92.
	25/26 July	Night Conference.	See p. 100.
	26 July	Morning.	See p. 103.
	26 July	Conference with Kluge.	See p. 103.
	? July	Unknown.	Short fragment in poor condition.
	4 Oct.	Morning.	Transcript only partially preserved and in poor condition. Contains reports by Jodl on fronts in Balkans and Italy, by a representative of the Navy on naval operations, and by Christian on air operations.

Date		Preservation and Contents of Transcript
1943		
26 Oct.	Evening.	Fragment. Reports on Eastern and Italian fronts and discussion of war production. Hitler angry at Finnish peace feelers.
19 Nov.	Morning.	Reports from all fronts and a brief mention of peace feelers by Hungary and Rumania. Hitler discusses technical details of a new tank. See p. 127.
? Dec.	Unknown.	Only a few sentences preserved.
20 Dec.	Evening.	Unconnected, single fragments. Concerns over-all military situation and
22 Dec.	Morning.	activities of resistance groups in occupied countries.
27 Dec.	Conference with Zeitzler.	See p. 139.
28/29 Dec.	Night conference.	See p. 151-2.
29 Dec.	Conference with Zeitzler.	See p. 151-2.
30 Dec.	Conference with Küchler.	See p. 151-2.
1944		
28 Jan.	Telephone conference between Hitler and Zeitzler.	Zeitzler recommends some withdrawal at the southern sector of Eastern front on the basis of fresh reports. Hitler refuses to allow withdrawal, and Zeitzler states that he will take up the question again at the evening conference.
? Feb.	Evening.	Badly charred fragment. Trend of discussion is not comprehensible.
? March	Morning.	Long fragment in poor condition. Survey of all fronts. Hitler complains about lack of exact information concerning effects of recent air attacks on London.
? March	Unknown.	Only a few lines comprehensible.
6 April	Morning.	Long fragment in very poor condition. Some remarks by Hitler refer to the American presidential elections, and to the confiscation of art works in occupied countries. Hitler objects to the fact that a statue excavated in Corfu or Corinth was given to the Greeks. 'Everything that is found by Germans must be brought immediately to Germany.' Hitler is asked whether he ordered that six old Spanish guns found in France be given to Franco. Hitler denies it: 'On principle I don't give historical objects as presents. Once I was asked to give Nefretete away as a present in order to establish better relations with Egypt. I refused. Then it was proved that we got Nefretete by some mean act. A Jew had committed some fraud to export Nefretete. Then I said, "All right, I'll hand back the Jew," but then they were not interested.'
18 May	Evening.	Fragment has large gaps. Concerns military situation in Italy and France.
18 June	Evening.	Only short fragments preserved.
31 August	Conference with Krebs and Westphal.	See p. 155.

Date		Preservation and Contents of Transcript
1944		
1 Sept.	Morning.	Long but very fragmentary transcript. Concerned with reports on the situation at all fronts. It contains the following remarks by Hitler. 'There is no worse defense zone than the Rhine,' and 'we have an institution for which all countries in the world envy us—the Armed Forces High Command [OKW]. Nobody else has that. People just don't realize it because the Army General Staff doesn't like it.'
17 Sept. 6 Nov.	Evening. Afternoon.	Long transcript, broken into incoherent fragments. Concerns presentation of reports on the military situation on all fronts. At the occasion of Christian's report on air activities, Hitler makes very critical remarks. In thinking over the activities of the air force he has come to a 'devastating result' concerning the effectiveness of its activities; Goering did not know what was going on. At the occasion of the report on events in the north, Hitler remarks that the Swedes are moving troops to the north for fear of the Russians, although their official reason is some frontier violation by the Germans. Hitler suggests reporting in the newspapers that the Swedes motivated the movement of a few divisions up north by saying that a German soldier had taken hay from a haystack; that they should not be so cowardly but frankly admit that they are afraid of the Russians. At the occasion of a pro-Allied declaration by Franco, Hitler remarks, 'What would he do if we announced that the whole thing did not come to anything only because we were not willing to violate the clause about the colonies?'
28 Dec.	Conference with Blaskowitz.	Transcript in very poor condition. Concerns plans to follow up Ardennes offensive with attacks in the Alsace and upper Rhine region.
29 Dec.	Conference with Thomale.	Concerns questions of replacement and equipment for troops in the West. Hitler complains several times about the lack of technical understanding in the German General Staff. Conference ends with a long speech by Hitler: 'Soldierly qualities show themselves only in the moral quality of holding out, in tenacity and persistency. That is the decisive thing in any success. . . People who have only ideas, thoughts, etc., but lack a firm character, persistency and tenacity won't achieve anything. They are just soldiers of fortune. . . You can't make history. You can make world history only if, above common sense, a lively conscience and continuous alertness, there is a fanatic tenacity, a strength of faith which makes a man a real fighter.'

Date		Preservation and Contents of Transcript
1945		
9 Jan.	Evening.	Report on the military events in East and West. A few interruptions of the report by Hitler.
10 Jan.	Afternoon.	Long but fragmentary transcript. Concerns the general military situation and the production of new weapons and of airplanes. Hitler expresses displeasure with the progress of arms production. He emphasizes the great importance of the enemy's bombing planes, expresses the wish to see a book written 'which gives a general technical consideration of all ways known to us since the ancient world. Then one would realize how frequently with quite few technically superior weapons wars have been decided. If Hannibal, when he passed the Alps, had had, instead of his seven or 13 or 11 elephants, 56 or 250, that would have been enough to conquer Italy.'
? Jan.	Unknown.	Incomplete transcript in poor condition. Remarks on airplane production, efficiency of the V-1 rocket, importance of railroads. Hitler says that the present situation shows how right he was in opposing retreats. Present production difficulties are result of lack of space and vulnerability of a small area.
27 Jan.	Afternoon.	See p. 165.
24 Feb.	Evening.	Brief report on the general military situation. Very few remarks by Hitler.
Feb./March	Unknown.	Short fragment in very poor condition. Concerns construction of bunkers and war production.
Feb./March	Unknown.	Disconnected, single fragments. Hitler wants to disregard the rules of the Geneva Convention: 'To hell with that. . . If I make it clear that I show no consideration for prisoners but that I treat enemy prisoners without any consideration for their rights, regardless of reprisals, then quite a few [Germans] will think twice before they desert.'
? March	Conference with Löhr.	Only a fragment preserved, in poor condition. Deals with situation in the Balkans, naval and air operations.
? March	Afternoon.	Brief fragment in poor condition. Concerns the Western front.
? March	Afternoon.	See p. 191.
23 March	Evening.	See p. 201.

BIBLIOGRAPHY

Badoglio, Pietro, *Italy in the Second World War*, London, 1948.

Boldt, Gerhard, *Die Letzten Tage der Reichskanzlei*, Hamburg Stuttgart, 1947.

Bonomi, Ivanoe, *Diaro di un Anno* [Italy], 1947.

Butcher, Capt. Harry C., *My Three Years with Eisenhower*, New York, 1946.

Cavallero, Ugo, *Comando Supremo*, Rocca S. Casciano, 1948.

Churchill, Winston S., *The Gathering Storm*, Boston, 1948.

Ciano, Galeazzo, *The Ciano Diaries 1939-43*, ed. Hugh Gibson, New York, 1946.

Ciano, Galeazzo, *Ciano's Diplomatic Papers*, ed. M. Muggeridge, London, 1948.

Dulles, Allen Welsh, *Germany's Underground*, New York, 1947.

Eisenhower, Dwight D., *Crusade in Europe*, New York, 1948.

Fuller, J. F. C., *The Second World War 1939-45*, London, 1948.

Goebbels, *The Goebbels Diaries 1942-43*, ed. Louis P. Lochner, New York, 1948.

Guillaume, A., *La Guerre Germano-Soviétique*, Paris, 1949.

Guingand, Sir Francis de, *Operation Victory*, New York, 1947.

Halder, Franz, *Hitler as War Lord*, London, 1950.

Hitler e Mussolini, *Lettere e Documenti* [Italy], 1946.

Hossbach, Friedrich, *Zwischen Wehrmach und Hitler*, Wolfenbuettel, Hannover, 1949.

International Military Tribunal, *Trial of the Major War Criminals*, Nuremberg, 1947.

Kordt, Erich, *Wahn und Wirklichkeit*, Stuttgart, 1947.

Liddell Hart, B. H., *The German Generals Talk*, New York, 1948.

Martienssen, Anthony, *Hitler and His Admirals*, London, 1948.

Montgomery of Alamein, *Normandy to Baltic*, London, 1946.

Rahn, Rudolf, *Ruheloses Leben*, Duesseldorf, 1949.

Roatta, Mario, *Otto Milioni di Baionette*, Milano, 1946.

Schmidt, Paul, *Statist auf Diplomatischer Buehne*, Bonn, 1949.

Sherwood, Robert E., *Roosevelt and Hopkins*, New York, 1948.

Shulman, Milton, *Defeat in the West*, New York, 1948.

Trevor-Roper, H. R., *The Last Days of Hitler*, London, 1947.

U.S. Office of Chief of Counsel for Prosecution of Axis Criminality, *Nazi Conspiracy and Aggression*, Washington, 1946.

U.S. Navy Department, *Fuehrer Conferences on Matters dealing with the German Navy*, Washington [N.D.].

U.S. War Department, *Biennial Report of the Chief of Staff of the U.S. Army*, July 1st, 1943, to June 30, 1945.

INDEX

Note: The names of persons who are not identified in the text or in footnotes are followed by a short explanatory note. When not otherwise indicated, titles and ranks are those of Nazi Germany. A number followed by an asterisk indicates the first page of a conference in which the person participates; further references to that person throughout the conference are not listed separately.

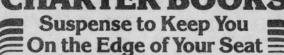